THE BENEFITS OF HEALTH
AND SAFETY REGULATION

THE BENEFITS OF HEALTH AND SAFETY REGULATION

Edited by

ALLEN R. FERGUSON
Public Interest Economics Foundation

E. PHILLIP LeVEEN
Public Interest Economics West

BALLINGER PUBLISHING COMPANY
Cambridge, Massachusetts
A Subsidiary of Harper & Row, Publishers, Inc.

This book was prepared with the support of NSP Grant #DAR77-12137. However, any opinions, findings, conclusions, and/or recommendations herein are those of the authors and do not necessarily reflect the views of NSF.

International Standard Book Number: 0-88410-721-3

Library of Congress Catalog Card Number: 80-20460

Printed in the United States of America

Library of Congress Cataloging in Publication Data

Main entry under title:

The Benefits of health and safety regulation.

Includes index.
1. Industrial hygiene—Law and legislation—United States—Cost effectiveness
—Congresses. 2. Industrial safety—Law and legislation—United States—Cost
effectiveness—Congresses. I. Ferguson, Allen R. II. LeVeen, E. Philip.
HD7260.5.B46   338.4.336311.0973   80-20460
ISBN 0-88410-721-3

CONTENTS

Appendixes

About the Editor

LIST OF FIGURES

LIST OF TABLES

PREFACE

At a time when regulatory activities in general, and those dealing with the quality of life in particular, are under heavy attack for being too costly, the Public Interest Economics Foundation (PIE−F) is publishing this book, derived from the proceedings of a conference funded by the National Science Foundation, to explore the assessment of benefits of health and safety regulation. The conference took place on October 12−13, 1978, in Berkeley Springs, West Virginia.

The primary purpose of the conference was to emphasize the role of assessing the benefits of health and safety regulation in setting priorities and developing regulations rationally. Second, the conference was intended to apprise decisionmakers of the best available techniques for benefit assessment, as well as their limitations. Concurrently, it gave leading academicians exposure to the real concerns of regulators.

The conference was relatively small, and the object was less to develop new scientific information than to increase the usefulness of available and future analytic work. The fifty-five participants were high level decisionmakers and their immediate subordinates from government agencies, prominent members of consumer and environmental groups, and academicians with extensive knowledge of governmental regulations. The conference consisted of plenary sessions and meetings of workshops of six members each.

The conference addressed three broad questions about the benefits of health and safety regulation: Why? How? For whom? The first session was concerned with the rationale for formally assessing benefits; the second, with the most advanced methods of assessment; and the third, with one of the least understood aspects of regulation, namely, the distribution of benefits.

There have been substantial efforts to estimate the total cost of regulation, to develop instrumentalities to control and systematize the regulatory process, and to make it more efficient and efficacious. However, national policy requires that judgment about the net public gain of regulation be based not only on estimations of cost but also on the benefits regulatory programs produce.

The benefits of health and safety regulation are defined as risks avoided: the risk of premature death, injury, or illness. For the most part regulation pertains to reducing (postponing) "statistical" deaths or avoiding "statistical" injuries or cases of disease. The benefits are a reduction in the probability that all members of some population group will encounter some specific form of suffering.

Frequently efforts have been made not only to estimate expected benefits but also to place a monetary value on them. Such a value would permit measuring the benefits of a regulation against its resource cost and ascertaining whether the costs exceed the benefits. However, that requires setting a monetary value on life and health. The questions of how to identify and measure the benefits of avoiding risks to health and safety, and whether and how to evaluate them, were central to the conference.

The experience at the conference confirmed that answers to these questions are neither simple nor obvious and indeed that the benefits of some programs may be very difficult to measure. For example, a program that is designed primarily to meet some physical or functional need of handicapped persons might also reduce their sense of isolation.

In the formal sessions and workshops, the dialogue ranged from broad generalizations and abstract concepts to discussion of studies and experiments seeking to measure and evaluate the benefits of specific programs and the practical obstacles to applying benefit analysis effectively. The papers laid out some of the potential benefits of health and safety regulation and the problems of achieving them, as well as the rationale for regulation and problems of attaining both equity and efficiency in regulation. As collected in this book, the papers encompass a brief review of much of the basic material in the area of cost-benefit analysis and its application to health and safety, including the concepts of economic efficiency that underlie all aspects of cost-benefit analysis, and a general review of the history of cost-benefit analysis. In addition, specific topics are rigorously addressed in considerable detail. It is our hope that this book will provide valuable information and pose challenges for new research and effective application of existing knowledge.

Allen R. Ferguson
President
Public Interest Economics Foundation and Center

Cynthia L. Figge
Former Director of Education
Public Interest Economics Foundation

ACKNOWLEDGMENTS

The Public Interest Economics Foundation (PIE−F) gratefully acknowledges the financial support of the National Science Foundation through Grant Number DAR77−12137, which made the entire undertaking possible. We particularly appreciate the deep interest and extensive involvement of Dr. Laurence C. Rosenberg who assisted in the planning of the conference, participated in it, and encouraged the publication of this book.

PIE−F relied on several members of its Board of Economic Advisors and others knowledgeable about regulation, particularly Professors Roger C. Noll, Allen V. Kneese, Robert H. Haveman, and Thomas C. Schelling, for their ideas as to scope and participants in the conference. Leonard Lee Lane, formerly of PIE−F, participated in the development of the initial ideas.

PIE−F is especially grateful to Cynthia Figge, former Director of Education, who was responsible for translating the ideas into reality by coordinating the conference activities, working with the panelists in preparing their materials, inviting speakers and other participants, making all necessary arrangements, and participating in initial preparation of conference materials for publication. The assistance of Sharon Higginbotham and Laura Layman of the PIE−F staff throughout the conference was indispensable. The efforts of Martha Ashelman and Audrey Ferguson also contributed to the smooth running of the conference.

The final preparation of this manuscript for publication could not have been accomplished without the efforts of Judith H. Behn, who assisted in editing the manuscript; Elizabeth Watson, present Director of Education, who coordinated the manuscript preparation; and Barbara Flagg, Anne M. Vezzi, and Helen Morrison of the PIE−F staff who were responsible for the production of the final manuscript.

1 ON THE BENEFITS OF HEALTH AND SAFETY REGULATION

*James W. Vaupel**

THE PROSPECTS FOR SAVING LIVES AND LIMBS

Nearly two million people will die this year in the United States, most of them from causes other than old age. Three-fifths of them will be younger than seventy-five, and over a third, younger than sixty-five. Some fifty thousand infants will die, as will over forty thousand children and teenagers, nearly fifty thousand young adults in their twenties, and more than half a million people in those prime and productive years between ages thirty and sixty-five (National Center for Health Statistics 1978).

This year, an average adult, aged seventeen or over, will suffer twenty "restricted activity days" and spend eight days sick in bed. A quarter of the adult population will visit a physician at least five times, and more than an eighth will be hospitalized at least once.

Over a full work week will be lost, on average, because of illness among the employed, and more than a tenth of this loss will be due to occupational injury and illness. In total, occupational injury and illness will cost some thirty-five million work days. Consumer-

*Associate Professor of Policy Studies and of Business Administration, Institute of Policy Sciences and Public Affairs, Duke University.

The author would like to thank Philip J. Cook, Associate Professor of Public Policy Studies and Economics at Duke University, for his substantial contribution to this chapter.

1

product-related injuries, caused by falling off stairs, slipping in bath-tubs, running into doors, cutting, burning, poisoning, and so on, will result in nearly nine million people rushing to be treated in hospital emergency rooms.

As a result of various accidents and diseases, more than half a million people currently are blind or so visually impaired that they cannot "carry on major activity" and nearly another half a million people are unable to carry on major activity because of paralysis.[1]

These macabre statistics hint at the staggering social losses and personal tragedies caused by the current incidence of mortality and morbidity in the United States—and the enormous potential benefits of trying to reduce them.

The Unequal Distribution of Losses

Three overlapping disadvantaged groups—blacks and other disadvan-taged nonwhites, the poor, and the poorly educated—suffer dispro-portionately from early death, sickness, and mutilation. For example, at current mortality rates, two black children in five will die before age sixty-five, compared with one white child in five (National Cen-ter for Health Statistics 1978). Various studies of mortality among the poor and the poorly educated have generally found death rates "between 50 and 100 percent higher in the lowest socioeconomic class than in the middle and upper classes."[2] Similar differentials exist for morbidity: the poor, for example, assess their health status as "poor" or "fair" far more frequently and suffer much higher rates of "restricted activity days," "bed disability days," and "work loss days" than persons with higher incomes (Public Health Service 1977).

The greatest difficulty of being disadvantaged may not be inferior material possessions but unhealthiness and the threat of early death—as well as the tragedies caused by the frequency of sickness, disabil-ity, and early death among relatives and friends.

Evidence that Mortality and Morbidity Could Be Reduced

These mortality and morbidity data imply immense costs that are regressively distributed over the population. Any improvements, therefore, could result in substantial benefits. Fortunately, the evidence suggests that substantial progress could be made.

Some of the evidence concerns the large health differentials, both in general and for specific causes of illness and death, between various groups—blacks versus whites, the poor versus the affluent, the poorly educated versus the well educated, males versus females, residents of Nevada versus residents of Utah, Japanese Americans and Seventh Day Adventists versus other Americans, and so on (see Vaupel 1978: 24−26). Although the differentials may be partially due to climate, genetics, or other factors largely beyond control, it does seem plausible that factors such as health care, hazardous behavior, and pollution levels that can be influenced by public policies play a major role.

Other suggestive evidence includes the long-term downward trends in mortality and morbidity rates. For example, the likelihood of early death—that is, the probability, at prevailing mortality rates, that a newborn will die before age sixty-five—fell from some 61 percent at the turn of the century to under 25 percent in 1976 (Vaupel 1978: 27−32). The rate of progress has been remarkably steady—a decline of close to half a percentage point each year. If this progress can be continued, in half a century the likelihood of death before age sixty-five would be reduced to virtually zero. This is, perhaps, not as impossible a goal as it may at first seem. In 1900, almost a quarter of the newborns in the United States could be expected to die before age fifteen, but today the likelihood of death before age fifteen has been reduced to under 2 percent (Vaupel 1978: 32).

The most striking evidence that the incidence of mortality and morbidity in the United States might be reduced substantially is given by comparisons with other developed countries. A good summary indicator here, as before, is the likelihood of early death, that is, death before age sixty-five. The United States falls near the bottom of the list of countries for which recent data are available, behind all other major industrialized nations, and behind a number of less-developed countries as well (Vaupel 1978: 32−42). In Sweden, which ranks first, the likelihood of early death is a third less than it is in the United States. If U.S. early death rates could be reduced to Swedish levels, nearly a quarter of a million early deaths could be averted every year (Vaupel 1978: 32).

Similar international differentials exist for specific causes of death or serious illness. For example, Swedish rates of infant mortality, fatal accidents, and fatal cardiovascular disease before age sixty-five are all less than two-thirds of U.S. levels (Vaupel 1978: 45–46).

The Range of Policy Options

Given the staggering aggregate losses and inequalities caused by illness, disability, and untimely death, and given the array of evidence that substantial progress could be made in saving lives and limbs, it is not surprising that enormous efforts are being made to achieve this progress. Our health and safety industry is huge, currently absorbing a tenth of the GNP, or roughly $200 billion.[3] And it is extremely diverse. On the federal level alone, there are scores of agencies concerned with different aspects of health and safety. State, local, and private agencies and organizations can be counted by the hundreds. One compilation lists 172 federal agencies and 248 federal grants and domestic assistance programs in medicine and health (Medical and Health Information Directory 1977). A listing of agencies and organizations involved in the promotion of transportation safety—one narrow category in the field of health and safety regulation—runs on for ten closely printed pages.[4]

The work of these various agencies, organizations, and programs can, broadly speaking, be classified into six categories: (1) medical care, (2) preventive medicine, (3) reduction of physical hazards, (4) alteration of hazardous personal behavior, (5) modification of the social environment, and (6) biomedical research. Scrutiny of any one of these six categories yields the same two conclusions. First, while much is being done in each area, there is much more that could be done. Second, there is very little hard evidence to indicate which of the many options within each area ought to be given priority. In fact, there is little known about the effectiveness of existing programs! In those careful studies that have been done—as in the case of the Occupational Safety and Health Administration, the Consumer Product Safety Commission, the Food and Drug Administration, with various surgical procedures, and with medical screening tests—the analysts have usually concluded that the apparent benefits are hardly worth the costs.[5] Even more generally, our lack of understanding extends to the very reason why mortality and morbidity have been declining. There is some evidence that most of the decline can be attributed to rising standards of living rather than to any particular program or regulation. It is not surprising that we do not know what we should do to further reduce accidents and disease.

The evidence that mortality and morbidity can be substantially reduced, together with the ignorance of how we ought to proceed, implies an adaptive, multipronged "learning strategy" based on extensive but judicious experimentation and thorough, careful evaluation of the costs and benefits of various options. Unfortunately, this strategy has not been followed. While there has been much experimentation, there has been almost no evaluation. Consequently, we have learned little from the experimentation. The current amount of evaluation being conducted is perhaps a tenth and maybe a hundredth of what it should be. According to an Office of Management and Budget estimate for fiscal year 1977, the total expenditures on evaluation by the Department of Health, Education and Welfare (now the Department of Health and Human Services) was only $83.5 million. The Department of Transportation spent only $14.5 million, and total federal expenditures on evaluation were only $243 million.[6] At a time when total government expenditure on health and medical programs amounted to $67 billion and the nation spent over $200 billion, these sums must be viewed as inadequate.

THE RATIONALE FOR HEALTH AND SAFETY REGULATION

In principle, three kinds of policy options are available: choice-augmenting, choice-improving, and choice-constraining policies. Choice-augmenting policies involve the least governmental interference with an individual's behavior. Such policies attempt to improve society's health and safety by increasing opportunities for health and safety. Thus, if government-sponsored research leads to a cure for a disease, or if governmental action—providing lifeguards, for example—makes a practice less risky, new opportunities for consumption may be created. Some choice-augmenting policies may produce unintended constraints on choice. For example, whereas a bicycle path may reduce the hazards of cycling and thus increase the options of cyclists, it might degrade a popular picnic spot. The rubric "choice augmenting," however, seems a useful one for classification purposes.

Choice-improving policies are designed to provide individuals with better information about the range of options available, thereby permitting better decisionmaking. For example, an antismoking campaign may seek to improve awareness of the link between smoking and lung cancer, allowing individuals to take this information into account when deciding whether or not to smoke.

The Current Regulatory Process
and Individual Liberty

There is more to life than death and illness. The reduction in premature mortality and morbidity are worthy goals of public policy, but they are not the only goals. We have limited resources and many pressing needs, and, in addition, we cannot neglect the importance of maintaining individual liberty. Unfortunately, many governmental regulatory decisions have been characterized by an extremely narrow viewpoint. For example, Richard Crout, former Director of the Food and Drug Administration's (FDA's) Bureau of Drugs, asserted:

> I would emphasize very strongly that the Food and Drug Administration regulates health policy, not economic matters. That is terribly important to understand. We do not pay any attention to the economic consequences of our decisions and the law does not ask us to (Crout 1975).

But reasonable policy does impell us to look at the question of costs. Money wasted is simply human resources wasted and thus, in a sense, lives wasted. In short, we cannot legitimately emphasize one goal of regulation to the exclusion of all other considerations.

The direct effect of choice-augmenting and choice-improving policies is to increase individual liberty by enlarging the choice domain, or by improving the choice process. Such policies give at least some people the opportunity to increase both the quantity of goods and services consumed, and their health and life expectancy. Choice-constricting policies push people toward health and safety at the expense of individual consumption, convenience, pleasure, and other desirable attributes of life.

It would be ideal if regulation could always take the form of the first two kinds of policy. That is, if the best policies for improving health and safety were those that do not conflict with individual liberty, they would always be preferred to choice-constraining policies.

A dilemma arises only when a choice-constricting policy would save more lives or would cost less than the best choice-augmenting or choice-improving policy. Under this set of conditions, the issue becomes whether the extra lives saved by the more effective choice-constraining policies are worth the loss of liberty and quality of life imposed by such policies.

This is a simple but important point often missed by policymakers. In deciding whether to adopt a choice-constricting policy, the decision is not a decision between that policy and nothing, nor even a decision between the best choice-constricting policy and nothing. Rather the decision is a five-fold decision among the best choice-constricting policy, the best choice-augmenting policy, the best choice-improving policy, nothing, or some combination of these.

Consider, for example, the FDA's proposed ban on saccharine. Originally the FDA apparently saw its choice as whether to ban saccharine completely or to do nothing—and because of the Delaney amendment, it was felt that if there were any evidence that saccharine might cause cancer, the ban had to be imposed. In the ensuing uproar it became clear that there was actually a wide range of alternatives. Instead of a total ban, the FDA suggested allowing the sale of saccharine by prescription—a somewhat less choice-constricting option. One choice-improving policy that was proposed was to require a warning label on all products containing saccharine. Some scientists noted that certain alternative sweeteners were being developed—including a sugar molecule that was too large to be absorbed by the digestive system—and that a choice-augmented policy that supported this research, or merely delayed the ban on saccharine, might produce an acceptable alternative to saccharine in a few years. Senator Edward Kennedy, chairman of the Senate health subcommittee, proposed a mixed approach that included: (1) an eighteen-month delay of the ban in order to permit the development and substitution of an alternative sweetener, (2) a ban on television and radio advertising of most saccharine-containing products during this period, (3) a ban on the sale in vending machines of diet drinks and other products sweetened with saccharine, and (4) a strong warning label on products containing saccharine (*Wall Street Journal* 13 June 1977).

There is a broad and deep stream of thought, espoused by such diverse philosophers as Locke, Kant, Mill, Rawls, and Nozick, that argues the importance of individual liberty as primary criterion for public policy, ahead of efficiency and equity. In the United States, freedom of individual choice is certainly a value especially strongly held. Consequently, regulatory policies that constrict an individual's domain of choices require special and clearly demonstrated justifications. Two basic justifications for choice-constraining policies are the existence of "externalities" and the need to help correct "irrationality" or inadequacies in information, wisdom, or decisionmaking ability.

The Externalities Argument

"Externalities" are the consequences of an individual's behavior that affect the welfare of people who did not voluntarily contract with the individual to receive these consequences. For example, some kinds of hazardous behavior pose direct physical threats to others. Much health and safety legislation is justified and motivated primarily by such externalities; examples include highway speed limits, laws against drunk driving, gun control regulations, and mandatory vaccinations.

Even in cases of self-hazardous behavior, however, like cigarette smoking in a nonpublic place or consumption of saccharine or laetrile, externalities cannot be ignored since deaths and injuries impose losses on others. Aside from the obvious impacts of illness, injury, or death on those who are directly related to the individual, such events may have important costs to the general society. For example, everyone who pays health insurance premiums is to some degree affected when disability imposes higher costs. Finally, the overall productivity of the society may be lowered by the loss of labor due to injury or illness. Thus, nearly everyone has some interest in the health and welfare of everyone else.

This discussion raises two important issues. First, when one individual's behavior affects the welfare of another, why should the rights of the individual producing the externality be given less weight than the rights of those affected by his or her behavior? (Nozick 1974). After all, if a ban on smoking substantially reduces the welfare of the smoker in order to improve the welfare of the nonsmoker, can we say unequivocally that the society is really better off? Second, even if it is granted that the society does have the right to intervene in the event of significant externalities, at what point does this intervention stop? We could probably reduce deaths by lowering speed limits to 30 miles per hour, by prohibiting alcohol completely, and by rationing consumption of meat, butter, eggs, and other high-cholesterol products—but is this good social policy and would the society be better off? Clearly there must be some criteria that would indicate when it is appropriate to limit an individual's rights, and when it is not.

One approach to evaluating rationally issues regarding the appropriate extent and level of intervention is the application of some form of cost-benefit analysis. The analyst would attempt to examine a regulation involving externalities by treating them as just one of many kinds of costs that must be incorporated into the calculations. Good social policy is policy that produces benefits in excess of the costs of policy. Thus, while reducing the speed limit will reduce deaths, it will also impose large costs in higher travel time, and this will have ramifications throughout the entire production process as well as directly upon consumers. Thus, the object of cost-benefit analysis would be to elucidate the nature of the trade-off between fewer traffic deaths and the higher costs associated with the consequent loss of time.

In a complete cost-benefit analysis, one of the costs that would be included in the evaluation of regulation is the loss of individual liberty resulting from the selection of the form of the regulation. Thus, choice-constraining regulations would be evaluated as being more costly to society than choice-augmenting regulations since the former impose greater costs in the form of loss of liberty than the latter. For this reason, choice-constraining policies would, all else being equal, generally be less desirable, especially if alternative regulatory procedures were readily available. Theoretically, at least, alternatives are often available. For example, instead of banning hazardous behavior, it might be possible to levy a tax or a differential charge that covers the costs of the externalities. Such taxes have been proposed for cigarettes and liquor and could be implemented on such activities as skiing. Similarly, in the case of cyclamates, an alternative to a ban would be a tax of a few pennies on soft drinks and other products containing cyclamates.

The purpose of these taxes would be to provide incentives to consumers and producers to switch to other products or activities and, at the same time, provide a source of revenue to cover the expected social costs of those individuals who continue to pursue the hazardous behavior. If such options were adopted, individual liberty would be less threatened than under regulations imposing an outright ban.

Finally, an alternative to some kinds of choice-constraining policies would be for the government to pay the costs rather than consumers or business. If, for example, air bags in automobiles reduce medical expenses that society now pays through higher insurance premiums and medical costs, then air bags benefit the society as a whole. To the extent that it seems fair that those who benefit from a policy should pay for it, an argument can be made that society ought to pay for at least part of the cost of air bags through government subsidies.

These arguments do not imply that externalities should not count—they should. The point is that factors other than externalities should also count, and that alternatives to restrictive policies should also be considered. This implies that policy decisions have to be based on careful calculations rather than the mere fact that externalities exist.

The Rationality Argument

Social scientists frequently assume that individuals make their choices rationally. Thus, if a person rides in a car with the safety harness unfastened, smokes two packs of cigarettes daily, and spends the weekends hang-gliding, it is asserted that these hazardous choices have been made because in each case they have been perceived as "better" than any of the available alternatives. If this is the case, and if the impact of this behavior imposes no serious costs on the rest of society, then from a utilitarian point of view, the welfare of both the individual and the society is greatest if government does not regulate such behavior.

The problem is that even if individuals are rational in their selection of activities, the decisions may not be made in the light of full information about the probabilities of disaster related to each activity and they may not have been chosen using the most systematic decision process. If individuals suffer gaps in knowledge, they may make decisions for which they will later be sorry. In this case, there may be an argument for government regulation on the grounds of offsetting inadequacies in the decisionmaking process.

Decisions about unhealthy or unsafe behavior hinge on small probabilities (e.g., one chance in ten thousand) of unusual or unique experiences—such as severe disability or death. There is considerable evidence that suggests that individuals, in making such decisions, tend to be especially poor decisionmakers.[7] Beyond this, individuals are often locked into hazardous behavior by the enormously powerful momentum of habit. Smoking, overeating, overdrinking, lack of exercise, and consumption of certain kinds of drugs, for example, have two types of ill effects—they have a cumulatively negative effect on health and life expectancy, and in each case they also tend to make it increasingly difficult for individuals to change their behavior. Making a well-informed decision about how much to eat, smoke, and drink takes a particular type of foresight—the ability to consider future changes in one's own tastes induced by current behavior. Who would start smoking if it caused the immediate onset of emphysema? Yet many people who suffer from emphysema as a result of twenty years of smoking find they cannot stop.

In such cases of inefficient individual decisionmaking, however, government intervention is not necessarily justified—government intervention might produce an even less efficient outcome. Government bureaucracies often act in the interests of their own members or in accordance with the dictates of organizational behavior, rather than in society's best interests. Thus, there is no guarantee that governments will adopt cost-effective programs. Furthermore, given the nature of bureaucracies, paternalistic policies that are justified on utilitarian grounds may conceivably be an opening wedge for unjustified restrictions of individual liberty.

In addition to these well-known and important imperfections of government, there are two other major reasons government intervention may produce a less efficient outcome than unrestricted individual decisionmaking. First, the policy instruments available for government intervention are limited in effectiveness and are often blunt and inflexible. Consider, for example, the limits on government intervention regarding bad habits:

1. Government policy to stop the acquisition of bad health practices is more readily justified than policy that interferes with those who have already acquired these habits. Yet most feasible policy instruments are too blunt to distinguish veterans from novices.

2. Many substances (e.g., food) are not harmful when consumed in small quantities—the health problem comes from excess con-

sumption. How can policy distinguish between moderate and excessive users?

3. Enforcement of such regulations as bans on cigarettes and alcohol would place an extraordinary strain on the criminal justice system. In considering such legislation, the costs to the system and to individuals who are punished for violating such regulations must be included in the utilitarian calculus.

Second, governments, like individuals, do not have full information. Government agencies may have an advantage in terms of information concerning some aspects of unhealthy or risky behavior—for example, statistical information concerning frequency of deaths and injuries—but individuals may have better information concerning other aspects of their behavior, such as their own personal tastes and their willingness to reduce consumption in order to purchase reductions in low probabilities of death or injury.

To summarize, the point of this section is simply that it is not enough to argue that people are presumably rational and therefore self-hazardous behavior should not be restricted. Since some collective agency, like the government, might be able to gather and process information more effectively than individuals can, it is possible that, for some kinds of decisions, it would be more efficient for the government to decide for its citizens rather than allowing each citizen to make the decision individually. As is the case with externalities, whether or not government intervention will increase social welfare is a matter of careful cost-benefit analysis.

THE BENEFITS OF HEALTH
AND SAFETY REGULATION

The phrase "careful cost-benefit analysis" covers a lot of territory. Policy alternatives have to be designed. Effects have to be predicted. Costs and benefits have to be assessed—the easiest job is assessing monetary costs, but even this is devilishly difficult. And some decision analysis has to be done to synthesize the predictions and assessments in order to determine which of the alternatives is most desirable. Benefits are usually more difficult to assess than costs because we understand the relationship between policy, health, and safety so poorly. Even given some kind of reliable causal connection between a regulation and a desirable outcome, we must be able to compare outcomes having very different consequences. How does one compare, for example, a policy that reduces injury with one that reduces the probability of premature death? These issues are discussed in this section.

Lives versus Limbs

The benefits of health and safety regulations are the deaths, injuries, and illnesses that have been averted. However, frequently an administrator must choose between two policies, one of which may avert an expected 10,000 serious injuries and 500 expected premature deaths, while another may avert 1,000 premature deaths and 5,000 expected serious injuries. Given limited budgets, it is necessary for society to make choices in the policies it will implement and such choices implicitly require that the administrator be able to make a choice between averting deaths and serious injury. How can such choices be made?

Such trade-offs are often made implicitly, by some hidden process of judgment; occasionally they are explicit. The Consumer Product Safety Commission (CPSC), for example, uses an index that starts at 10 (for a sprained ankle) and goes up to 2,516 (for a serious injury or death) (Kelman 1974: especially pages 93−94). The index has been justly criticized. How can a serious injury be the equivalent in undesirability to a death? Is a death really equivalent in undesirability to 252 sprained ankles? Originally the CPSC's index assigned a value of 34,721 to a death, so that it was equivalent to 13.8 serious injuries and 3,472 sprained ankles. Perhaps this weighting seems more reasonable, but putting such a high weight on deaths implies that those policies aimed at averting death would almost always be preferred to policies intended to avert injury or lesser consequence. The CPSC decided that this weighting of deaths and injuries was therefore not reasonable and lowered the value of death. But is *this* reasonable? How lives should be weighted against limbs is an important and unresolved question in benefit analysis.

The Benefits of Averting a Death

Regardless of the exact trade-off between death and injury of lesser magnitude, it is clear that the single most important factor in evaluating the benefits of health and safety regulation is the number of deaths averted. Not surprisingly then, the question of the value of saving a life has received more attention than any other question related to benefits of health and safety policies. Much has been learned, but a great deal of controversy and uncertainty remains.

The most important point in the evaluation of the impact of regulation on mortality is that lives are never "saved" but only prolonged. Policies can avert early death, and hence can increase the number of years of life for some members of society. Public programs cannot, at least at current levels of knowledge, avert the inevitability of death. Therefore, for the purposes of policy analysis it is useful to evaluate the numbers of deaths averted in terms of mere numbers, but in terms of the various age groups they involve. From this perspective, reducing the incidence of early death is more important than simple comparisons of numbers of early and late deaths suggest, essentially because early death deprives an individual of life—and society of the individual—for more years than late death. In examining the losses from death, we can group them into two broad categories: losses to decedents and losses to surviving individuals. In both cases, the losses due to death tend to be more severe for early deaths.

Consider first the losses to decedents. Young persons whose lives are saved will generally receive a larger benefit than older people for two reasons. First, the young person receives a benefit of more years of life, and second, the quality of the years of life given him or her is probably higher than that of older people. As Swift wrote, "Every man desires to live long, but no man would be old."[8] To adjust for these factors, it has been proposed that the years of prolonged life be quality adjusted.[9]

Second, early death tends to impose greater costs on surviving individuals. All deaths cause sadness among friends and relatives, but death in older people is regarded as natural whereas for young people, tragic. Society thus generally regards the loss of an individual in the prime of life as more significant a social problem than the death of elderly people. Policies to reduce the possibility of the loss of the young are therefore likely to produce greater social benefits than those designed to prolong the life of the senior citizen. Early death also creates more adjustment problems for the decedent's family, which is deprived of the income or services of a mother or father, than is true in the event of the loss of a grandparent.

Finally, death also creates anxiety among the survivors who must contemplate their own mortality. A high rate of early death increases this anxiety. As Epictetus asked: "How are you desirous at the same time to live to old age, and not to see death of any person whom you love."[10]

In short, the losses due to death should be measured not in terms of the number of deaths but with some index that captures the amount of quality-adjusted life years lost and the amount of grief, social deprivation, and anxiety that results. Unfortunately, so little systematic research has been done on the exact nature and size of these losses that it is presently infeasible to devise a precise and persuasive index of this kind.

Monetary Measures of the Value of a Life

The "human capital" or "livelihood" measure of the loss due to a death is given by the discounted present-value of future earnings lost. It is by far the most commonly used formal method for assessing the value of reducing mortality. Although much criticized, the human-capital measure has some advantages—it is easily calculated and it may well have approximately the right shape over age. The measure assigns a moderate value to deaths in infancy, rises to a peak of above three times this value at roughly age thirty, and then tapers off to very low values in advanced old age.[11]

Used as a rough index to compare deaths at various ages, the human-capital measure may be satisfactory, but use of the measure to determine how much more valuable whites are than blacks, men than women, the rich than the poor, or college-graduates than high-school dropouts is, to say the least, highly controversial.

An alternative to the human-capital measure is the "willingness-to-pay" measure. Essentially, the value of a program that reduces the risk of death or injury is calculated by summing the amounts of money all the affected parties would be willing to pay for the program. This approach is conceptually appealing to many analysts, but the practical difficulties of carrying out the required surveys are so difficult that no adequate attempt has ever been made.

Some scattered theoretical and small-scale empirical efforts, however, tend to indicate that the willingness-to-pay measure, if it could be calculated, may well place the value of saving lives twice as high, and possibly ten or more times as high, as the human-capital measure. To the extent that this is true and to the extent that the willingness-to-pay measure more adequately captures the benefits of saving lives, the reliance on the human-capital measure may be leading to substantial underestimates of the benefits of health and safety regulation.

Equity and Distribution

Cost-benefit analyses of the effect of policies on aggregate social welfare are commonly supplemented by some analyses of distributional impacts. To many, the question of who gets what is as important as the question of whether society as a whole is made better off. The concern here is about "equity," which may be a concern about equality, or about fairness. This section considers five issues concerning equity that are of special importance in the evaluation of the benefits of public health and safety policies:

1. The distinction between process equity and outcome equity.
2. The equity rationale for absolute prohibitions and requirements.
3. The equity of the distribution among individuals of the direct benefits and costs of a policy.
4. The equity of valuing different lives differently.
5. The equity of the process for deciding how and whether to save lives and limbs.

Process versus Outcome Equity.   The costs of too-safe behavior are relatively small per person and are more or less evenly distributed among the people who choose or who are required to be too safe. The costs of hazardous behavior, on the other hand, are extremely high and are concentrated on the few unfortunate people who die or are disabled.

Consider, for example, the decision whether to fasten a seat belt on some particular car ride. There may be only one chance in a million that a fastened seat belt will be of any use. Fastening the seat belt may be somewhat troublesome and once fastened, may feel uncomfortable. Consequently, for some people it may be fully rational not to fasten seat belts. If these people are numerous enough and if the people who erroneously fail to fasten their seat belts are few enough, then it may not be efficient to require people to fasten their seat belts.

However, such nonintervention will lead to very unequal outcomes: those people without fastened seat belts who do survive without injury will be slightly better off as a result of not having to obey an arbitrary government regulation; those who die will be infinitely worse off. This asymmetry calls attention to the difference between process and outcome. An equitable process that allows individuals to decide for themselves whether to engage in risky behavior may lead to extremely unequal outcomes. To avoid this kind of outcome inequality, society may prefer to prohibit some kinds of hazardous behavior, even if, at the time the hazardous decision is being made, the aggregate benefits are not quite worth the aggregate costs. Indeed, if concern for outcome equality is sufficiently great, society might be willing to prohibit hazardous behavior that is fully rational for every individual—thus violating that most hallowed of economists' tenets, the Pareto Principle.[12] How important concern for outcome equality is to the American people is a largely unanswered question that deserves attention.

The Equity Rationale for Absolute Requirements.   There seems to be a strongly held feeling in some quarters that in certain areas of health and safety the rich, clever, or determined should not be allowed to do what the poor, less clever, or less determined are denied. For example, when Illinois banned the sale of certified raw milk, no exceptions were made for people who strongly favored drinking such milk, who were willing to sign an affidavit testifying that they understood the risks they were taking, or who were willing to pay any resulting medical costs themselves. In a similar vein, the proposal that a high tax be imposed on cigarettes has been opposed as inequitable compared with a ban on cigarettes, as a high tax would discourage the poor from smoking more than the rich.

In this last example, the feeling is that the rich should not be allowed to engage in self-hazardous behavior that is denied to (or, at least, is more restricted to) the poor. In some other examples, the feeling is that the poor should not be allowed to engage in self-hazardous behavior that the rich might not engage in. For instance if air bags in automobiles are optional, the proportion of people buying them would probably decline with income. As a result some poor people would lose their lives. This seems inequitable. But while that may be true, it is not a sufficient reason for requiring everyone to invest in some health or safety good. Such a policy may make poor people even worse off by forcing them to buy something that they would rather not buy and perhaps (if a careful decision analysis were done) that they should not buy, given their other pressing needs, and the present unequal distribution of wealth.

The Distribution of Direct Net Benefits.   The two previous equity arguments favored choice-constricting policies; there is a third equity argument that runs against such policies. For example, consider again the requirement that air bags be installed on all cars. The basic issue is whether low risk consumers (those who do not drive very much, drive safely, faithfully fasten their safety harnesses when they drive, etc.) should be forced to pay for air bags simply because there are some high risk drivers. As a second example, consider a ban on cigarette smoking. Smoking apparently is of little risk to those who smoke infrequently and to those who start smoking late in life. Should the pleasure of smoking be denied to a prudent sixty-year-old who would like to begin having a single cigarette after dinner in order to prevent a reckless sixteen-year-old from smoking two packs per day?

The basic question here concerns the distribution of net benefits. Even if aggregate net benefits are positive, a policy may be undesirable if some individuals gain most of the benefits while other individuals gain little or no benefit but suffer substantial costs. Equity considerations of this sort favor less choice-constricting policies. In the case of air bags, for example, consumer education or public provision of air bags would be suggested. Similarly, in the case of cigarette smoking, consumer education or a heavy paternalistic tax might be indicated.

The Allocation of Death and Disability.   The resources society spends on saving lives and limbs are not allocated equally—more is spent on some people than on others. The wealthy drive safer cars and receive better medical treatment than the poor. The well-educated make better use of life-prolonging programs than the poorly educated. The federal government pays for renal dialysis but not for treatment of hemophilia. Society may spend millions of dollars to rescue a trapped coal miner while it does not spend a million dollars to build a railroad overpass to save ten, currently unidentified, lives.

These differential expenditures imply that society acts as if different people's lives were of different worth. This seems inequitable.

But what weight should be given to this consideration in determining how much of its scarce resources society should spend to avert the deaths and illnesses of different kinds of people in different situations?

Process as Part of the Outcome. The optimal amount and allocation of health and safety expenditures depend not only on the outcome of such expenditures in terms of deaths and illnesses averted and resources spent, but also on the process by which the expenditure decisions are made. One process, even if it saves more lives at less cost, may be inferior if it seems illegitimate, indecent, unjust, or inequitable, or if it seems to deny the sacredness and "pricelessness" of human life. For example, cost-benefit studies may show that society spends millions of dollars to prolong, for a few months at most, the lives of the victims of some exotic disease, while ten thousand dollars will not be spent to put a traffic light at a deadly intersection. While such a resource allocation is inefficient, it is also symbolically important not to let a hospitalized person die because of financial constraints.

In short, it may be optimal for society to adopt an inefficient resource-allocation process (i.e., to sacrifice lives and resources), if this process preserves important symbolic values and meets various legal, constitutional, moral, and cultural constraints. This said, the question still remains: Is a more efficient process for allocating life-prolonging expenditures possible within the present framework of values and constraints?

CONCLUSION

It is clear that we could substantially, if gradually, reduce the tragically high incidence of death, disability, and illness in the United States—but it is not clear how. The desirability of any particular health and safety policy can be determined only by careful prediction of its effects with regard to the following triple criteria: efficiency (aggregate social welfare), equity (the distribution of costs and benefits), and liberty (the right of an individual to make choices, independent of the wisdom of what is chosen). To determine better how best to allocate politically and economically constrained resources, far more cost-benefit analysis should be done. There are some important unresolved questions concerning how this analysis should be accomplished—these perplexing questions diminish but by no means negate the value of analysis. One particularly puzzling set of questions concerns how the benefits of health and safety regulations should be addressed. These questions include:

- How should externalities be handled?
- How good are individuals at making health and safety decisions?
- What is the trade-off between lives and limbs?
- What is the value of a life?
- What is the importance of various kinds of equity and distribution considerations?

The following chapters are intended to help to clarify and resolve some of these important questions.

NOTES TO CHAPTER 1

1. These various statistics are from *Health, U.S.A. 1976–1977* (Public Health Service 1977).
2. See Vaupel (1978: 19 and 20) for references to this literature.
3. Extrapolated from Vaupel (1978: 127).
4. "Department of Transportation and Related Agencies Appropriations for 1978: Hearings before a Subcommittee of the Committee on Appropriations, House of Representatives, 95th Congress, First Session," Part 1: Hearings on the National Transportation Safety Board: 185–194.
5. See Vaupel (1978: 73–118) for a survey.
6. Noted in *Current Public Policy Research* (November 1977: 1–2).
7. See Tversky and Kahneman (1974: 1124–1131); Simon (1969: Chapter 2); Behn and Vaupel (1976); Vaupel and Cook (1978).
8. Jonathan Swift, "Thoughts on Various Subjects," quoted in Bartlett, *Familiar Quotations* (1955: 295).
9. See Zeckhauser and Shepard (1976) for further discussion of this point.
10. Epictetus, *Discourses*, III, 24, quoted in Adler and Van Doren, *Great Treasury of Western Thought* (1977: 40).
11. See Cooper and Rice (1976: 21–36) and, for a critique, Acton (1976).
12. Cf. Keeney and Raiffa (1976: 532–536).

BIBLIOGRAPHY

Acton, Jan. 1976. "Valuing Lifesaving—Alternatives and Some Measurements." *Law and Contemporary Problems* 40, no. 4 (Autumn).

Behn, Robert D., and James W. Vaupel. 1976. "Why Decision Analysis is Rarely Used and How It Can Be." Institute of Policy Sciences and Public Affairs, Duke University. Unpublished paper.

Cooper, Barbara S., and Dorothy P. Rice. 1976. "The Economic Cost of Illness Revisited." *Social Security Bulletin* (February): 21–36.

Crout, J. Richard. 1975. "Discussion." In *Drug Development and Marketing*, edited by Robert B. Helms. Washington, D.C.

Current Public Policy Research. 1977. II, no. 2 (November): 1–2.

"Department of Transportation and Related Agencies Appropriations for 1978: Hearings before a Subcommittee of the Committee on Appropriations, House of Representatives, 95th Congress, First Session." Part 1: Hearings on the National Transportation Safety Board, pp. 185–194. Washington, D.C.: Government Printing Office.

Epictetus, *Discourses*, III, 24. In *Great Treasury of Western Thought*, edited by Mortimer J. Adler and Charles Van Doren, p. 40. New York: Bowker, 1977.

Keeney, Ralph L., and Howard Raiffa. 1976. *Decisions with Multiple Objectives.* New York: Wiley.

Kelman, Steven. 1974. "Regulation by the Numbers—A Report on the Consumer Product Safety Commission." *The Public Interest* no. 36 (Summer): 83–102.

"Kennedy Backs Delay in Saccharine Ban, Seeks 18 Months for Study of Drug Law." 1977. *Wall Street Journal* (June 13): 4, column 1.

Medical and Health Information Directory. 1977. Detroit: Gale Research Company.

National Center for Health Statistics. 1978. "Final Mortality Statistics, 1976." *Monthly Vital Statistics Report* 26, no. 12 (March 30).

Nozick, Robert. 1974. *Anarchy, State and Utopia.* New York: Basic Books.

Public Health Service. 1977. *Health, U.S.A. 1976–1977.* Washington, D.C.: Government Printing Office.

Simon, Herbert A. 1969. *The Science of the Artificial.* Cambridge, Mass.: M.I.T. Press.

Swift, Jonathan, "Thoughts on Various Subjects." In *Familiar Quotations*, 13th ed., edited by John Bartlett, p. 295. Boston: Little, Brown, 1955.

Tversky, Amos, and Daniel Kahneman. 1974. "Judgment under Uncertainty: Heuristics and Biases." *Science* 185, no. 4157 (September 27): 1124–1131.

Vaupel, James W. 1978. "The Prospects for Saving Lives." Institute of Policy Sciences and Public Affairs, Duke University.

Vaupel, James W., and Philip J. Cook. 1978. "Life, Liberty and the Pursuit of Self-Hazardous Behavior." Institute of Policy Sciences and Public Affairs, Duke University. Unpublished paper.

Zeckhauser, Richard, and Donald Shepard. 1976. "Where Now for Saving Lives." *Law and Contemporary Problems* 40, no. 4 (Autumn).

INFORMATION AND
BENEFIT ASSESSMENT

2 DESCRIPTIVE AND PRESCRIPTIVE ASPECTS OF HEALTH AND SAFETY REGULATION

Paul R. Kleindorfer*
Howard Kunreuther*

There has been a lively debate in recent years over the benefits and costs of regulating products that affect the health and safety of the population. Those who favor regulation contend that specific directives are necessary to protect uninformed consumers and workers from the health and safety hazards of products that they use and produce. Those opposed to regulation claim that it restricts consumers' and producers' freedom and leads to inefficient allocation of society's resources. For example, in the case of the introduction of new prescription drugs, those favoring strong regulation by the Food and Drug Administration (FDA) claim that it is necessary because the complexity of modern drugs precludes full knowledge by doctors and patients of the safety and efficacy of these products. Those opposed to governmental intervention argue that drug companies themselves have powerful incentives to exercise care in introducing new drugs and that increased safety regulation will only hinder product innovation.[1]

Economists have found it much easier to develop a case against regulation than for it since the costs associated with regulation are more explicit than the benefits. This chapter takes a step in redressing this balance by proposing a framework that emphasizes the impacts that limited information or misinformation have on behavior.

*Both authors are Professors of Decision Sciences at the University of Pennsylvania.

25

When the decision process is formally considered as part of the problem, regulation may turn out to be a more attractive alternative than it otherwise would seem.

The merits of health and safety regulation can be better appreciated if we consider the interrelationship between descriptive models and prescriptive policy analysis. The descriptive models characterize the actual decision process of consumers and firms in response to particular policies. They are a fundamental input to the prescriptive phase, which is concerned with the evaluation of the social merits of alternative policies. We now summarize these two phases, indicating problems of interest to policymakers:

Descriptive Phase. Given any specific problem, this phase provides a description of the historical context of the problem as well as of the institutional arrangements that define informational and authority relationships among parties involved. A historical perspective often provides insight into why policymakers have questioned whether normal market mechanisms or other existing arrangements are working sufficiently well. For example, the 1962 Amendments to the Food, Drug, and Cosmetic Act, which tightened drug regulations, were stimulated by the adverse effects the use of thalidomide by pregnant mothers had on the babies. These changes in legislation are at the heart of the current controversy over the appropriate role of the FDA in regulating new prescription drugs.

Perhaps the most important aspect of descriptive analysis, and certainly the most neglected, is understanding the decision processes of each of the actors involved. We define decision processes here to mean the collection, processing, and dissemination of specific types of information in determining and promoting a specific course of action. A central focus in this chapter is the interaction between process and policy. To illustrate this, consider the problem of evaluating proposals regarding seat belts. It is clearly important to understand how consumers evaluate the probability and losses associated with wearing or not wearing a seat belt so that we can predict the likely impact or behavior of different measures.

Fortunately we know considerably more today about the decision processes of individuals than we did a decade ago. Recent empirical studies in field and in controlled laboratory settings have shed light on the behavioral processes associated with collecting and utilizing information and the impact that these phenomena are likely to have on policy prescriptions. In particular, Tversky and Kahneman (1974) have shown that individuals exhibit systematic biases in their processing of information. One of these biases, availability, implies that individuals judge the probability of an event by the ease with which they remember similar past events. Such a heuristic implies that past experience will be a critical variable in individual decisionmaking. This finding suggests that individuals are likely to underestimate their chances of being affected in the future by low-probability events that have not personally affected them in the past. Calabresi (1970: 56) makes a similar point by observing that "such things always happen to the other guy and no amount of statistical information can ever convince the individual that they can happen to him."

In discussing problems of product safety, Fischhoff (1977) suggests that individuals tend to ignore information about overall accident rates because they feel they are different or more careful. He cites studies that reveal that 75 to 90 percent of the drivers believe that they are better than average drivers, and that if they have had an accident it was the other person's fault.

In evaluating the decision processes of individuals and firms it is also relevant to learn from what sources decision-aiding information is obtained. The extensive literature on the diffusion of innovations (see Rogers and Shoemaker 1975) indicates that the mass media are normally the initial source of knowledge about a product, but that information from more personal sources is usually obtained prior to its adoption. This pattern of behavior is one consistent with one of the classic studies in this area, Coleman, Katz, and Menzel (1966), on the adoption of a new medical drug by doctors in four midwestern communities. The study indicates that salesmen and direct mail were the most frequent source of original knowledge about the drug, but just prior to adoption the doctor was most likely to seek out a colleague or consult a professional journal article. Another general finding in the empirical literature on innovations is that individuals are reluctant to spend much time collecting and processing information. The accuracy of their own data to a large extent will be dependent on those of their colleagues and friends. From a prescriptive point of view these findings suggest that informal contacts may play at least as important a role in providing information as the market system.

Finally, there is literature emerging that indicates that individual attitudes toward risk are affected by the way information is diffused and processed. Kunreuther et al. (1978), in a field survey of 3,000 homeowners in flood- and earthquake-prone areas, found that people's decisions to purchase insurance were determined by past experience and interpersonal contact with other policyholders rather than by a comparison of the event in relation to the benefits of insurance. In a complementary set of controlled laboratory experiments on insurance, Slovic et al. (1977), found that individuals preferred to insure themselves against high probability, low loss events rather than against catastrophes that had a very small chance of occurrence. These findings imply that individuals may view uncertainty and risk in a different way than has traditionally been assumed by economists. They also have important implications with respect to the benefits of regulations, as discussed below.

Prescriptive Analysis. To undertake any prescriptive analysis one first has to specify a set of alternative policies that the government may want to consider. Regulatory policies may involve assessing the quality of a product (e.g., new drugs) or imposing a set of standards on the manufacturer (e.g., requiring the installation of a specific type of seat belt in new cars). At the other end of the spectrum, the government can decide to do nothing to encourage or hinder specific actions by the supplier. Between these two extremes the policymaker may want to design a set of informational and price incentives to promote specific behavior.

Once a set of policies has been specified, it is then necessary to use the results of the descriptive phase to understand and evaluate the consequences of each alternative for different individuals. We cannot overemphasize the importance of this phase of the analysis. For example, suppose a case for more stringent drug regulation was based on the assumption that consumers and doctors are less informed on the safety of these products than the drug manufacturers, who then take advantage of their superior knowledge in pursuit of profit. The policymaker needs to know whether or not such asymmetric information exists and if so, whether the predicted behavior by the manufacturer actually occurs.

As a final step in the prescriptive phase it is necessary to evaluate the set of alternative policies and make a choice. The outcome of this process clearly depends on how the preferences of individual consumers or firms are weighted in determining a social ranking of alternatives. If, for example, policies are evaluated by one individual, then the ranking procedure and the outcome may be considerably different from the one determined by a group involving some or all of the affected parties or several government agencies. Before policymakers can predict the consequences of different alternatives they must understand what behavioral rules individuals and firms follow. Maximizing expected utility or profit is such a rule—the one normally assumed by economists. In practice, individuals may follow rules of thumb or other heuristics that economize on information and produce a different set of responses than those predicted by utility theory.

Individuals also may be misinformed on the consequences of their decisions. The framework developed in the next section recognizes two phenomena concerning misinformation by consumers: felicity in error and decision by default. We will discuss each of these concepts below as they may have important implications for prescriptive analysis.

The first consequence of being misinformed, *felicity in error,* occurs when a person chooses actions on the basis of incorrect information, which he or she later regrets when more accurate information is revealed (e.g., when the *actual* consequences of the decision become manifest). We have used the term "felicity" here since the empirical evidence suggests that people tend to misperceive and underestimate negative consequences, especially when the events leading to them occur infrequently. An informed policymaker may have the correct information with which to evaluate the ex post consequences of these individuals' actions; and, if losses due to misinformation are sufficiently high, the policymaker may choose an action that provides individuals and firms with an incentive to act more in consonance with the true consequences than they otherwise might. For example, consider individuals who do not wear seat belts because they consider the probability of having an accident as being so small as to be negligible. Some of these individuals will be victims, much to their dismay, as well as society's. Policymakers may consider these losses to be sufficiently high that they provide incentives to consumers or the automobile industry to promote the wearing of seat belts. This could take the form of a fine, should a person be caught on the road with an unbuckled seat belt, or the government could pass a regulation requiring the installation of passive seat belts that automatically buckle up when you sit in the car.

The second concept we have termed *decision by default.* You may want to speculate on the number of individuals who do not even consider the consequences of some of the actions they take. Why do they avoid a decision? Is it desirable to change their behavior? If so, can one change their actions through specific information or incentive systems, or is regulation a more desirable alternative? We will return to these questions after we develop a more explicit characterization of the social choice problem.

A FRAMEWORK FOR ANALYSIS

We begin here to set out a framework for dealing with some of the issues raised above. Consider a benevolent, selfless policymaker who is trying to determine in what ways, if any, the government should intervene in the provision of some good. Aside from the *government*, represented by our policymaker, the following actors also play a role: the *supply industry*, which produces the good; the *consuming public*; and finally, the *nonconsuming paying public* who help finance the costs of government intervention but receive no direct benefits from the provision of the good.

The problem confronting the policymaker is to select an action that reflects the values of the society. There are obviously a number of problems in choosing between alternative policies. First, some measure(s) of welfare must be agreed upon to help rank alternative policies. Second, since such welfare measures can be expected to depend on the actual behavior of consumers and industry, one must also understand what each actor's behavioral response to alternative governmental policies will be. These problems of representation of welfare and of predicting behavioral adjustment are central to public policy analysis. Therefore, before proceeding, it may be instructive to sketch the traditional framework for dealing with these issues.[2]

In the traditional approach of neoclassical economics, individuals and firms are assumed to be rational.[3] This means that each person or firm (labelled i below) acts as if it were maximizing utility or felicity. Such felicity depends on

x = typical consumer's behavior;

y = typical firm's behavior;

z = government policy;

s = uncertain state of the world.

For each individual or firm i, felicity is expressed by a utility function $U_i(x, y, z, s)$. A simple example will serve to illustrate what is involved here. In the case of health insurance, x might represent the amount of coverage purchased by the typical consumer, y the premium charged by the insurance industry, and z a governmental policy variable representing, for example, guarantees on catastrophic losses. The variables would then represent the probabilities and consequences of contracting various diseases. According to the standard model of rationality, consumers and firms estimate such probabilities and consequences reasonably accurately and use these data in determining optimal levels of coverage and in designing optimal premium schedules.

With the above general assumptions concerning behavior we may summarize the traditional approach as follows:

Descriptive Phase. Suppose the government fixes the policy z and that, for its given policy, consumer and industry perceptions of probabilities and consequences of outcomes are given by $s = s(z)$. In response to z and s consumers and industry adjust their behavior until a steady-state or equilibrium behavior is achieved. We denote this equilibrium by $(x, y) = (x(z, s), y(z, s))$ to convey its dependence on z and s. The adjustment process is typically characterized by assuming that actors behave as if they were maximizing their expected felicity (as measured by $U_i(x, y, z, s,)$), taking everyone else's behavior as fixed. This explains how x, y, and z are determined. The so-called ex ante felicity[4] is just the expected felicity each actor experiences, given his or her perceptions. The felicity, or misfortune, actually experienced by each actor is realized when the previously uncertain state s becomes known. The basic data required for the traditional descriptive analysis are the perceptions and associated utility functions of each party. Given this information, all else is assumed to follow as per the above scenario.

Prescriptive Phase. The traditional theory assumes that each economic agent involved is the best judge of his or her own felicity. Therefore, the choice of a socially optimal policy is based on a measure of welfare, denoted W below, which depends on x, y, z and s only through the utility functions of the actors involved. If we label these actors $1, 2, \ldots, N$, a simple measure of welfare would be just the sum of the utility functions of all the actors, that is,

$$W = U_1(x, y, z, s) + U_2(x, y, z, s) + \ldots + U_N(x, y, z, s),$$

where the utilities in the above welfare function are to be evaluated ex ante based on the expected behavior $(x(z, s), y(z, s))$ in response to the policy z and ex ante perceptions s. There are, of course, many problems in choosing a welfare function and these issues have been the subject of considerable debate in the economics literature.[5] The literature seems to be in general agreement on one important point, however: the utilities in the welfare function are evaluated under the assumption that individuals and firms are well-informed and rational.

Now, as we indicated in the first part of the chapter, there is growing evidence that many individuals and firms are neither well-informed nor rational. Therefore, it seems important to inquire how departures from these assumptions might influence the analysis and conclusions of this theory and what the implications of these findings are for regulatory policies. Two implications are immediate in this regard. First, consumer and industry behavioral responses to particular policies will change if their decision processes or perceptions change. Since the welfare function, W, is evaluated on the basis of expected behavior, we see that such process changes have implications for the outcome of policy analysis. For example, if many individuals underestimate the chances of certain low probability events, they may not take voluntary protective action (e.g., purchase insurance) where objective data would suggest this to be an attractive option. Second, if consumers or firms are misinformed, reasonable objections can be raised to evaluating policies solely in terms of the expected felicity as expressed by these consumers and firms themselves. That is, some form of regulation may be called for to counteract misinformation.

To illustrate these remarks we will focus on departures from the rational-man model due to misinformation, but we will continue to assume that each actor behaves as if he or she were maximizing expected felicity as measured by a utility function $U_i(x, y, z, s)$. Thus, the only change we will make from a technical point of view is to assume that each actor may have different perceptions of s and that some of these may be inaccurate. Obviously many other departures from the rational-man model on the decision process side are also possible, but we will neglect them here. Two phenomena are of some interest under these circumstances.

Felicity in Error. The actors misperceive the consequences of uncertain states, usually optimistially.

Decision by Default. The actors do not understand the relationships between their actions, possible states of the world, and their felicity, and end up maximizing ex ante expected utility by choosing a null decision (e.g., the do-nothing decision). Although decision by default could have deeper psychological grounds, we will treat it here, like felicity in error, as being purely the result of misinformation about the probabilities and consequences of uncertain states of the world.

We may now proceed directly to the prescriptive phase by assuming that the traditional theory still holds as the descriptive model of choice but that the consumers are either misinformed or uninformed about the uncertain states of the world. In this case we will want to tabulate not only the ex ante expected welfare as viewed by consumers but also the actual levels that they obtain given the policymaker's assumptions about probabilities and consequences of outcomes. In determining a socially optimal policy a trade-off must be made between the consumers' felicity in error and the policymaker's estimate of "felicity in fact." The concept of felicity in fact is simply the expected social welfare evaluated using actual probabilities and consequences of states of the world.

A simple example should clarify the difference between felicity in error and felicity in fact. Consider the problem of evaluating whether a passive restraint feature such as air bags should be required as standard equipment for all new automobiles. Suppose that the welfare measure of interest is the expected number of fatalities per year.[6] Table 2–1 presents illustrative data for this case. For each of the two alternatives (mandatory versus optional installation of air bags), we tabulate the welfare consequences of different informational patterns (evaluating welfare by using the behavior of the average consumer).[7] For ease of exposition we neglect the automobile industry in this analysis and assume, moreover, that all consumers share the same (mis-)information.

Consider Part A of Table 2–1. When consumers evaluate the probability of a dangerous accident as $\hat{p} = .001$, they will behave (i.e., they will drive and use active safety restraints) in such a way that expected welfare, as they see it, will be $W_E = 9$.

Suppose, on the other hand, that consumers estimate the probability of a dangerous accident to be $\hat{p} = .001$ when in reality our policymaker Zeus knows that it is $p = .002$. In this case consumers' estimate of fatalities remains at $W_E = 9$ while the actual figure has now

Table 2-1. Illustrating welfare analysis when actors are misinformed.

A. Air Bags Mandatory			B. Air Bags Optional		
	ZI			*ZI*	
CI	$p = .001$	$p = .002$	*CI*	$p = .001$	$p = .002$
$\hat{p} = .001$	$W_E = 9$	$W_E = 9$	$\hat{p} = .001$	$W_E = 15$	$W_E = 15$
	$W_F = 9$	$W_F = 20$		$W_F = 15$	$W_F = 33$
$\hat{p} = .002$	$W_E = 15$	$W_E = 15$	$\hat{p} = .002$	$W_E = 25$	$W_E = 25$
	$W_F = 8$	$W_F = 15$		$W_F = 12$	$W_F = 25$

Key:

p = actual probability of a dangerous accident (per auto/per year)

$\hat{p}$ = consumer's estimated probability of a dangerous accident (per auto/per year)

CI = consumer's information or beliefs

ZI = Zeus's information

W_E and W_F are estimated and actual fatalities per year in thousands

increased to $W_F = 20$. A similar explanation applies to other entries in Table 2-1. In constructing these figures we have assumed that consumers drive more carelessly as their estimate of p decreases, thus compounding the welfare losses. This assumption is reflected in Table 2-1 by the higher actual fatalities (W_F) when $\hat{p} = .001$ than when $\hat{p} = .002$. As we have stressed throughout the chapter, all welfare measures (W_E and W_F) are based on the actual behavior followed by consumers.[8]

To finish this example, we may ask what action a policymaker should take here. To make matters simple we will assume that the policymaker knows that $p = .002$ and that $\hat{p} = .001$. Then from Table 2-1 the following welfare measures are relevant for policy choice:

Air Bags Mandatory	Air Bags Optional
$W_E = 9$, $W_F = 20$	$W_E = 15$, $W_F = 33$

The consumers estimate that 6,000 lives will be saved per year if air bags are mandatory whereas, in fact, 13,000 will be saved. At an add-on price of, say $100, the citizenry might be willing to make air bags mandatory, if it knew and believed the actual figures, but it might be opposed to such action in its current, misinformed state. In this instance, the policymaker would have to determine how much weight to give to consumers' felicity in error and how much to give to their felicity in fact in deciding whether to push for mandatory installation of air bags or not.[9] One would expect that a decision to go against current opinion (i.e., put a high weight on W_F relative to W_E) would be accompanied by an information campaign to attempt to correct the misinformation or probability of fatalities and provide a rationale for the new regulation. For example, one might encourage a better appreciation of the dangers of automobile driving over a twenty-year period than over a period of one year. Support for this conjecture comes from Slovic et al. (1977) who found that subjects were more willing to appreciate the importance of wearing seat belts when presented with the probabilities of death and injury on 40,000 trips rather than with those probabilities on a single trip.

In summary, the basic thrust of our framework is that the actual behavioral rules and beliefs of agents involved, and not some hoped for rationality, must be the basis of policy prescription. In capsule form, the procedure we suggest would entail the following steps:

1. For each alternative, predict consumer behavior and likely consumer beliefs.
2. Determine expected welfare as estimated by the various actors involved (W_E) and as viewed by an omniscient observer (W_F) under various possible conditions.
3. Depending on the accuracy of the policymaker's information, a trade-off between W_E and W_F is performed and policy choice proceeds accordingly.[10]

The trade-off between W_E and W_F is, of course, not a simple matter. A major issue here is to determine what is politically feasible in persuading a reluctant public to take medicine for a disease it does not believe it has. Also important is who has to bear the costs of felicity in error, the consumers, or, primarily, the nonconsuming paying public. In a similar vein, it would be easier to make a credible case for disregarding felicity in error if it resulted from behavior and beliefs that reflected primarily decision by default rather than if it were the result of firmly held beliefs. In the next section we speculate further on these points and offer a few hypotheses on the implications of the above framework for regulatory policy.

IMPLICATIONS OF FRAMEWORK FOR REGULATION

The framework developed and illustrated in the previous section suggests that policy analysis must be based on the actual decision processes and beliefs of the economic agents involved. In particular, if individuals or firms underestimate the probability or consequences of negative events, or do not estimate them at all, then their felicity in error, or their ignorance, must be accounted for in policy evaluation and choice.

This viewpoint complements recent work by economists on policy problems associated with imperfect information. Up until now, past studies have focused on situations where the supply industry is assumed to know less than consumers. This is the case, for example, in problems of adverse selection, which is frequently cited as a reason for market failure. As explained by Arrow (1963) and Akerlof (1970), adverse selection in, for example, health insurance, exists because coverage at any given premium will be demanded primarily by the group in poorest health. This results in a selected biased sample with consequences for the insurance industry.

The main thrust of this chapter has been to add to the list of informational problems for market imperfections those problems associated with misprocessing and nonprocessing by consumers. The empirical evidence discussed previously suggests that such "nonrational" behavior may be quite common, especially for low probability, complex events such as those involving health and safety hazards. The question of whether the government ought to move to reduce or underwrite the resulting felicity in error is one of the major issues raised here. In addressing this question, let us first list a few attributes that may be important in this regard:

1. The complexity of the product or hazard considered;
2. The magnitude of potential losses, and especially, whether human life is at stake;
3. The degree to which the results of misprocessing or nonprocessing of information are borne by decisionmakers as opposed to noninvolved taxpayers; and

4. The familiarity of consumers and firms with the product or hazard involved.

Let us now turn to some hypotheses on the government's role in dealing with "nonrational" behavior. In formulating these, when we speak of stronger or weaker government intervention, we will have in mind the following hierarchy of possible interventions:

1. Informational intervention—collecting and disseminating information to consumers and firms;
2. Positive incentives—payouts by the government to induce certain behavior;
3. Negative incentives—fines and special taxes levied to discourage certain behavior; and
4. Formal directives or regulations: laws requiring specific behavior.

Now to a few hypotheses. These are to be viewed as preliminary and provocative only, intending to stimulate discussion and research on the potential benefits of regulation.

Hypothesis 1: The more complex a product or hazard is, and the less familiar it is, the more likely consumers will opt for decision by default, and the more receptive they will be to some form of governmental intervention.

A prime example of this is prescription drugs. Since neither consumers nor doctors are in a position to evaluate new products, strong FDA regulations may be viewed as desirable. With respect to automobile safety, a nationwide public opinion survey by the Institute for Highway Safety in July 1976 indicated that 77 percent of car-buying Americans favored an increase in crash protection that would be completely, or at least partially, automatic.

A corollary to this hypothesis is that protective measures are not likely to be voluntarily adopted by consumers unless they perceive the probability of the occurrence of some hazardous event to be above a threshold level. The lack of interest in voluntarily purchasing flood or earthquake insurance, wearing seat belts, or engaging in preventive health activities is consistent with this conjecture.

Hypothesis 2: As individuals' perceived probability of an event decreases, they will tend to reduce their estimates of the ex ante loss from an accident or disaster. Furthermore, their ex post valuations following an event will be greater than their ex ante estimates.

This hypothesis implies that for low probability events individuals will underestimate the potential losses to themselves or their property. In such cases we would expect felicity in error to be much lower than felicity in fact. A person would thus be expected to estimate the cost of an injury in an automobile accident to be much lower prior to its occurrence than after it happened. Oi (1976), in his discussion of product safety problems, makes the point that an individual attaches a much higher value to his or her arm after losing it in an accident than when accepting the lower risks prior to the accident.

Hypothesis 3:   The higher the impact of felicity in error or decision by default on the nonconsuming paying public, the more ready society will be to disregard uninformed felicity in favor of (society's) felicity in fact, and to accept stronger governmental intervention.

Thus society is willing to have government play only an informational role with respect to cigarette smoking, yet a much stronger role in dealing with other habit-forming drugs (e.g., heroin). This is both because of the more serious consequences of hard drugs for the individual as well as because the nonconsuming paying public ends up, as a victim of drug-related crime, footing the bill for many addicts.

Hypothesis 4:   The greater the perceived catastrophic potential (in terms of lives lost suddenly through no proximate fault of their own) and the greater the frequency of a hazard, the more willing society is to accept governmental intervention.

This hypothesis reflects the empirical results of Otway et al. (1978) and of Slovic et al. (1978) concerning individuals and societal evaluations of risk. Based on experimental studies, these authors conclude that social opposition to hazards, which we will equate to social willingness to have the government intervene, is primarily a function of perceived frequency of occurrence and catastrophic potential (e.g., nuclear power hazards) and is not affected by judgments of social cost.

The above hypotheses are intended to illustrate when misprocessing and misinformation may be expected to occur and when government regulation may be beneficial and socially acceptable. These hypotheses require further empirical testing. As a prelude to such research, the following reflections may be useful.

First, it may be safely assumed that there are real benefits to an unhealthy life style. Some smokers confronted with the option of giving up the habit and adding a number of years to their lives, may process this data (perhaps incorrectly) and then decide that they enjoy cigarettes enough to want to continue smoking. Similar arguments could be raised with respect to the decision by some individuals not to wear seat belts because of an uncomfortable feeling they may have of being strapped in. Both the individual and society may have to pay a price for this ex ante behavior in the ex post world. A principal justification for regulation and government incentives would be to bring ex ante and ex post felicity into greater balance. In doing so, however, the policymaker should determine when this "ex ante–ex post" difference is due to an informed choice of an unhealthy lifestyle and when it is due to felicity in error or decision by default. Regulation will be less desirable if a conscious decision is made by consumers to follow unhealthy or unsafe lifestyles.

A second caveat concerns the level of expert's knowledge concerning uncertain events. As Holdren (1976) indicated in discussing nuclear power hazards, there may be just as wide a level of practical uncertainty for experts as for laymen about highly uncertain events. In the absence of sufficient experience to provide reasonable estimates of probabilities and consequences, policymakers would do well to recognize their own information and process limitations. The same caveat extends, of course, to policymakers' knowledge about constituent values (measures of utility or felicity) and perceptions of risk. Regulation will become a less desirable alternative as policymakers' knowledge of uncertain events becomes more uncertain.

As a final point, our analysis above discusses gaps between actual and imagined felicity as though these were fixed. In fact, however, one of the first steps a policymaker might undertake is to narrow such gaps through information dissemination programs.[11] Before developing such strategies for coping with informational distortions, the policymaker should identify the nature and magnitude of these errors and their relationship to individuals' decision processes. As always, to appreciate the benefits of regulation one must undertake both descriptive and prescriptive analyses.

NOTES TO CHAPTER 2

1. See Peltzman (1973) for a further elaboration on the costs and benefits of regulation in the context of new drug regulation.

2. See Stokey and Zeckhauser (1978) and Mirrlees (1974) for a discussion of the economic literature related to evaluating risky projects from a social point of view.

3. There has been a recent trend toward reexamining the traditional theory of rationality in economics. This reexamination (see Lesourne 1977) has attempted to provide tractable analytical models that are better descriptive models of human behavior than the traditional model. We restrict attention here to the traditional theory, though a similar analysis could be carried out for other theories of rational behavior.

4. See Starr (1973), Mirrlees (1974) and Deschamps and Gevers (1977) for a discussion of ex ante and ex post felicity in economics.

5. For a recent, readable summary of this debate see Hicks (1975).

6. The reader will note that this departs from our previous conception of using welfare measures that are to be maximized. Note also that we do not include the costs of installation in our welfare measure, delaying until later a discussion of the trade-offs between such costs and fatality reductions.

7. These figures are only illustrative, although they reflect those reported in Lave and Weber (1970) and The Insurance Institute for Highway Safety (1978).

8. Although recent studies do not bear this out for driving habits (see The Insurance Institute of Highway Safety 1978: 22), such changes would be quite credible. In a related paper, Colantoni, Davis, and Swaminuthan (1976) have provided an interesting analysis of regulatory policy when consumers have imperfect information. They evaluate the impact of the adoption of different auto safety features from the consumer's point of view but do not make the distinction between ex ante and ex post felicity.

9. The cases for weighting only felicity in error or only felicity in fact were stated, for the air bags issue, as follows:

   Representative E.G. Shuster (R-PA), speaking against air bags:

   > It is a national tragedy that only 44 percent of the people wear safety belts. It is downright foolish not to buckle up, but free people have a right to do foolish things. . . . This air bag edict is a very small piece of a dark and heavy blanket, gradually being lowered over a free people by their paternalistic government.

   Representative J.H. Scheuer (D-NY), speaking for air bags:

   > We shall share the cost of accidents through higher taxes and insurance premiums; the diversion of police, for ambulance, medical and other resources urgently needed elsewhere. We all pay for Medicaid, Medicare

and other forms of public health care. We all pay the Social Security disability and survivor benefits, welfare benefits, pensions, and unemployment insurance which traffic accident victims and/or their families may require.

The above are excerpts from the interesting piece written by P. J. Ognibene for the *Washington Post Parade Magazine* (August 28, 1977) on the controversy surrounding proposals to make air bags mandatory.

10. Thus, in effect, a new social welfare function W is constructed as:

$$W = aW_E + (1-a)W_F \qquad (0 \leq a \leq 1),$$

where W_E and W_F are the welfare levels corresponding to agents' information and policymaker's information, respectively, assuming the latter is accurate, both evaluated at participant's actual behavior. The question of how a is chosen is discussed below.

11. See Fujii (1975) for a discussion of the campaign on the health hazards of cigarette smoking and The Institute of Highway Safety (1978) for a review of the work on information dissemination on the use of seat belts. Neither of these advertising campaigns was particularly successful.

BIBLIOGRAPHY

Akerlof, G. 1970. "The Market for 'Lemons': Quality Uncertainty and the Market Mechanism." *Quarterly Journal of Economics* 84: 488–500.

Arrow, K. 1963. "Uncertainty and the Welfare Economics of Medical Care." *American Economic Review* 53: 941–973.

Calabresi, G. 1970. *The Costs of Accidents.* New Haven: Yale University Press.

Colantoni, C., Davis, and Swaminuthan. 1976. "Imperfect Consumers and Welfare Comparisons of Policies Concerning Information and Regulation." *Bell Journal of Economics* 2: 602–615.

Coleman, J.S., E. Katz; and H. Menzel. 1966. *Medical Innovation: A Diffusion Study.* Indianapolis: Bobbs–Merrill.

Deschamps, R., and L. Gevers. 1977. "Separability, Risk-Bearing, and Social Welfare Judgements." *European Economic Review* 10: 77–94.

Fischhoff, B. 1977. "Cognitive Liabilities and Product Liability." Report 77–9. Eugene, Oregon: Decision Research.

Fujii, E. 1975. "On the Value of Information on Product Safety: An Application to Health Warnings on the Long Run Medical Implications of Cigarette Smoking." *Public Finance* 3: 323–332.

Hicks, J.R. 1975. "The Scope and Status of Welfare Economics." *Oxford Economic Papers*: 307–326.

Holdren, J.P. 1976. "The Nuclear Controversy and the Limitations of Decision Making by Experts." *Bulletin of the Atomic Scientists* 32: 20–22.

Insurance Institute for Highway Safety. 1978. *To Prevent Harm.* Washington, D.C.

Kunreuther, H.; R. Ginsberg; L. Miller; P. Sagi; P. Slovic; B. Borkan; and N. Katz. 1978. *Disaster Insurance Protection: Public Policy Lessons.* New York: Wiley & Sons.

Lave, L.B., and W.E. Weber. 1970. "A Benefit–Cost Analysis of Auto-Safety Features." *Applied Economics* 2: 265–275.

Lesourne, J. 1977. *A Theory of the Individual for Economic Analysis.* New York: North-Holland Publishing Company.

Mirrlees, J.A. 1974. "Notes on Welfare Economics, Information and Uncertainty." In *Essays on Economic Behavior Under Uncertainty,* edited by M.D. Balch, pp. 243–258. New York: North-Holland Publishing Company.

Ognibene, P.J. 1977. "Should Air Bags Be Mandatory for Your Car?". *Washington Post Parade Magazine* (August 28): 20–21.

Oi, W.Y. 1978. "Products Liability and Products Safety." *Interagency Task Force on Product Liability.* Washington, D.C.: U.S. Department of Commerce.

Otway, H.J.; D. Mauford; and K. Thomas. 1978. "Nuclear Power: The Question of Public Acceptance." *Futures* 10: 109–118.

Peltzman, S. 1973. "An Evaluation of Consumer Protection Legislation: The 1962 Drug Amendments." *Journal of Political Economy* 81: 1049–1091.

Rogers, E., and F.F. Shoemaker. 1975. *Communication of Innovations.* New York: The Free Press.

Slovic, P.; B. Fischhoff; and S. Lichtenstein. 1978. "Perceived Frequency and Cost of Death as Determinants of Social Evaluation of Hazards." (Draft).

_____ . In Press. "Accident Probabilities and Seat Belt Usage: A Psychological Perspective." *Accident Analysis and Prevention.*

Slovic, P.; B. Fischhoff; S. Lichtenstein; B. Corrigan; and B. Combs. 1977. "Preference for Insuring Against Probable Small Loss: Implications for the Theory and Practice of Insurance." *Journal of Risk and Insurance* 44: 237–258.

Starr, R. 1973. "Optimal Production and Allocation Under Uncertainty." *Quarterly Journal of Economics* 87: 81–95.

Stokey, R., and R. Zeckhauser. 1978. *A Primer for Policy Analysis.* New York: W.W. Norton & Company.

Tversky, A., and D. Kahneman. 1974. "Judgment Under Uncertainty: Heuristics and Biases." *Science* 185: 1124–1131.

3 THE BENEFITS OF BETTER BENEFITS ESTIMATION

George Eads *

We are approaching a watershed in environmental, health, and safety regulation in this country. The public, stimulated by the research of numerous individuals and groups, as well as by its own observations, has begun to perceive that such regulation can potentially impose substantial costs as well as substantial benefits. In the course of their daily lives, citizens have begun to encounter with increasing frequency examples of regulations that, despite their good intentions, generate perverse effects or are just plain absurd. One needs to travel only a short distance out of Washington to sense a growing climate of mixed amusement and anger at the federal government's attempts to protect citizens from the seemingly endless array of hazards to which modern American life has become subject.

In spite of what some may have hoped, the result of this "revolt" has not been a cry to abolish regulation. Those waiting for such are likely to be disappointed. What the public seems to be asking is not that the government cease to regulate, but that it use more common sense in designing and implementing its regulation.

*At the time of writing, Dr. Eads was Research Program Director of Regulatory Policies and Institutions Program at The Rand Corporation. The opinions expressed here are strictly those of the author and do not necessarily reflect the views of The Rand Corporation or any of its sponsors.

Dr. Eads was appointed to membership in the Council of Economic Advisors in June 1979.

The challenge to the status quo has not gone unrecognized, but to date, the response has been predictable—and misdirected. To the claim that regulation raises costs to consumers, regulators have either responded by saying "that is nonsense," or they have attempted to minimize the impact by relating it to that great leveler, the Gross National Product. To the charge that they are engaged in trying to control behavior they do not understand, the regulators have introduced palliatives in the form of "increased public participation" and, wonder of wonders, commitments to write their regulations in "plain English."

I believe the solution lies elsewhere. As far as I can tell, the public is willing to bear significant costs in the name of a cleaner environment, safer consumer products, and a safer and healthier workplace—but only if these results are indeed achieved. Thus, the origins of present dissatisfaction lie not so much in the magnitude of the costs regulations may impose as in the perception that the benefits received are not commensurate with these costs.

One solution is to work to reduce the costs of regulation. Those who urge that increased attention be given to the use of economic incentives rather than command and control techniques are proceeding in that direction. What I write here should not be taken as denigrating the importance of that effort. Indeed, I wholeheartedly applaud it. What I wish to do instead is suggest a complementary avenue for those who seek to improve the functioning of the regulatory process. This is a plea for greater attention to the benefit side of the equation.

I do this with some trepidation. Being an economist, I am prone to consider costs as "concrete" and benefits as "squishy," lending themselves to infinite manipulation. I have precedent to support my concern. Whenever I hear those who defend current regulatory practices arguing, correctly, that our current techniques of benefit estimation omit certain intangibles such as "improved quality of life," I am reminded of the "make weights" created by the Bureau of Reclamation and Corps of Engineers as they sought to boost water projects of dubious merit over a cost-benefit hurdle by employing closely analogous concepts. One of the purposes of this book, a purpose that I support wholeheartedly, is to explore how better benefit measures can be developed. But we should always keep this unfortunate previous experience in mind.

I am more sympathetic to the observation that many of the benefits of environmental or health and safety regulation, while tangible, are nonetheless likely to be observable only in the very long run. The damage to chemical workers' health from long-term, low level exposure to certain substances has taken a long time to show up; the effects of reductions in this exposure will require a similarly long time to become manifest.

Fortunately for the argument I wish to make, the public's anger seems not to be directed so much against regulations that are designed to protect it from persistent, longer term hazards as at those that promise immediate, observable results but that fail to deliver. With regard to the former, the public understands that complex scientific judgments, about which there must always be uncertainty, are involved. However, in judging the latter, the public feels comfortable in applying a "reasonable man" standard, and it is when judged against such a standard that many such regulations appear unreasonable.

I will leave it to others to debate whether new and more esoteric techniques can be developed that will permit us to approach the ideal of quantifying all the positive aspects of regulation. My plea is for something much more simple and straightforward—that, through better and more effective use of the tools and information now at hand, regulatory agencies pay greater attention to the task of identifying and evaluating benefits.

This seems like a strange plea to have to make. What is more natural than for the agencies charged with promulgating regulations designed to protect consumers, workers, and the environment to wish to stress the value of what they are doing? Certainly such agencies already go to great lengths to claim how much their activities benefit the public. The problem is in the credibility of these claims. It is toward improving this credibility that my plea for better benefit estimation is directed.

What do I mean by benefit estimation? For one, it is *not* equivalent to hazard identification—something we already seem to be quite good at. The Consumer Product Safety Commission (CPSC) knows a great deal about which household products are associated with various injuries. The Occupational Safety and Health Administration (OSHA) knows which occupations are relatively hazardous and which are relatively safe. The Environmental Protection Agency (EPA) and the Food and Drug Administration (FDA) seem to have identified more hazards than we can count.

Although benefit measurement must start with hazard identification, it involves a great many more steps. First, the nature of the process by which the hazard is generated must be well understood.

Second, the theoretical effectiveness of a proposed remedy must be determined. Third, this theoretical effectiveness must be modified to take account of "real world" considerations. Only when all these steps are carefully carried out can one claim to have obtained an accurate measure of the likely benefits of a proposed regulatory action.

These steps may seem trivial, and sometimes they indeed are. At other times they require a major analytical undertaking. The important thing, however, is that where they are not undertaken in a serious manner, the outcome is generally predictable.

Consider, for example, a regulation I had some direct involvement with when I was at the Council on Wage and Price Stability several years ago—Motor Vehicle Safety Standard 121—Truck Air Brakes. The idea for this standard originated with the observation that a significant proportion of accidents involving trucks were brake-related and that the incidence of these accidents might be significantly reduced if trucks had more effective brakes—in particular, brakes that did not "lock up" when applied. The technology to produce such braking systems had long been utilized in the aerospace industry and showed promise of being adaptable to the somewhat different operating environment of trucking.

But how big was the improvement in safety likely to be? (Forget whether the improvement, whatever its magnitude, could be considered "worth" the costs it would impose.) A number of pieces of information were available to the National Highway Traffic Safety Administration (NHTSA) on this issue. First, engineering tests showed in how much shorter a distance trucks equipped with properly functioning antilock systems could be expected to stop. Second, detailed data described the circumstances surrounding most significant accidents involving trucks. These data would have permitted the estimation of the number of accidents that might conceivably be avoided by properly functioning antilock systems. Third, experience was available concerning the problems posed when complex technical systems are introduced into the field. Therefore, all the elements were present that would have permitted NHTSA to determine far in advance whether the proposed antilock systems were likely to improve safety significantly and, if there were doubts, what experimental evidence was needed to resolve them.

Unfortunately, the bulk of this information was *not* utilized by NHTSA. Relying almost exclusively on engineering test results, the agency determined to its satisfaction that the standard would measurably improve safety. Only in the context of an extremely "quick and dirty" benefit-cost analysis (undertaken, it appears in retrospect, to confirm a previously made decision to proceed with the standard—not to evaluate its wisdom) was the second body of evidence tapped—and then, only superficially. Finally, as far as I am able to tell, absolutely no thought was ever given to the possibility that theoretical levels of performance might be degraded in the field.

The agency, in spite of numerous protests, undertook a "universal experiment" by promulgating regulations that, in effect, mandated antilock systems. The field experience with the equipment proved disappointing. Questions have even been raised as to whether the net result has been a *reduction* in safety. The standard continues to be embroiled in controversy. Yet this could have been avoided had adequate attention been paid, at the time the standard was first being considered, to benefit estimation using simple analytical techniques and readily available evidence.

Someone is bound to contend that the example I have cited is atypical. I can provide no statistical proof on this point, but my experience in reviewing regulations indicates that it is not. Too often, what passes for benefit estimation is nothing more than hazard identification with an engineering fix thrown in. It is little wonder that the public questions the government's sanity.

In certain areas of regulation the courts, previously tolerant of vaguely drawn links between a demonstrated, or even hypothesized, harm and proposed remedies, are beginning to take a tougher stance. In its recent *Aqua-Slide* decision, the Court of Appeals put the Consumer Product Safety Commission on notice that it would have to heed the requirement in its legislation that it demonstrate both the presence of an unreasonable risk of injury, and that a proposed standard would be likely to significantly reduce that risk.[1] The matter at issue was the reasonableness of proposed swimming pool slide regulations. The CPSC had demonstrated that adults who slid into water headfirst on these slides encountered a one in ten million chance of spinal injury and paralysis. The proposed remedy was a recommendation that the slides be moved to deeper water and a requirement that labels be affixed to the slides warning against improper use. Finally, in recognition of the fact that moving slides to deeper water might increase the risk of drowning, the attachment of a ladder chain to the end of the slide was to be required.

The court agreed that the CPSC had met the burden of showing that an "unreasonable risk" existed. Although the probability of an accident was indeed low, the consequences of such an accident were extremely severe. However, after reviewing the evidence the CPSC used in determining that its proposed remedies would be effective in reducing this risk, the court concluded that the burden had not been borne. The court remarked:

> The Commission did not test its warning signs. It did not establish that users would need them and "belly slide" in the proper manner. It deprived the public of any meaningful chance to challenge its investigation into the possibility that the signs were so explicit in their mention of "paralysis" that they might unnecessarily frighten away those who would be willing to buy them if they knew how remote the risk actually was. The Commission has not adequately demonstrated the ability of the ladder claim to avert the serious danger of drowning that placing slides in deeper water could create.[2]

Therefore, it set aside the standard. Significantly, the court took pains to note that it was not suggesting that an elaborate cost-benefit analysis was required; merely that the CPSC ". . . shoulder the burden of examining the relevant factors and producing substantial evidence to support its conclusion that they weigh in favor of the standard."[3]

The kind of evidence that might prove convincing in such a case, plus the relative ease with which such evidence can be assembled, is suggested by the preliminary results of a study being conducted by a group of engineers and lawyers at Carnegie–Mellon University.[4] This study examined both the process by which a CPSC lighter flame height standard was established and the evidence (that, as in the case of NHTSA, appears not to have been utilized) concerning the probable effectiveness of the proposed remedy in mitigating the identified hazard. A series of forty-six, in-depth CPSC accident reports involving lighter accidents were examined by the researchers. Each accident was classified into one of six categories depending on the likelihood that its occurrence would have been influenced by the existence of the standard. In about one-third of the cases, risk reduction was considered "probable." This seems to indicate that the standard was "reasonably necessary." But the assessment also showed that in an almost equal proportion of cases, it was considered "impossible" for the "fix" proposed by the standard to have affected the accident. This suggests that, if the risk really was considered "unreasonable," remedies in addition to the one chosen should have been considered.

The previous example points up another positive feature of systematic benefit estimation. If treated as an important part of developing a regulation it can, by itself, focus needed attention on alternatives and side consequences and can even eliminate consideration of courses of action that once had seemed extremely promising.

Research The Rand Corporation carried out for the EPA, investigating the economic impact of potential controls over nonaerosol fluorocarbon emissions, demonstrates just that. A ban on aerosol emissions was set in 1978. But nonaerosol emissions are approximately equal in magnitude to aerosol emissions (at least in the United States), and their magnitude is growing rapidly. Hence, the EPA's concern. But before getting to the subjects that are normally considered the meat of such an investigation—costs, prices, employment impact, and so forth—nearly a year was spent developing a better understanding of the emissions process that characterizes certain fluorocarbon-using products and how certain actions are or are not likely to affect it. In my mind, this is properly classified as benefit estimation.[5]

The most dramatic examples of the kind of results mentioned above concern fluorocarbon solvents and fluorocarbon-containing rigid polyurethane foams. In the former case, research, again by The Rand Corporation, has led to three important conclusions, all of which are at variance with previous beliefs. First, results point up the importance of workplace practices in determining actual, as opposed to theoretical, emissions from solvent-using devices. This suggests that regulations mandating equipment characteristics may promise less in the way of emission reduction than strategies designed to make conservation consistent with good business. Second, analysis has revealed, quite unexpectedly, that one control strategy previously thought to offer great promise—the external recycling of fluorocarbon solvent waste—can, at best, make only a minor contribution to reducing solvent emissions. Third, it has demonstrated that all the control options under consideration—mandated conservation, use or emissions fees, and marketable permits—are, in fact, simply variants of the same underlying strategy. Thus, in subsequent economic impact analysis analysts can separate issues relating to the level of control from those relating to control instruments or techniques.

The results of the analysis in rigid urethane foams are likely to have an even greater impact on any regulation that is ultimately undertaken. Previously thought to be only a minor emissions source, this product, which is used primarily as thermal insulation, was analyzed as presenting a major regulatory problem. By carefully modeling the previously neglected post-manufacturing emissions process, it was demonstrated that most fluorocarbons being used in these products are "banked," perhaps for decades. Indeed, rigid urethane foams obtain their excellent insulating properties primarily from the fact that they retain fluorocarbons for such a long time. Aside from actions that would discourage the use of the foam itself, thereby imposing a substantial energy or cost penalty due to the need to use less effective or more costly insulating material, most "interesting" regulatory strategies involve a shifting of emissions over time. Work has been done to specify these choices in greater detail.

I have no idea how EPA and the other government agencies will resolve the thorny issues surrounding nonaerosol fluorocarbon emissions. I do believe that the benefit estimation work performed for them in the above cases, *prior* to beginning a formal "economic impact analysis" is likely to prove as important in determining the outcome as the economic impact analysis itself.

I should note, however, that in contrast to the examples I cited earlier, the work at Rand, especially with regard to rigid foams, has required the use of relatively complex statistical and analytical tools. It has not been easy. Yet, once completed, it may provide a model of how much can be learned if an interdisciplinary team of analysts (in this case, a team consisting of three economists, an engineer, and a chemist) is permitted to focus seriously on the issue of benefits.

What about those areas where not even an acceptable surrogate for benefits can be identified? Must we abandon the attempt to understand and evaluate the link between what agencies are considering and what the effects are likely to be?

I have already indicated that, in the case of fluorocarbons the true benefit measure, reduction in the incidence of skin cancer, can be estimated only imprecisely and involves complex scientific judgments. It seems that in such cases, the most the public is asking of the regulators is that the *process* by which such judgments are made be reasonable. By "reasonable" I mean that the agency considers the body of scientific evidence bearing on an issue, applies reasonable techniques for dealing with uncertainty inherent in the decision, is open to modifying its judgments if new and better information becomes available, and is not blind to the side effects its actions may cause. While these seem like simple criteria, I believe it can be demonstrated that our current regulatory processes fail to meet them.

Failure to observe the last of these criteria was what seems to have generated public outcry in the case of saccharine. The recent argument over what to do about nitrites in cured meats seems to reflect that lesson.

Precisely how our processes for making decisions involving risk could be brought into better conformance with these ideals is a matter of some dispute. The notion of setting up a "science court" to adjudicate issues of "scientific fact" may appeal to some scientists, but it has little appeal for me. Other improvements in processes such as the use of commissions made up of "hard" scientists, social scientists, and lawyers may deserve more serious attention, but are still probably not the answer. The increased use of formal scientific advisory committees as recommended to the EPA by the National Academy of Sciences seems to run squarely in the face of recent court decisions sharply limiting the ability of regulators to rely on such advice.[6]

This is not the place to address this issue in detail. Suffice it to say that it could stand careful examination. One critical thing to be kept in mind in any such evaluation is that, like it or not, our regulatory processes are, in essence, legal processes. Scientists indeed have an important role to play in them, but they need to be run according to the rules of science. Unfortunately, finding anyone willing to support such research is likely to prove extremely difficult.

Economists, no doubt, will note that I have not yet mentioned the issue on which many of them have likely bent their spears—the "proper" value that should be placed upon a human life in evaluating the benefits of health and safety regulatory programs. The omission is intentional. Some years ago I argued that estimates of the deadweight loss of regulation were likely to be irrelevant in convincing regulators or legislators to reform traditional economic regulation. I believe that my contention has been fully borne out by subsequent history. So would I, here, maintain that the "value of life" debate, while intellectually interesting, is largely irrelevant to policy and, indeed, may be counterproductive. Simple calculations showing the value that regulators are implicitly placing on human life as a consequence of their proposed actions are likely to prove much more useful—and lack the "how many angels can dance on the head of a pin" quality of much of the "value of life" research. As is true in the case of economic regulation, economists need to talk the regulators' language before they can be full-fledged participants in the policy debate—just as "deadweight loss" was a foreign language to economic regulators, so is "value of life" a foreign language to health and safety regulators.

I have also successfully avoided mentioning that body of work that purports to demonstrate through the tools of regression analysis that major health and safety regulatory programs are, in toto, ineffective, whatever that means. Ineffective they may be, although I doubt it, but researchers will never build a convincing case that way.

My prescription for those who would challenge the "effectiveness" of regulation is, ironically, identical to my recommendation to regulators who are seeking to counter a growing public disenchantment with their activities—look to the benefits side of the balance sheet.

NOTES TO CHAPTER 3

1. *Aqua Slide 'n Dive Corp.* v. *CPSC*, Court of Appeal, 5th Circuit, March 3, 1978.
2. Ibid., pp. 2500–2501.
3. Ibid., p. 2495.
4. Research was sponsored by the National Science Foundation. Unfortunately, support has been terminated. I am extremely grateful to Professor Henry Piehler of Carnegie–Mellon for making their preliminary results available to me and for giving me permission to cite them.
5. I hasten to add that I fully recognize that we are dealing with a surrogate measure of benefits—reduction of fluorocarbon emissions, not cases of skin cancer prevented. I will leave it to the scientists to prove or disprove the links between the two. However, I understand the results so far may have complicated their task by throwing some of their previous calculations of historic fluorocarbon emissions into some doubt.
6. *Seacoast Anti-Pollution League* v. *Costle*, No. 77–1284, 1st Cir., February 15, 1978.

DISCUSSION OF PART I

Allen Ferguson: (Moderator) Kleindorfer and Kunreuther's chapter raises some extremely interesting questions of the importance of information deficiencies, and the social impact of limited information or misinformation of consumers and firms. The authors give a specific evaluative method and offer a set of hypotheses on the government's appropriate role in dealing with health and safety hazards. My questions to the discussants are: (1) Do you find the hypotheses valid? (2) Do you see the method as being useful? (3) What is its relevance to your operations?

George Eads has emphasized the need to begin with the identification of the hazards avoided by regulation and the need for regulations to make effective use of the limited information that is available. He also stresses the problem of predicting the effects of proposed regulations. Here, the questions we must ask are: (1) What is the operational importance of identifying hazards? (2) Is there sufficient information available to develop "reasonable" regulations and to determine the efficacy of regulations?

Robert Elder: My interpretation of the two chapters is biased by my experience within the Food and Drug Administration (FDA). Based on this experience, I offer the following observations.

The Drug Act, as amended in 1962, is a law requiring benefit-risk analysis and efficacy studies. In no case, however, does the legislative record indicate that we should consider benefits in terms of economic advantage to the individual or to the country. Although Congress has called on us to defend our reasons for approving some drugs, we have yet to be called on to defend our disapproval of a drug. I think there is a reason for this apparent lack of concern for benefits.

In analyzing the intent of a law or of the Congress we have to recognize that the principal justification for passing the original legislation was the protection of the general public from involuntary acceptance of risk. As Chauncy Starr has written, the consumers are willing to assume a thousand times greater risk when they make the decision than when the decision is made for them. In situations where the consumer has no choice, such as in food additives, the consumer, through Congress, has mandated a very low tolerance of risk. This accounts for the Delaney Clause[a] and for the generally very restrictive legislation under which we operate. In short, we cannot pursue the kinds of benefits analysis as proposed in these chapters, for the issue is only whether there is a risk present, not whether the risk is large or small, or economically desirable or undesirable.

For these reasons, then, I would not want to be forced to attach economic values to risk probabilities, and I would not want to defend such an analysis in front of Congress and the general public. I might add that an additional problem I face is that my audience does not understand the concept of probability and would certainly have great difficulty following any benefits assessment such as that presented by Kleindorfer and Kunreuther. Such analysis is far too sophisticated, and would not gain acceptance.

Finally, I would like to add that in recent years, I sense that the general public is becoming less preoccupied with involuntary risk and that some of the criticism of our regulation is now directed at what the public sees as overly protective laws. The cases of saccharine and nitrites illustrate the changing mood. Saccharine is found to be cancer causing and hence, under the Delaney Clause, it must be banned. It is regulated as an involuntary exposure. However, many individuals apparently want to expose themselves to this risk, as indicated by their continued interest in purchasing diet soft drinks. Thus the phi-

---

a. The Delaney Clause prohibits the use of direct food additives that have been shown through appropriate tests to cause cancer in humans or laboratory animals.

losophy under which the Delaney Clause was enacted and that of the nation today appear to be changing. We must implement the law, but perhaps we are out of tune with what the population wants.

Nitrite presents an even more difficult situation, because it has both benefits and risks. It has huge commercial implications to the nation. If nitrites are banned, the energy demand for refrigeration may become phenomenal. Perhaps the law should allow a consideration of these benefits as well as the risks posed by nitrites. This is a situation not anticipated by the Delaney Clause.

I would close with the following comment. Decisions such as those relating to nitrites and saccharine are unusual. For the most part, our work consists of making many decisions of much smaller consequence, such as whether to permit a new emulsifier that works in fifteen seconds rather than thirty seconds. Such decisions would be very costly to analyze, using the kinds of procedures outlined in the two chapters. I wonder if we can even begin to estimate the benefits of an emulsifier that works fifteen seconds faster. Is it a good idea to force all decisions such as this through a benefit-risk analysis? If so, we need much more guidance on how to proceed than we now have available.

Roy Gamse: I have been involved in economic analysis for the Environmental Protection Agency (EPA) since 1972, a time during which the emphasis has been on the costs side of the equation. We have encouraged people first to identify costs and benefits, and then to derive a benefit-cost balance. Benefits are harder to assess than costs.

George Eads stresses the need for more effective benefits estimation. His examples of truck air brakes and swimming pool slides are excellent illustrations of this point. However, I feel it is much harder to test the effectiveness of EPA's regulatory actions since one cannot run experiments in very many of the individual cases.

For example, although Eads has figures on effectiveness in controlling fluorocarbon emissions, he does not have them on effectiveness in limiting skin cancer, which is the main concern. To make any assessment of whether the regulations are worthwhile, which is basically the benefit-cost balancing that we would like to do, we must deal only with effectiveness in limiting the pollutant.

A more typical case might be the limitation of emissions of an air pollutant, such as sulfuroxides, or a water pollutant, such as mercury. In such a case, if we are to make a judgmental comparison of costs and benefits, we must go beyond the total amount of emission. We have to study the emission's effect on the water or air quality in order to tell whether there are dangerous amounts of pollutants. It is difficult to do this in most of the regulatory areas that we affect and, thus, it is difficult to be sure that we are accomplishing what we think we are.

Kleindorfer and Kunreuther's chapter focuses on the gap between actual and perceived benefits. It provides food for thought on the question of when government should regulate. Should it do so in situations where consumer choice is involved or where providing information may be an alternative? I think many times people thinking about the pros and cons of regulation do not appreciate what information consumers have, and how able they are to make a choice. Both regulators and critics of regulators need to think about this issue.

George Eads is concerned with the same issue in a different way. He talks about perceived versus actual effectiveness, not so much in the eyes of the consumer, but in the eyes of the regulator, who, in many instances, is making the choice for the consumer.

EPA's problem right now is the difficulty we have in coming up with measures that allow benefit-cost comparison. Decisionmakers at EPA must deal with a lot of uncertainty in making the balancing decision, because there is no clearly identified actual impact. There are many uncertain steps between having a regulation on the books and actually getting the clean air or water. It does not automatically happen. And if we do not understand the differences between actual impacts and benefits and perceived impacts and benefits, we can write bad regulations.

Paul Kleindorfer: I find it useful to structure the discussion of benefits of health and safety regulation into two major areas: one describes what is going on and the other evaluates the results. The major point that Howard Kunreuther and I make is that both of these areas require explicit consideration of the way consumers, firms, and administrators actually make (or fail to make) decisions.

To understand and describe what is happening in a particular sphere, the decision processes of consumers and firms are clearly an essential feature. The evaluation and policy choice question is harder to relate to the decision process. The basic idea is that the generally accepted maxim that individuals are the best judges of their own welfare indicates that social felicity has to be based on some aggregate of individual felicities, and the latter clearly depend on individual perceptions, beliefs, and decision processes. This leads us to the problems and hypotheses advanced in our chapter.

What I think is missing in most of the theoretical literature on benefits assessment is precisely this link between what consumers and firms believe is good for them and what governmental administrators and legislators are trying to achieve in the name of the public. Trying to link these two more closely, through a more participative evaluation or through survey instruments, is very important if regulatory action, both in substance and scope, is to be at all representative of public tastes.

One of the main problems in setting up a more participative evaluation process is that many consumers and firms are, in fact, uninformed or misinformed on the very questions on which we are seeking their value judgments. Indeed, given the complexity of modern society, the body politic may see the prime benefit of health and safety regulations as relieving it of the difficult task of assessing and controlling hazards. While the benefits of health and safety regulation in obtaining socially more efficient information processing and decision procedures are to be emphasized, we must also be clear on the impact of an uninformed public, both in terms of its behavior in the face of health and safety hazards and in terms of how well off it perceives itself to be. In the end, there would appear to be some trade-off between the informational efficiencies of (benign) paternalism and the social and political costs of felicity-in-error and decision by default that paternalism, benign or not, may encourage. A reasonable assessment of the benefits of regulation will have to face this trade-off directly.

Howard Kunreuther: The comments of the discussants emphasize the importance of understanding what information individuals collect and how they process the data as a basis for prescribing policies. The discussants have, for example, indicated that there is a lack of consumer knowledge with respect to low probability, high-loss events and they have raised interesting questions as to the types of biases we must think about in designing policies. Both of these points deserve further attention in evaluating the appropriate role of regulation by government today.

It is more evident now than five years ago that considerably more research must be undertaken to understand what information both consumers and regulators have utilized to assess the costs and benefits of alternative decisions. In some cases, such as natural hazards, there is considerable evidence that most individuals are unconcerned about potential disasters because they estimate that the chances of such an event occurring is relatively low. For other potential disasters, such as nuclear power explosions, there appears to be grave concern expressed by a vocal segment of the public for the potential consequences of such a disaster and little discussion on the probability of such an event. We need to gain a better understanding of why individuals behave so differently with respect to these two types of low-probability, high-loss events to determine the relative merits of regulations in relation to more market-oriented incentive systems.

With respect to regulatory agencies, we need to determine the types of data available to them and how this information is utilized in their design of policies. For example, Bob Elder made the point that the Food and Drug Administration may not have as much information as it would like in designing its regulations. What other data would this agency and other regulatory groups like to collect in order to make better decisions? How do they utilize the data they now have in designing policies? What would they be likely to do with the additional information should they collect it? If regulators are subject to the same types of limitations as consumers, then one has to take this factor into account in analyzing the basis for certain regulations.

If regulatory bodies are able to obtain relevant information on the probability and consequences of certain negative events, then one of their important functions is to provide such data to the public in a form that influences behavior. This requires an understanding of how presenting information in different forms will influence behavior. For example, if the National Highway and Traffic Safety Administration has accurate statistics on the chances of serious injuries with and without a seat belt, they must consider how the data should be presented to automobile passengers so as to influence their decisions. If these probabilities were presented on a per trip basis, then people might be less likely to buckle up than if the chances of injury with and without a belt were presented on an average annual car mileage.

Finally, some thought should be given to the costs and benefits of providing information to consumers and letting them make their own choice or, alternatively, enforcing specific regulations, such as banning a product or requiring seat belts. The case for regulation is strongest when the regulatory body has more accurate information on probabilities and losses than consumers or firms, the cost of enforcement is relatively low, and individuals and firms exhibit wide disparities between ex ante and ex post felicity.

George Eads: I would like to reemphasize two points I tried to make in my chapter. First, although you never have all the information available when making a decision, in general, you have a lot more than you think you do. Therefore, rather than wringing your hands about the lack of information, make use of the information that you do have available.

Second, regulations designed to produce immediate, plausible, and observable effects are presenting some of the biggest problems today. When people do not see these immediate and supposedly observable effects, they tend not to trust the regulators' ability to deal with the big and long-term problems.

Clarence Davies: I would like to know how one analyzes the implicit values that are inherent in the regulatory decisions.

Roy Gamse: If we can identify the effects of our regulatory actions in terms of the number of deaths averted, or the number of health hazards we are no longer exposed to, and if we can identify the costs of the regulation, then by comparing these we can identify what the implicit cost to the person affected is. If we also have the basis for determining the costs of other ways of protecting people, we can put the regulation into some perspective. Instead of going through a soul-searching analysis of what a life is worth, doing an analysis of what the cost of a particular regulatory action is may make it clear whether it is cheaper to do A or B. Then, we could probably figure out whether the regulatory action is indeed warranted.

The weakness of taking this approach is simply the weakness involved in the data on the effects themselves. But where we can get decent assessments of what the effects are, we can start identifying these implicit values and making comparisons. I think that within EPA this is just starting to be a useful tool for decisionmakers. We are seeing the first examples where we are able to measure effects well enough to provide some perspective to decisionmakers, who would otherwise be much more confused about what they were causing to happen.

Often regulators are bound by statutory constraints that hinder their ability to make use of the data on effects for the best result. Having this information, however, allows us to regulate where we have the flexibility to do so.

William Nordhaus: Implicit values are descriptions of what you are doing. That is to say, what is the Department of Defense currently paying to protect its pilots? What is the Department of Transportation, or the state of California, currently paying to protect people from accidents? These costs incurred to protect life constitute the value of life implicit in those programs.

Nicholas Ashford: A question that has not been addressed is what the decision rule is with regard to avoiding risk, that is, the construction of a risk averse function. One may be very concerned about the small probability that a catastrophic number of deaths occur. That may be on the fringes of the acceptable theories that calculate the distribution of risks or the risk profile.

Rather than using the expected rate of return for a regulation, or the most likely damage prevented, regulators are operating under a rule that is more like a minimizing of the maximum regret of not providing enough protection than delivering to the consumer or worker the maximum of net benefits.

We are talking about benefits, the issue of measurement, and about the difficulties of perceiving the benefits as they exist. Suppose we were to correct that situation. Suppose that we expect workers to trade off their wages for their health. Should the fact that they are the ones making that trade, at a price that reflects their bundle of goods, their assets, concern us? This would mean that the supply term of the market on selling lives comes from a group of people whose wealth is lower than the average. They are selling their lives cheap. Should we accept that valuation in a place where we want such regulation?

Unidentified Speaker: That last remark was an interesting comment for it raises the question of how regulators live in a world of grossly inequitable distribution of wealth. Do we act as if this does not exist, or do we try to use regulation responsibly?

Robert Elder: I would like to respond because I think you have hit upon an important point. Look at the way we regulate carcinogens today. One of the basic precepts of life in the United States is that everyone gets to live a long natural life, and die whenever the body collapses—and, in our philosophy, cancer is not part of that collapse. We are under considerable pressure at FDA concerning the high costs of testing the carcinogenic effects of toxics on workers. The price is $400,000 or $500,000 for each substance.

One of the fundamental risks addressed in regulating radiation is mutation, which will affect future generations. If this meeting should reconvene twenty years hence, carcinogens might no longer be the basic issue of regulation in the United States—it could well be mutagens. I bring this up to emphasize our implicit distributional decision in regulating to protect the people alive today, versus the people of tomorrow.

Kathleen Sheekey: George Eads points out in his chapter that, like it or not, our regulatory processes are in essence legal processes. In that regard, Eads' regulator is to examine all sides of the issue, and then act as a final decisionmaker in that process. The problem with that, however, is that it leads to an unbelievably disproportionate influence of industry in the regulatory process.

In 1976, for example, $1.2 million was spent by the airline industry in proceedings before the Civil Aeronautics Board. There is only one public interest group concerned with those problems that ever gets before the Civil Aeronautics Board. And the total annual operating budget of that group, through 1976, was $20,000. I think the future is very, very bleak for correcting these processes. We must think about this very great imbalance. Sometimes the regulatory agencies, themselves, contribute to the dilemma.

I was rather disturbed also by Dr. Elder's comment on how the Delaney Clause is not in tune with what the population wants. I think that the FDA dealt the Delaney Clause a staggering blow. I am not defending the Delaney Clause; I am not sure that it should survive. But there was no effort on the part of the FDA to explain the widely accepted scientific methodology for testing the carcinogenicity of substances in laboratory animals, and how the short life spans of these animals precipitated the use of large dosages.

The FDA really played into the hands of the Calorie Control Council, which was the group that sprung up overnight, financed by the soft drink industry, and the very next day had a full-page ad in *The New York Times*. That ad, decrying the saccharine ban, cost fifteen thousand dollars! Certainly no public interest group represented here today can afford to take out such an ad in *The New York Times*. The imbalances are just staggering. We ought to address this problem in our discussion.

METHODS OF BENEFIT ASSESSMENT

4 BENEFIT ANALYSIS AND TODAY'S REGULATORY PROBLEMS*

Allen V. Kneese**
Ralph C. d'Arge***

Benefit-cost analysis is a well-established mode of applied economics extensively used for the evaluation of public investment projects. It is now also being employed increasingly to evaluate new technologies, scientific programs, and environmental policies. These applications present special difficulties. Before turning to these more explicitly, it will be useful to say a little about the history of benefit-cost analysis.

The technique was initially developed to evaluate water resources investment made by the federal water agencies in the United States, principally the U.S. Bureau of Reclamation and the U.S. Corp of Engineers. The general objective of benefit-cost analysis in this application was to provide a useful picture of the costs and gains from making investments in water development. The intellectual "father" of benefit-cost analysis is often said to be the nineteenth century

*This chapter relies mostly on material found in *Methods Development for Assessing Tradeoffs in Environmental Management*, a four volume draft report published by the Environmental Protection Agency, February 1979. The research was supported by USEPA Grant No. R805059010 to the University of Wyoming. The principal investigators are Shaul Ben-David, David Brookshire, Thomas C. Crocker, Ralph C. d'Arge, Allen V. Kneese, and William Schulze. The contents of the chapter are solely the responsibility of the authors and do not necessarily reflect the views of the sponsoring agency.

**Allen V. Kneese is a Senior Fellow at Resources for the Future.

***Ralph d'Arge is Professor of Economics at the University of Wyoming.

Frenchman, Jules Dupuit, who in 1844 wrote a study "On the Measure of the Utility of Public Works." In this remarkable article he recognized the concept of consumer surplus and saw that consequently the benefits of public works are not necessarily the same thing as the direct revenues that the public works projects will generate.

Early contributions to development of benefit-cost analysis as a practical technique did not come from the academic or research communities but rather from government agencies. The agencies responsible for water development in this country have been aware of the need for economic evaluation of projects for a long time. In 1808, Albert Gallatin, Jefferson's secretary of the treasury, produced a report on transportation programs for the new nation. He stressed the need for comparing the benefits with the costs of proposed waterway improvements. The Federal Reclamation Act of 1902, which created the Bureau of Reclamation and was aimed at opening western lands to irrigation, required economic analysis of projects. The Flood Control Act of 1936 proposed a feasibility test based on classical welfare economics, which requires that the benefits to whomsoever they accrue must exceed costs. In 1946 the Federal Interagency River Basin Committee appointed a subcommittee on benefits and costs to reconcile the practices of federal agencies in making benefit-cost analyses. In 1950, the subcommittee issued a landmark report entitled "Proposed Practices for Economic Analysis of River Basin Projects." While never fully accepted either by the parent committee or the federal agencies, this report was remarkably sophisticated in its use of economic analysis and laid an intellectual foundation for research and debate that set it apart from other major reports in the realm of public expenditures. This document also provided general guidance for the routine development of benefit-cost analysis of water projects that persists to the present day.

Following this report came some outstanding publications from the research and academic communities. Several books that have appeared over the past two decades have gone much further than before in clarifying the welfare economics concepts applicable to our water resources development and use, and in exploring the fundamental rationale for government activity in the area. Otto Eckstein's *Water Resource Development: The Economics of Project Evaluation,* which appeared in 1958, is particularly outstanding for its careful review and critique of federal agency practice regarding benefit-cost analysis. While a bit dated, this book is still well worth reading.

One report produced in the early 1960s that was especially notable for its deep probing into applications of systems analysis and computer technology within the framework of benefit-cost analysis was produced by a group of economists, engineers, and hydrologists at Harvard. It was published under the title *Design of Water Resource Systems* in 1962. The intervening years have seen considerable further work on the technique, and a gradual expansion of it to areas outside the water resources field. The most recent book containing a full discussion of the theoretical basis for benefit-cost analysis and some illustrative applications is *Economic Theory of Natural Resources* by Orris Herfindahl and Allen Kneese (1974).

The most striking development in benefit-cost analysis in recent years has been an increasing application of the technique to the environmental consequences of new technologies and scientific programs. For example, the Atomic Energy Commission (before the Energy Research and Development Administration and the Department of Energy were created) used the technique to evaluate the fast breeder program (*Updated (1970) Cost Benefit Analysis of the U.S. Breeder Reactor Program*). The technique has also been applied to other potential sources of environmental pollution and hazard. Two studies that come to quite contrary conclusions have been made of the Automotive Emissions Control Program. The first, reported in "Air Quality and Automotive Emissions Control," was prepared by a committee of the National Academy of Sciences (1974). The other study (Jackson et al. 1976), was produced by General Motors Corporation. Other studies have been or are being conducted in the area of water quality analysis, emissions from stationary sources, and toxic substances.

Even while the benefit-cost technique was limited largely to the relatively straightforward problem of evaluating water resources investments, there was much debate among economists about the proper way of handling both empirical and conceptual difficulties with the technique. Some of the discussion surrounded primarily technical issues, for example, ways of computing consumer surplus, and how best to estimate demand functions for various outputs. Others were more clearly value and equity issues, such as whether the distribution of benefits and costs among individuals needed to be accounted for or whether it was adequate to consider only aggregates, and what is the appropriate rate of time discount to use on water projects.

Application of the technique to issues such as nuclear radiation, the storage of atomic waste, and the regulation of toxic substances aggravate both the empirical and value issues that existed in water resource applications. There are several reasons for this. We will focus on one of them in this chapter.

While water resource applications often involve the evaluation of public goods (in the technical economic sense of goods exhibiting jointness in supply), the bulk of outputs pertain to such things as irrigation, navigation, flood control, and municipal and industrial water supplies, which usually could be reasonably evaluated on the basis of some type of market information. In the newer applications we are dealing almost entirely with public goods and market surrogates are much more difficult to establish. The problem of finding justifiable monetary values of outcomes of the projects or regulatory decisions is a very difficult one.[1]

BENEFIT ANALYSIS AND THE NEW GENERATION OF ENVIRONMENTAL PROBLEMS

The next large task of environmental regulation in this country is to manage the flow of toxic and hazardous materials into our environment in some socially optimum manner. To the extent that this effort is to be aided by explicit benefit-cost analyses the capabilities of the technique will be stretched to its limits, as pointed out above. This is not to say that decisions should not be guided by an orderly effort to assemble and develop information in a format that gives attention to both the benefits and the costs of a regulatory action.

Indeed several pieces of new legislation aimed at control of the toxic substances problem explicitly require such comparisons. A look at Table 4–1 indicates that the Occupational Safety and Health Act (OSHA), Toxic Substances Control Act (TOSCA), Federal Insecticide, Fungicide, and Rodenticide Act (FIFRA), and Safe Drinking Water Act (SDWA) require a weighing of costs and benefits. On the other hand, the hazardous substances provisions of both the Clean Air Act and the Federal Water Pollution Control Act do not. Additional examination of the table would reveal other inconsistencies, but it is not our purpose here to pursue them. The point is that the society and its regulatory agencies are faced with an exceptionally difficult evaluation problem with these substances. In most instances

Table 4–1. Federal legislation regulating toxic substances.

Legislation	Definition of Toxic or Hazard	Type of Regulation	Degree of Protection	Burden of Proof	Balancing of Costs
1970 Clean Air Act Amendments	"an air pollutant . . . which . . . may cause, or contribute to an increase in mortality or an increase in serious irreversible, or incapacitating reversible, illness" Section 112(a)(1)	Emission standards	". . . an ample margin of safety to protect the public health . . ." Sec. 112(b)(1)(B)	EPA	No
Federal Water Pollution Control Act	". . . pollutants which will . . . cause death, disease, behavioral abnormalities, cancer, genetic mutations, physiological malfunctions . . . or physical deformations." Sec. 502(13)	Effluent standards, ambient standards	". . . ample margin of safety." Sec. 307(a)(4)	EPA	No
Occupational Safety and Health Act	Not defined	Exposure standards	"adequately assures to the extent feasible that no employee will suffer material impairment of health or functional capacity . . . Sec. 6(b)(5)	OSHA	Yes, Sec. 6(b)(5)

Table 4–1. continued

Legislation	Definition of Toxic or Hazard	Type of Regulation	Degree of Protection	Burden of Proof	Balancing of Costs
Toxic Substances Control Act	those substances "... presenting an unreasonable risk of injury to health or the environment ..." Sec. 6(a)	Premarket notification and testing; prohibitions on manufacturing, processing, and distribution; information on chemical components must be supplied to EPA	Not specified	Proponent	Yes, Sec. 2(b)(3)
Food and Drug Administration	Not defined	Labeling; bans on products deemed "unsafe"	"... necessary for the protection of public health ..." Sec. 406 [346]	Proponent for drugs and food additives; FDA for cosmetic ingredients	No, in case of food additives; yes, for drugs and cosmetics
Federal Insecticide, Fungicide, and Rodenticide Act and the Federal Environmental Pesticide Control Act	One which results in "... unreasonable adverse effects on the environment or will involve unreasonable hazard to the survival of a species declared endangered ..."	Registration of all pesticides and uses; permits for applicators; cancellation or suspension of specific pesticides or uses	Not specified	Proponent	Yes, Sec. 6(b)(2)

Safe Drinking Water Act	"... contaminant(s) which ... may have an adverse effect on the health of persons." Sec. 1401(1)(B)	Maximum contaminant standards	"... to the extent feasible ... (taking costs into consideration) ..." Sec. 1412(a)(2)	EPA	Yes, Sec. 1412(a)(2)
Resource Conservation and Recovery Act	one which "may cause, or significantly contribute to an increase in mortality or an increase in serious irreversible, or incapacitating reversible, illness; or, pose a ... hazard to human health or the environment ..." Sec. 1004(5)(A)(B)	Standards for generators, transporters of hazardous waste; permits for treatment, storage or disposal of hazardous waste	"that necessary to protect human health and the environment ..." Sec. 3002–3004	EPA	No

Source: Reprinted with permission from Paul Portney, "Toxic Substances Policy," in Paul Portney, ed., *Current Issues in Environmental Policy,* published for Resources for the Future by the Johns Hopkins University Press, Baltimore and London, 1978. Copyright Johns Hopkins University Press, 1978.

there will be two central questions: How does one obtain a dose response function? and What value does one place on risks to life and health?

In this chapter we review three recent experiments concerning these questions. All three pertain to the effects of toxic levels of air pollution.

A PRECIS OF THREE EXPERIMENTS

The research efforts cited at the outset, and briefly sketched here, represent a variety of attempts to elevate the state-of-the-art in assessing the benefits of environmental quality enhancement. There are two primary areas of emphasis. First, new experimental techniques for measuring the value of air quality improvements are developed and tested for a specific area, the South Coast Air Basin of southern California. Second, the analytical and empirical methods of economics are used to develop hypotheses on disease etiologies and to value labor productivity and consumer losses due to air pollution-induced mortality and morbidity. Since the major focus for each area of emphasis has been on methodological development and experimentation, all the reported empirical results are only properly regarded as tentative and ongoing rather than definitive and final. For policy applications, these results require further refinement.

Nevertheless, they do suggest that previous studies may have substantially underestimated the economic losses caused by the impacts of air pollution, and, by implication, benefits of improvements in air quality. Furthermore, they represent some real progress in the use of data and method and hold out the hope that at least limited, but helpful, evaluations of environmental risk can be made. We turn first to what we call the epidemiology experiments.

EPIDEMIOLOGY EXPERIMENTS

These experiments focused on developing methodology for valuing the benefits to human health associated with air pollution control. Air pollution may affect human health in three ways: (1) by increasing mortality rates; (2) by increasing the incidence of chronic illness (morbidity); and (3) by increasing the incidence of acute illness (morbidity).

Two approaches for determining health effects and valuing them in economic terms were developed within the study. First, if a dose-response relationship is known between mortality rates and air pollution, economic losses can be approximated. In this case, one must know how the population at risk values increased safety. Thus, if air pollution control reduces risk of death from air pollution-related disease, studies of the value consumers place on safety in other situations—on the job, in transportation, and so forth—can be applied to measuring the benefits of pollution control programs. Note, however, that valuing safety for small changes in risk is very different from the alternative of valuing human life through lost earnings as has been done in previous studies. That approach is rejected in this study. Rather, the focus is on examining the value of safety to individuals, that is, how much consumers are willing to pay for safety obtained through pollution control. The appendix to this chapter presents a short, methodological discussion of the vital issue of how to value appropriately environmental risk.

A second approach for valuing the effects of air pollution on human health is to attempt to observe the direct effect of air pollution on economic factors, thus avoiding the necessity of developing dose-response relationships. If one can develop relationships employing data on wages, wealth, socioeconomic and health status characteristics, as well as pollution exposures, consumer willingness to pay to avoid illness can be derived. We term this second methodology the willingness-to-pay approach. It is based on traditional microeconomic theory.

In regard to these approaches two experiments were conducted. First, a data set on sixty U.S. cities was explored to determine if some of the problems of aggregate epidemiology—epidemiology using aggregate data on groups of individuals as opposed to data on individuals—can be overcome. The study attempted to estimate a human dose-response expression in which 1970 city-wide mortality rates for major disease categories are statistically associated with population characteristics such as doctors per capita, cigarettes per capita, information on dietary patterns, race, age, and air pollution. The study is unusual in two respects. First, it is the first aggregate epidemiological study of the effect of air pollution on mortality to include dietary

Table 4-2. Summary of two-stage linear estimates of factors in human mortality: hypotheses not rejected at the 97.5 percent confidence level (one-tailed t-test, $t \geq 2.0$).

Variable (sign of hypothetical effect)		Total Mortality Rate	Vascular Disease	Heart Disease	Pneumonia and Influenza
Doctors per capita[a]	(−)	−	−	−	
Median age	(+)	+	+	+	+
Percent nonwhite	(+)	+		+	
Cigarettes	(+)	+	+	+	
Room density	(+)	+			+
Cold	(+)	+			+
Animal fat	(+)			+	
Protein	(+)	+			
Carbohydrates	(?)				
NO_2	(+)				
SO_2	(+)				
Particulates	(+)				+
R^2		.82	.60	.77	.54

a. Two-stage estimator employed.

Source: Ben-David, Shaul; David Brookshire; Thomas C. Crocker; Ralph C. d'Arge; Allen V. Kneese; and William Schulze. *Methods Development for Assessing Tradeoffs in Environmental Management.* Four volume draft report to the EPA.

variables that, along with smoking and medical care, prove to be highly significant statistically. Second, the study accounts for the fact that human beings will attempt to adjust to disease by seeking out more medical care. Thus, cities with higher mortality rates are likely to have more physicians per capita. This adjustment process has in the past prevented an estimate of the direct effect of physicians on the prevention of disease. An estimation technique for the actual contribution medical care makes to reducing mortality rates is employed. The result of including these new variables in the analysis is substantial. In fact, the total effect of air quality on mortality is

Table 4–2. continued

Emphysema and Bronchitis	Cirrhosis	Kidney Disease	Congenital Birth Defects	Early Infant Diseases	Cancer
−		−			−
	+	+			+
	+	+		+	+
					+
	+	+			
					+
+					+
−					
				+	
.39	.64	.54	.22	.55	.86

about an order of magnitude smaller than other estimates.[2] Rather small but important associations are found between pneumonia and bronchitis and particulates in air, and between early infant disease and sulfur dioxide air pollution. The direction of the associations that were found among all the variables is shown in Table 4–2.

The sixty-city study does, however, have a number of remaining problems. These include biases introduced by using aggregate as opposed to individual data, the exclusion of data on radiation, exercise, and migration of individuals between cities, and the possibility that individuals may die from combinations of causes.

Given these qualifications, it is possible to construct benefit measures using the methodology outlined in the appendix to this chapter. That methodology is briefly summarized in Table 4–3.

Table 4-3.   Methodology for health benefits assessment.

Benefits = (Population at Risk) × (Value of Safety) × (Reduction in Health Risk)

Value of Safety Based on Consumer's Willingness to Pay

Low estimate:	$340,000
Source:	Thaler and Rosen (1975) (see the chapter appendix for details)
High estimates:	$1,000,000
Source:	Smith (1974) (see the chapter appendix for details)

First, to obtain national estimates, it is necessary to know the population at risk. Since the sixty-city sample is entirely urban, and since toxic air pollution is principally an urban problem, a population at risk for 1970 of 150 million urban dwellers was used. As a range for the value of safety, Thaler and Rosen's estimate of $340,000 (in 1975 dollars) was used as a lower bound and Smith's estimate of $1,000,000 as an upper bound. Finally, to provide an estimate of reduced risk from air pollution control, an average 60 percent reduction in ambient urban concentrations was assumed both for SO_2 and particulates. Then, using the mean concentration of these pollutants in the sixty-city sample as a basis for calculation, it was possible to derive the average reduction in risk of pneumonia mortality for a 60 percent reduction in particulates, and the average reduction in risk of infant diseases for a 60 percent reduction in SO_2 from the estimated dose-response functions for these diseases.

Multiplying the population at risk by the assumed value of safety and then by the *average* reduction in risk gives a crude approximation of the benefits for a 60 percent reduction in national urban ambient concentrations of particulates and SO_2, respectively. National urban totals and the value of the average individual risk reduction are shown in Table 4-4.

The second major experiment focused on morbidity rather than mortality.[a] It employed data on the health and the time and budget allocations of a random sampling of the civilian population nationwide. The sample, which was collected by the Survey Research Cen-

a. The results of this study should be regarded as even more preliminary than those of the previous experiment. Not much weight should be put on them before a substantial body of additional research is completed and they are sustained.

Table 4–4.   Urban benefits from reduced mortality: value of safety for 60 percent air pollution control.

Disease	Pollutant	Average Individual Safety Benefit (dollars/year)	National Urban Benefits (billion dollars/year)
Pneumonia	Particulates	29–92	4.4–13.7
Early infant disease	SO$_2$	5–14	.7– 2.2
Total		34–106	5.1–15.9

Source: Shaul, Ben–David; David Brookshire; Thomas C. Crocker; Ralph C. d'Arge; Allen V. Kneese; William Schulze. *Methods Development for Assessing Tradeoffs in Environmental Management,* 4 vols. U.S. Environmental Protection Agency.

ter of the University of Michigan, consisted of approximately 5,000 heads of households for nine years starting in 1967. Generalized measures of acute illness, stated in terms of annual days ill, and chronic illness, stated in terms of years of illness duration, were available. The measures of illness were substantially less than ideal. For example, individuals who died between the reference year of the interview and the time of the interview are not included.

For most of the dose-response expressions estimated using regression analysis in the study, air pollution appears to be significantly associated with increased time being spent acutely or chronically ill. Air pollution, in addition, appears to influence labor productivity, where the reduction in productivity is measured by the earnings lost due to reductions in work time. The reduction in productivity due to air-pollution-induced chronic illness seems to be much larger than any reductions due to air-pollution-induced acute illness.

The analysis suggests that the representative individual who instantaneously adjusts from an extremely polluted location to an extremely clean one might expect to acquire about $20 (in 1970–71 dollars) in additional annual earnings from potential reductions in air-pollution-induced acute illnesses. This same individual would annually acquire several hundred dollars by the reduction in chronic illness obtained from a similar adjustment. Both these results assume that wage rates do not change in response to a cleaner environment.

The willingness of the representative individual to pay for the annual hours of acute illnesses that could be avoided by being in a clean rather than a relatively polluted environment is, for the two samples for which we obtained estimates, between \$300 and \$500 annually. In these willingness-to-pay calculations, wage adjustments that may occur between clean and relatively polluted locations are taken into account.

A summary of the results of the two experiments is shown in Table 4–5. The table shows the potential health benefits of a 60 percent average ambient reduction in air pollution concentrations (particularly SO_2 and particulates) for a U.S. urban population of 150 million individuals. Although the experimental analyses sketched here were undertaken primarily for development of methodology, the results on health effects, as shown in Table 4–5 under the urban benefit column, can be very crudely extrapolated. We present our speculations here but with the caveat that they represent extreme extrapolations from the detailed analyses contained in the full report of the research project. With these qualifications in mind Table 4–5 is nevertheless rather suggestive.

First, the safety benefits of air pollution control (associated with reduced mortality) are similar in amount to the estimates provided by Lave and Seskin (1977). This occurs in spite of the fact that mortality effects of air pollution reported in this study are about an order of magnitude smaller. However, a representative consumer's value of safety, which is used here, is an order of magnitude larger than the "value of life" based on lost earnings used by Lave and Seskin. This accounts for the rough parity of the benefit estimates.

Second, little previous work has been done on the morbidity benefits associated with air pollution control. Thus, the benefits of air pollution control have been derived almost solely on the basis of mortality effects. Yet, it is clear from the range of estimates in Table 4–5 that benefits of reduced morbidity may possibly outweigh the benefits of reduced mortality several fold. Finally, the possible total health benefits alone of a high degree of pollution control (60 percent control for ambient concentrations of certain pollutants) would seem to be quite large—possibly as much or more than 43 billion dollars annually.[3]

Table 4–5. Health benefits for a 60 percent control of ambient air pollution: U.S. extrapolations (*1978 dollars per year*).

Study	Effect	Low Measure (high measure)	Benefit per Capita (dollars per year)	Total Urban Benefit (billions of dollars per year)
Sixty-City	Mortality	Low value estimate for safety	34	5.1
		High value estimate for safety	(106)	15.9
Michigan Survey Experiment	Chronic morbidity	Worker productivity	240	36
		(Willingness to pay)	(400)	60
	Acute morbidity	Worker productivity	16	2.4
		(Willingness to pay)	(280)	42
	Totals		290	43.5
			(786)	117.9

Source: Ben–David, Shaul; David Brookshire; Thomas C. Crocker; Ralph C. d'Arge; Allen V. Kneese; and William Schulze. *Methods Development for Assessing Tradeoffs in Environmental Management.* Four volume draft report to the EPA.

THE SOUTH COAST AIR BASIN
URBAN EXPERIMENT

The South Coast Air Basin of southern California was selected to test some benefit measures of air pollution control. In this case both health and aesthetic considerations were involved. For the household sector, two distinct approaches to valuation of environmental quality have emerged from recent research. The first involves the analysis and observation of how some pertinent actual market prices, such as real property prices, are influenced by environmental quality attributes. The second tries to induce individuals to reveal directly their actual preferences, in monetary terms, for environmental attributes. Clearly, there should be a well-defined relationship between what people do pay through differences in property values and what they say they will pay, provided there are no incentives for them to distort their bids. New survey techniques include ways of testing whether there are distortions in what people say they will bid.[4]

During the past few decades, the general air quality in the Los Angeles area has deteriorated substantially. However, in some neighborhoods deterioration has been slight, such as in communities adjacent to the Pacific Ocean, while in others, the deterioration has been relatively severe as measured by concentrations of NO_2 or total oxidants. The researchers believed the Los Angeles area, therefore, would be a good location to make test comparisons of the effects of air quality on housing prices and individual stated preferences, as the comparisons could be contained within a single large metropolitan area.

The South Coast Air Basin urban experiment consisted of an attempt to value air quality through examination of differences in property values and through an interview survey instrument designed to elicit willingness to pay for improved air quality.

Six pairs of neighborhoods were selected for comparison purposes. The pairings were made on the basis of similarities of housing characteristics, socioeconomic factors, distance to beach and services, average temperature, and subjective indicators of the "quality" of housing. Thus, for each of the pairs, an attempt was made to exclude effects on property values other than differences in air quality. A survey of randomly selected residents of single-family dwellings was then conducted for each paired neighborhood to discover attitudinal preferences.

A naive statistical comparison of these paired neighborhoods indicates that property value differentials between poor and fair air quality locales may be as high as $140 per month per household. Utilizing more advanced economic models, which better take into account factors other than pollution that may influence property values, differentials are about $40 per month. As a reasonably comparable estimate, the attitudinal survey results showed an *average* bid of slightly less than $30 per month. Thus, there is comparability between the magnitudes obtained between the survey and property value study estimates. Given various assumptions on income, location, aggregation by areas, specific housing characteristics, and knowledge of the health effects of air pollution, both the survey and property value studies will yield estimates ranging from $20 to $150 per month per household. These preliminary results indicate that air quality deterioration in the Los Angeles area has had substantial effects on housing prices and that these negative price effects on housing are comparable in magnitude to what people say they are willing to pay for improved quality.

Crude estimates can be made to deduce willingness to pay for improved air quality throughout the South Coast Air Basin. Difficulties are encountered in making data sets or groups of diverse individuals exactly comparable. Differences are observed between the survey and property valuation groups in average income, age (the mean age in the survey exceeded 42 years), and other socioeconomic factors. These differences have not been controlled for in the following estimates of the aggregate willingness to pay for air quality improvement in the South Coast Air Basin.

In Table 4–6 are recorded estimates of monthly bids by households and, by aggregation, estimates of the benefits for an approximate 30 percent improvement in air quality within the South Coast Air Basin. It should be noted that these experimental measures, while reflecting approximate valuations, need further refinement before they can even cautiously be applied to environmental policymaking. Nevertheless, they do suggest that dollar benefits from an improvement in air quality in the South Coast Air Basin are very large.

From the methodological standpoint it appears from these preliminary results and comparisons that attitudinal survey studies will tend to give a lower valuation of air quality improvement than observations based on what happens in an extremely volatile property market. However, only after substantial further statistical examination and comparability checks between the two methods will the research-

Table 4-6. Alternative estimates of monthly bids by household, and aggregate benefits for air quality improvement in the south coast air basin (*approximate 30 percent improvement in ambient air quality*) 1977 dollars.

	Property Value Study		Survey Study
	Paired Communities	Calculated Marginal Willingness to Pay[b]	Mean Bid
Bid per household per month, in dollars	$135	$42[a]	$29[c]
Annual benefits, in billions of dollars (selected areas and groups of the South Coast Air Basin)	$3.96	$.95	$.65

a. Best estimate. The possible range is from $26 to $63 per month.

b. This benefit calculation is considered an improvement over the paired sample approach since explicit account is made for a number of housing and neighborhood variables not captured in the paired communities comparison.

c. Based on maximum total bid with an adjustment for the number of years to achieve improvements in air quality.

Source: Ben-David, Shaul; David Brookshire; Thomas C. Crocker; Ralph C. d'Arge; Allen V. Kneese; and William Schulze. *Methods Development for Assessing Tradeoffs in Environmental Management.* Four volume draft report to the EPA.

ers be able to state unequivocally how these relationships may turn out. The results compiled in this study, however, suggest that survey instruments, when compared to property value techniques, provide a reasonable mechanism to obtain environmental quality benefit estimates. The survey approach has the advantages that: (1) data can be collected at low cost on specific environmental problems (the investigator is not tied to the availability of existing data sets); and (2) benefit measures can be disaggregated across individuals, and sources of benefits from various characteristics such as aesthetic experiences and perceived health can be obtained.

As a final caution, it should be kept in mind that the South Coast Air Basin studies were conducted in an area where individuals have both an exceptionally well-defined pollution situation, and a well-developed property value market for clean air. The effect of clean air on property values, and in turn, on the degree to which people are aware of increased housing prices in high air quality areas, appears to be exceptionally well specified at this time in the South Coast Air Basin. Also worthy of note is that 1970 property values on the basis of earlier studies have shown a much weaker association with air quality than those that were obtained utilizing the 1977–78 air quality data set used here. We feel that this change reflects a substantial shift in interest and concern over air quality for this regional population. Therefore, it should be recognized that the results of this experiment may not be generalizable to other situations where the environmental commodity, that is, air quality, is not so well specified, either through actual market prices or human perception.

CONCLUSIONS

Benefit-cost analysis has proved itself to be a very useful applied economics technique. But even in its conventional applications it has never been free from problems of both a conceptual and empirical nature. In its newer applications these problems are exacerbated, but there is promising research going on that should help to adapt the technique to new circumstances and new problems.

With respect to evaluating the benefits of regulating the flow of toxic and hazardous materials into the environment there are two chief problems, (1) establishing dose-response relationships, and (2) evaluating risks to health and life. In regard to the former, research reported in this chapter indicates that econometric technique can, in some instances, be helpful in estimating the needed relationships. The main obstacle is the absence or crudity of available data. In regard to the latter, it is now understood that the objective is the evaluation of small changes in risk spread over large numbers of people. The objective is not to attach a value to life itself. In this connection there has been some interesting work on observed behavior (e.g., in the labor market and the property market) and there is apparently consistency between values that can be inferred from such behavior and the results of the newest survey techniques. Such results are strictly valid, however, only for circumstances where risks are reasonably well defined and understood. Extrapolation of results to situations where they are not inevitably contains some element of arbitrariness. Extraordinarily knotty difficulties remain but research on these matters has accomplished considerable progress in our understanding of them in recent years.

Appendix: Value of Life versus Value of Safety

The evaluation approach that some economists have used to estimate the mortality costs of diseases resulting from environmental exposures is straightforward but difficult to quantify fully.[5] First, the population at risk must be known. Second, the increased risk of mortality associated with environmental exposures must be quantified either through epidemiology or through extrapolation from animal experiments. Third, the amount of money or the value that individuals place on safety (avoiding the risk of death) must be known. Multiplying these three values together then gives an approximation of the incremental benefits of reducing such exposures. This benefit is not in any way related to a "value of life" that is most likely unmeasurable, but instead focuses on a concept of the value of safety (or "cost of risk") to individuals where risks are statistically small.

Economists in the past have attempted to value human life as the sum of the present value of future earnings over an individual's lifetime.[6] This approach, however, is no longer viewed as acceptable. In the first place, it assumes that the value of life can, in fact, be measured—a point certainly open to debate. Second, it implies that the lives of children, housewives, retired, and other unemployed individuals are worth less than the lives of employed heads of households.

Two measures can be used to value safety or risk to life that are based on the economic concepts of equivalent variation (EV) and compensating variation (CV). An EV measure of the value of life is the amount of money an individual would pay to escape from or prevent certain death; in theory, a rational individual would part with all available wealth to save his or her life. CV, in contrast, measures the compensation required to induce an individual to accept voluntarily a situation where the probability of death is increased. As the probability of death approaches unity, the CV measure can be taken as an estimate of the value the individual places on his or her life. Logically, though, the value of life measured this way must be infinite, because as the probability of death approaches certainty, the probability of enjoying any compensation offered, and thus the value of the compensation, approaches zero. Thus, neither EV (which requires coercion) nor CV (which makes the value of life immeasurable) provides a wholly satisfactory way of estimating the dollar costs of mortality in real world situations that involve risk. An elaboration of the CV concept, however, can provide a useful measure of the compensation necessary to induce an individual to accept a slight increase in the probability of death.

Mishan (1971) was the first to distinguish between the concept of cost at risk, which is ethically appealing, and earlier efforts to value human life based on lost earnings, which as a methodology, has strange and intuitively objectionable features. The latter measure of the "value" of human life has been rejected by economists both on theoretical and, to some extent, on ethical grounds.

Thaler and Rosen (1975) were the first to estimate explicitly the value of safety, using wage differentials between jobs varying in the level of job-associated risk of death. In other words, workers in high risk jobs receive higher wages, and a value of safety can be imputed by examining risk related wage differentials. Unfortunately, however, their study dealt with a high risk class of individuals. The Thaler and Rosen estimate suggests that in current dollars a small reduction in risk over a large number of individuals that saves one life is worth about $340,000. Another study (Blumquist 1977) that examines seat belt use suggests that the figure might be $260,000. This study first estimates how people value their own time and then imputes a value of safety from the amount of time a sample of individuals spent in buckling up seat belts. These results may be biased downward because individuals seem not to perceive risks properly that involve an element of personal control, such as driving an automobile. Finally, Smith (1974), in a study similar to Thaler and Rosen's relating industrial wages to job-related risks, has suggested that, for a more typical population and for job-related risks, the figure may exceed one million dollars. Clearly, the cost of risk is not precisely known, and perhaps will never be, since attitudes—risk preferences—presumably can change over time, among groups, and can even vary in different situations. But, we at least have a range of values with which to make order of magnitude estimates of the cost of environmental risks. This range of values does not, however, overlap the value of life estimates based on lost earnings. For example, Lave and Seskin, in their 1977 book cited previously, use a value in the thirty to forty thousand dollar range for a life lost. The Thaler and Rosen value of safety is, for example, about an order of magnitude larger than the Lave and Seskin lost earnings number.

The theoretical basis of a value of safety or cost of risk concept can be shown briefly as follows: Assume that an individual has a utility function, $U(W)$, where utility is an increasing function of wealth, W. If risk of death is π, expected utility is $(1-\pi) U(W)$. If we hold expected utility constant, we have $(1-\pi) U(W) = constant$, and the total differential of this equation is:

$$-U(W) \, d\pi + (1-\pi) U'(W) \, dW = 0 \qquad (A.1)$$

where the prime denotes differentiation. Holding utility constant then implies that the increase in wealth, or income, necessary to off-set an increase in risk is:

$$dW/d\pi = U/U'(1-\pi) \ . \qquad (A.2)$$

This is the compensating variation measure of the cost to an individual attributable to an increased risk of death. Analysis of the last expression can be simplified if we assume a constant elasticity of utility with respect to wealth, η, such that $U(W) = \eta$ and consequently $\eta \frac{dU}{dW} \frac{W}{U}$. Then equation A.2 can be rewritten as:

$$dW/d\pi = W/\eta (1-\pi) \ . \qquad (A.3)$$

The right hand side of Equation A.3 suggests several interesting points about the value of safety or cost of risk. First, if we assume that the elasticity of utility is less than one, people are risk averse. This in turn implies that since the risk of death is positive ($\pi > 0$) that $dW/d\pi > W$. In other words, if individuals are risk averse, their lives, in terms of the risk premium necessary to get them to accept risk, are worth more to them than their wealth. Second, from Equation A.3, as wealth increases, the risk premium required to accept an increase in risk voluntarily, $dW/d\pi$, increases proportionally. Finally, if we take η as constant, then, since risk of death, π increases with age for adults, $dW/d\pi$ must increase with age, *ceteris paribus*. Then, one would expect older people to act in a more risk averse manner than younger individuals (require greater compensation to voluntarily take a risky action), both because of increased income and age.

This model contrasts for a number of reasons with the value of lost earnings approach previously used in economic analysis. First, if lost income itself is the measure, the "value of life" measured through lost earnings obviously cannot exceed wealth. Second, increased wealth will increase the lost earnings measure as well as the cost of risk measure. However, the cost of risk measure may not increase proportionately if a different utility function is used. Third, the lost earnings measure must decrease with age at some point as individuals get older because the expected remaining earnings must decrease, while the cost of risk, as we argued above, is likely to increase. Finally, it is clear from Equation A.3 that as π approaches unity, $dW/d\pi$ approaches infinity. In other words, the compensation required to induce an individual to accept a certainty of death voluntarily is infinite. The lost income measure has no similar property. Nevertheless, the implication is that small increases in risk may be valued in terms of compensation required to induce individuals to accept such risks voluntarily. Individuals, of course, rationally accept small risks on a daily basis, presumably on the basis of some monetary or psychic return.

Given the analysis above, the current methodology of multiplying value of safety numbers times experimentally or epidemiologically determined environmental risks can then be justified as follows: Assuming a utility function $U(W)$ where W is wealth, if risk of death is π, the marginal cost of risk as derived earlier, is $(dW/d\pi)\,\bar{U} = U/U'$ $(1-\pi)$. If risk, π is a function of pollution, X, where utility functions are identical for N individuals, one would wish to maximize expected utility,

$$N\,[1-\pi(X)]\,\,U(W)\,\,, \qquad\qquad (A.4)$$

subject to a constraint on total wealth, $\bar{W}$, or income of society

$$\bar{W}\,-\,NW\,-\,C\,(X^\circ-X)\,=\,0 \qquad\qquad (A.5)$$

that is allocated to individual wealth, assumed identical for purposes of exposition, (NW), and costs of controlling environmental pollution from the initial level of X°, $[C\,(X^\circ-X)]$. Noting that $\pi_X > 0$, and $C' > 0$, the first order conditions are (where λ is the multiplier on Equation A.5 and L denotes the Lagrangian)

$$\partial L/\partial W\,=\,N\,(1-\pi)\,U'\,-\,N\lambda\,=\,0$$

$$\partial L/\partial X\,=\,-N\pi_X\,U\,-\,\lambda C'\,=\,0$$

and imply

$$N\cdot\,[U/U\,(1-\pi)]\,\,\pi_X\,=\,C' \qquad\qquad (A.6)$$

or that the number of individuals, N, times the marginal cost of risk, $[U/U' \, (1-\pi)]$, times the marginal effect of pollution on risk, π_X, equals the marginal cost of control, C'. Clearly, this model abstracts from many welfare theoretic problems but it does imply that estimation of the left hand side of Equation A.6, as suggested at the beginning of this section, is a legitimate approximation of the incremental benefits of environmental control.

In summary, the direct cost of mortality has the advantage of focusing attention on one positive output of environmental agencies that has clear economic value—safety. It is important, however, to distinguish between the value of safety to consumers that does have measurable economic value—environmental agencies may be viewed as selling safety to the public—and techniques that claim to measure the value of human life. Benefit-cost arguments for environmental programs should and can rest on demonstrable increases in public safety delivered at costs comparable to what the public is willing to pay for safety, and not on specious claims as to the value of human life. However, the assessment of the risk of mortality associated with environmental exposures such as air pollution—whether based on animal experiments or epidemiological studies—remains difficult and uncertain and is central to the valuing of risk.

NOTES TO CHAPTER 4

1.   Other major problems are as follows:

First, such matters as nuclear radiation and toxic materials relate to exposure of the whole population or large subpopulation to very subtle influences of which they may be entirely unaware. It is difficult to know what normative value individual preferences have under these circumstances.

Second, we are in some cases dealing with long-lived effects that could extend to hundreds of thousands of years and many, many generations. This raises the question of how the rights and preferences of future generations can be represented in this decision process. Realistically the preferences of the existing generation must govern. The question is whether simple desires of existing persons are to rule or whether it is necessary to persuade the present generation to adopt some ethical rule or rules of a constitutional nature in considering questions of future generations. Such a proposed rule is found in John Rawls, *A Theory of Justice* (1971). Another related question of great importance is whether it is legitimate to discount benefits and costs over these long periods, thus effectively ruling out the future beyond a relative few years, and if it is legitimate what the proper rate is.

These issues are being studied by several members of the team that produced the research sketched in this chapter under a grant from the National Science Foundation's Ethics and Values in Science and Technology program.

2. See, for example, Lester B. Lave and Eugene Seskin, *Air Pollution and Human Health* (1977).

3. As a matter of perspective it should be noted that the analysis suggests that air pollution is a quite small factor in total mortality relative to other environmental factors.

    We can summarize the results as follows: If we *increase* each of the following significant variables by 1 percent over their mean values in our sample, from the estimated total mortality equation the following percentage change in mean total mortality results: (1) for doctors per capita a .76 percent *decline* in mortality rate; (2) for per capita cigarette consumption a .32 percent *increase* in mortality rate; and (3) for per capita protein consumption a 6.7 percent *increase* in mortality rate. These results suggest several observations. First, medical care, smoking, and diet appear to be enormously important factors in human health. Second, if one looks to a 100 percent decrease from mean levels for these variables, that is, the impact on average total mortality of setting these variables to zero, one obtains a 76 percent increase in mortality for a zero level of doctors per capita, a 32 percent decrease in mortality for no smoking and a 670 percent decrease in mortality for no protein in diet. Obviously, the last of these effects is impossible and suggests that we may only have linear approximations of highly nonlinear effects. Further, some protein is required to sustain life. Thus, the estimates of mortality effects are likely to be valid only for relatively small changes in explanatory variables. Finally, the air pollution variables are insignificant in the total mortality equation — as one might suspect if air pollution has only a small effect on mortality rates. This is verified by the fact that the significant estimated effects of particulates on pneumonia and influenza and of SO_2 on infant diseases are very small in terms of total mortality as compared to the effects of doctors, smoking, and diet.

4. For example one possible form of bias is known as "starting point bias." This is the possibility that the final bid will be influenced by the starting bid suggested by the interviewers — the higher the latter the higher the former. A test for this is to start with several different initial bids for different interviewees and then test to see whether the final bids are different in a statistically significant sense. Such tests indicated that starting point bias was not a large problem in the research reported here.

5. See, for example, Allen V. Kneese and William Schulze, "Environment, Health, and Economics — The Case of Cancer," *American Economic Review* 67, (February 1977): 26–32.

6. See, for example, Lester B. Lave and Eugene Seskin, *Air Pollution and Human Health* (1977).

BIBLIOGRAPHY

Blumquist, G. 1977. "Value of Life: Implications of Automobile Seat Belt Use." Unpublished paper, March.

Eckstein, Otto. 1958. *Water Resource Development: The Economics of Project Evaluation.* Cambridge, Mass.: Harvard University Press.

Harvard University. 1962. *Design of Water Resource Systems.* Cambridge, Mass.: Harvard University Press.

Herfindahl, Orris, and Allen V. Kneese. 1974. *Economic Theory of Natural Resources.* Columbus, Ohio: Charles Merrill.

Jackson, Clemant J., et al. 1976. "Benefit-Cost Analysis of Automotive Emissions Reductions," CMR 2265. Michigan: Research Laboratory, General Motors Corporation (October 15).

Kneese, Allen V. and William Schulze. 1977. "Environment, Health and Economics—The Case of Cancer." *American Economic Review* 67 (February): 26–32.

Lave, Lester B., and Eugene Seskin. 1977. *Air Pollution and Human Health.* Baltimore: Johns Hopkins University Press.

Mishan, Ezra J. 1971. "Evaluation of Life and Limb: A Theoretical Approach." *Journal of Political Economy* 79 (December): 687–705.

National Academy of Sciences. 1974. "Air Quality and Automotive Emissions Control." *The Costs and Benefits of Automotive Emissions Control* 4, Serial No. 19–24. Washington, D.C.: Government Printing Office, September.

Rawls, John. 1971. *A Theory of Justice.* Cambridge, Mass.: Harvard University Press.

Smith, Robert. 1974. "The Feasibility of an Injury Tax Approach to Occupational Safety." *Law and Contemporary Problems* (Summer–Autumn).

Thaler, Richard S., and Sherwin Rosen. 1975. "The Value of Saving a Life: Evidence from the Labor Market." In *Household Production and Consumption,* edited by Nestor E. Terleckyj. New York: Columbia University Press.

U.S. Atomic Energy Commission, Division of Reactor Development and Technology. 1977. *Updated (1970) Cost Benefit Analysis of the U.S. Breeder Reactor Program.* Washington 1184, January.

5 PRINCIPLES FOR SAVING AND VALUING LIVES

Richard Zeckhauser *
Donald S. Shepard **

Many of the most pressing decisions of society directly or indirectly involve the saving or expenditure of lives. Energy planning, national health insurance, and occupational health and safety regulation, as well as national defense policy, represent major issues that invariably bring us back to the question: Which lives should be saved? Or, to reflect the process of life-saving more accurately, the question might be rephrased: Where should we spend whose money to undertake what programs to save which lives with what probability? Fifteen years ago, merely asking this question explicitly would have seemed unethical or at least repugnant to many, though its central issues were addressed implicitly in a whole range of individual and collective decisions. Today variants of this question are studied by theologians and sociologists, as well as economists and policymakers. The question of how lives should be valued is now an acceptable one for intellectual inquiry, although it is true that for some the answer cannot come through academic discovery processes.

Though study of the issue has begun, the economists who write on the issue of valuing life do not appear to speak to the regulators and interest-groups who deal with the issue, at least in an implicit fash-

*Richard Zeckhauser is Professor of Political Economy, Kennedy School of Government, Harvard University.

**Donald S. Shepard is Adjunct Research Associate, Kennedy School of Government; Economist, Veterans Administration; and Lecturer, Harvard School of Public Health.

91

ion, on a day-to-day basis. Economists are accused, sometimes with justification, of concluding too quickly that policy choice to promote the saving of lives is merely a question of setting an appropriate price. Regulators are charged, often with merit, of ignoring (sometimes deliberately) the contribution that can be made by analytic approaches to policies for the preservation of life. The critical question is how to inject a bit of the thinking and concerns of each group into the approaches of the other.

This chapter integrates and substantially abridges two previous papers: "Procedures for Valuing Lives," Zeckhauser (1975) and "Where Now for Saving Lives," Zeckhauser and Shepard (1976). These papers provide numerous examples and references; they also address a number of technical issues not covered here.

Our discussion here is directed for the most part to the realm of public decisionmaking. The decisions to which it is relevant are those by which a public decisionmaker allocates resources to enhance the probabilities of survival of private citizens. The resources involved may be public, as with highway safety railings; private, but those of an unaffected party, as when radiation standards are established for industrial processes; or private and specifically those of the individual whose survival is affected, as with seat belt legislation.

Given a limited amount of resources to be spent in saving lives, it is clearly desirable to allocate these resources as efficiently as possible. The efficient use of resources for saving lives is particularly important during times of budgetary stringency, since expenditures for life-saving, like all other expenses, are subject to more probing budget reviews. Moreover, the ability of government agencies to shift life-saving expenditures to either individuals or business has been curtailed by the concern over inflation and the continuing fervor for regulatory reform. This suggests that even agencies that feel that present expenditures on life-saving are too low will benefit from rationalizing their interventions. And, pragmatically, the resource costs involved with saving lives inevitably enter into decisions. Agencies that attempt to insulate themselves from such considerations may find themselves overridden.

An analytic approach using only simple tools can help make the regulatory process more efficient. Decisionmaking could be substantially improved for instance, if agencies were required to generate information on the costs of their life-preserving programs and the benefits that they convey. The generation of such information, even if never introduced as a formal part of the decision process, would tend to make decisions more rational.

The concern of this chapter is with the analytical aspects of the life-saving decision process, and approaches that can provide useful inputs into the process. We divide the process into four areas: (1) *Valuation.* What values do we attach to the inputs to and outputs from our policies? (2) *Prediction.* What levels of outputs can we expect alternative policies to generate; what levels of inputs can we expect them to consume? (3) *Accounting.* How should we add up these values so that we do not misinterpret a quantity, miss anything of value, or double count? (4) *Incentives and the locus of decisionmaking.* Recognizing the interests of all affected parties and the likely differential access to information, who should be making the appropriate decisions?

We do not attach any hierarchy of importance to these questions; each is considered below. However, we believe that future progress in formulating effective policy regarding life-saving activities will require significantly greater attention to questions of prediction, accounting, and incentives.

PROCEDURES FOR VALUING LIVES

The perplexing problem of how we should value lives that might be saved, injured, or expended through public or private decision has not yielded to the substantial efforts of economists and others. Why has it proved so difficult to frame a mere question of value: What is a life worth? Some factors can be identified speculatively. First, unlike traditional economic commodities, there is only the slightest degree of standardization for lives. Second, unlike most commodities we value, lives are not bartered on markets. Indeed, it is against the law to sell them. Third, and perhaps partially explaining the second, the question of whose life should be saved at what cost involves many of the most fundamental values of our society. Fourth, there are many different producers of the commodity "increased probability of preserving a life." Individuals can do it for themselves; we can impose traffic laws and vaccination regulations to help protect them from other individuals; or society can provide incentives to induce them to preserve their own lives. Finally, through a variety of societal programs their lives can be saved for them. There are numerous other factors awaiting cataloguing in an eventual intellectual history of the life-saving discussion.

There is no unambiguous procedure for valuing a human life; indeed, evidence suggests that life valuation should not be approached as a search for an elusive number. Lives are different from other commodities that our society produces, expends, or merchandises. The valuation of lives involves and reflects many of the most basic beliefs and institutions of our society. With lives, it is not just the outcome of the valuation process that is important. The legitimacy and acceptability of the process itself may exert a significant influence on welfare.

The Potential for Analytic Approaches

It might seem, then, that economists would have little to contribute to the life-valuation discussion. This chapter argues the contrary. The complexity of the problem enhances the potential contribution of the organizing concepts of economics. Insights culled from the examination of a number of other sticky issues can be applied with profit. This chapter attempts to provide some of these insights.

It is critical that policymakers realize that there is no unambiguous procedure for valuing a human life. Not only do we lack a general approach that will apply in all circumstances; there is rarely any circumstance for which a specific approach could receive universal approval.

Because there is no possibility for a scientific discovery of the loss inherent in the cancer-induced death of a 40-year-old father of two, for example, a major purpose of a study such as this should be to foster agreement on methodology. The next stage would be to gather some empirical materials that could be fed into such a methodology. With the aid of these supporting materials, some significant narrowing may be achieved among the estimates of different assessors. With present knowledge and in the context of the existing debate, great advances can be made merely by securing agreement on ground rules. Indeed, even within the theoretical literature there are extraordinary areas of nonagreement. (The term disagreement is really not appropriate, for the conflicts are rarely explicitly addressed. With a few exceptions, such as Mishan's "Evaluation of Life and Limb: A Theoretical Approach" (1971), there has been little attempt to resolve the issues at debate.)

Failure to arrive at unambiguous estimates in the past reflects neither slack efforts nor stunted imagination. The assessment procedure is extraordinarily difficult. This suggests that whatever estimates are derived, whatever procedures are developed to secure estimates, there should be a continuous review process to note their successes and their implications. The valuation process may be simply too complex to reason through from beginning to end. An apparently attractive procedure may lead to valuations that are totally out of line with what seems to be intuitively reasonable. If so, it would be worthwhile to retrace the steps of the logic to search for possible deviation from what was truly intended. It is possible, of course, that the valuation procedure was not in error, and that our original intuition guiding its methodology was more refined than our expectation of its outcomes. In other words, it seems ill advised to make the valuation process merely a once-around proposition from agreed-upon procedure to accepted result. This may be the way of logicians, but it does not lead to sensible policy analysis.

Too often when analysts approach the problem of valuing life, they concentrate on philosophical issues that are inherently unresolvable. Sometimes they begin by identifying the difficulties. Then, if they have been scrupulously honest with themselves, they will tend to give up when they discover the most basic problems. At the other extreme, the analyst grinds out some numbers, however questionable. Such calculations are unlikely to have a positive effect. They will be effectively challenged by politically oriented individuals who oppose the actions they recommend, and by methodologically oriented decisionmakers who recognize inadequacies in their derivation.

If recognition of the difficulties leads to a surrender, and if plowing ahead leads to a discarded output, what should be done? Fortunately, a great deal can be accomplished. Most significantly, analysts can provide some basic building blocks so that the ultimate decisionmakers—and decisions are made every day, though frequently by inadvertence—can have some inputs for what they are doing. Sometimes these analytic inputs will make their greatest contribution by bolstering confidence. They may show, for example, that the choice between two options will not be affected by whether a human life is valued at X or at $100X$.

Willingness-to-Pay and the Valuation of Lives

Ask an economist how much a commodity is worth to an individual, and the likely answer is: The amount of other resources that the individual will sacrifice to secure it. The validity of a willingness-to-pay valuation is obvious when individuals are choosing goods for themselves. In the public sphere, however, goods are chosen for others, and payment as such will rarely be secured from the beneficiaries of public decisions. Nevertheless, the willingness-to-pay approach to valuation retains some attractive features. Most particularly, if willingness-to-pay amounts are employed to value outputs, and if programs are sought that provide the maximum excess of benefit over cost, then an efficient outcome will be secured. Conversely, if some selected programs are at variance with the maximization of net benefits using willingness-to-pay valuations, an inefficient outcome will be the inevitable result. As should be expected, the willingness-to-pay approach has been employed by those designing public programs for a range of goods from recreation days to waiting time for medical appointments. But the application has not been widespread.

Private Decisions. When the decisionmaker is also the payer and the predominant beneficiary (the person whose life is at stake), there is fairly widespread agreement that the decisionmaker's valuation should be the determining one. The analogy is made to market decisionmaking. Whenever the consumer is the only one affected by his or her purchases, and if markets are functioning perfectly, a socially desirable outcome is achieved by allowing each person to make his or her own choices. The consensus from economists about such situations is an important one: The government should not intervene.

In the private decision context, the willingness-to-pay criterion is relatively unquestioned. Thomas Schelling, in an essay entitled "The Life You Save May be Your Own" (1968), argued eloquently for this criterion. He hoped to help individuals get their thinking straight when allocating resources to their own benefit and to the benefit of others who value their continued survival.

If individuals are willing to pay some amount to increase their probability of survival, or the survival of someone else, then they should be allowed to pay that amount and reap the benefits. If there are other interested parties, and if social arrangements can be worked out so that these others contribute as well, then the sum total that interested individuals are willing to contribute should be spent to that purpose. No necessary connection is implied between willingness-to-pay and social value or intrinsic worth. Indeed, willingness-to-pay as it is traditionally employed to gauge the value of the outputs of policy choice is not even the subject of inquiry. Rather, individuals are merely being asked how much they will pay to secure something they value. The recommendation is being made that they be allowed to purchase it.

Public Decisions. The context of the problem changes when the decisionmakers are public, not private, and the lives at stake are not those of the decisionmakers or of others close to them. In general, public mechanisms for allocating resources do not allow for individual purchases by which a citizen who values an output highly can pay more for it and be assured of securing it. Most public resources are generated through tax mechanisms; taxes are rarely imposed on a benefits-received basis.

Still, a rich town may choose to spend more per capita than a poor town on public health or highway safety, thereby offering higher probabilities of survival for its wealthy citizens. It is frequently alleged that within cities with wide disparities in income, health-promoting services such as garbage collection are superior in rich areas. Because the rich would probably pay more for these services, such an outcome—whether the result of political influence, a desire to attract well-to-do citizens, or whatever—is closer to the hypothetical market outcome than an equal provision of services.

What is noteworthy is that many citizens, including some of the rich, find this unequal provision of services inequitable and undesirable. When decisions are made in the public domain, the normative significance of what would be produced by a private market is diminished. This lesson, coupled with observations about the distinctive qualities of life-preservation as an output, suggests that determinations of willingness-to-pay should not be widely accepted as sufficient guides to public decision in the life-preservation area. Nevertheless, willingness-to-pay calculations can provide a useful input to the decisionmaking process, and they represent the motivating philosophy for most analytic approaches to life valuation.

Identifying the Affected Parties. The willingness-to-pay approach suggests that to value lives appropriately, one should merely inquire what individuals would pay in a variety of contexts to save the particular lives at risk. When this process is undertaken, it should be recognized that the "interested parties" may be a diverse group with very different concerns.

The logical starting place is the individual whose life is to be saved. The reason for starting here, quite simply, is the expectation that his or her valuation will probably be the greatest, though this is not necessarily the case.

The second class of individuals who are likely to be interested is the family and friends of the individual. If the potential deceased is a breadwinner, then this will include the primary beneficiaries from the deceased individual's estate. If the individual at risk is a child, it will include people who would be required to support him or her.

The third category of individuals is society at large, consisting mostly of individuals who have only indirect connections with the potential deceased. Some indication of the magnitude of society's concern might be given by the amount that the individual would contribute to or drain from society. By this standard, a big taxpayer would be valued more highly than a welfare mother. However, it would seem that in American society, given the expressions of political feeling observed in other circumstances, net dollar contribution is not a good indicator of the valuation of the general society. In most circumstances, following the argument just made, it would be a substantial underestimate.

From an analytic standpoint, a life preserved bears many aspects of any good that may offer significant externalities. If the preservation of a specific life were up for sale, and if those who benefited from saving it could be charged in proportion to their benefits, everyone would be better off if the life were purchased for a price less than the sum of the valuations of all affected parties: the individual, the individual's family and friends, and the rest of society.

Alternative Procedures to Assess Willingness-to-Pay. Identifying the affected parties is a useful start to get a total willingness-to-pay figure. Next, dollar valuations must be secured. A number of analysts have attempted to make these assessments; their results are instructive, though few of them at this juncture would expect their empirical observations to be used in policy application as a well-justified and fair assessment of the value of a life.

Jan Acton (1973) prepared and disseminated a questionnaire that attempted to determine how much individuals would pay for a mobile cardiac unit that would decrease the probability of death if they had a heart attack. His results suggested that individuals had difficulty responding to the types of questions he posed, though they provided answers that were not obviously unreasonable. In response to questions about willingness-to-pay to avoid 1/1,000 and 1/500 risks of death, Acton concluded that "large groups of people would be willing to pay $28,000 and $43,000, respectively, for each life saved at the stated probabilities" (1973: 109–110).

It should be noted that Acton's question assesses the value of a post-heart attack life, indeed one for which the attack would have been fatal. The quality of such a life and its expected length are likely to be reduced relative to an individual who had not had a heart attack. As a general principle in valuing lives, it is important to identify their expected quality and duration should they be preserved. We shall address this issue at length in the section on Prediction.

Thaler and Rosen (1974) have looked to the labor market to see how it rewards occupations that involve varying risks of injury and death. Inserting appropriate qualifications, they conclude that workers "estimate the value of a life to be in the neighborhood of $200,000" (1974: 38). Their interesting methodology begins with consideration of prices revealed in the market, rather than an interview technique.

Frequently Proposed Alternative Measures of the Values of Lives

Although conceptually oriented economists have given most attention to the willingness-to-pay criterion as a means to approach the life valuation issue, a number of alternative measures have been presented in both the economics and public policy literature.

Discounted Consumption. One frequently employed approach is to look at discounted consumption as the total gain that an individual receives for remaining alive. There are a variety of objections to this indicator. First, it in no way assesses how pleasurable the individual finds his or her existence, or indeed whether additional funds would make much of a difference. Some people commit suicide, after all. Others might be willing to give up a substantial amount in terms of survival probability for an increase in yearly income. The major difficulty with relying on discounted consumption is that it really has no connection with the quantity that is to be determined—willingness-to-pay for reduced probability of death. Total consumption is determined more by an accounting relationship with lifetime net income plus net transfers than it is by any marginal optimization procedure.[1]

Discounted Production.   An equally popular, though no more compelling, measure of the value of life is discounted production. In theory discounted production takes into account the resources that the society as a whole would lose if the individual ceased to exist. Once again, however, the concept has no connection to tastes or preferences.

Do we really want to prevent a risk-sharing pool of individuals from spending 1 percent of their net production to protect themselves against a 1/10 of 1 percent loss? Admittedly, if sure death were the consequence being prevented, and if no one else cared, discounted production might be the upper bound on valuation. But fortunately that is not the situation, at least where such matters as the control of environmental risks are concerned. At the time that decisions are made on what levels of control to employ, no individual faces more than a small fraction as a probability of death. This implies that monetary amounts significantly in excess of lost productivity could be extracted to eliminate the radiation peril, at the same time increasing everyone's welfare above what it otherwise would be.

The key to this apparently paradoxical result is the absence of significant income effects. For large probabilities of loss, the constraint on payment imposed by one's discounted lifetime income may become a significant factor in limiting one's willingness to pay. There is an additional, more psychological phenomenon at play as well. Individuals seem to be willing to pay substantial amounts to protect themselves against any identified risk, however small its probability. Insurance companies capitalize on this tendency by offering actuarially unfair double indemnity coverage for very unlikely ways of dying. Once the salesman suggests, "And if your death should be by so-and-so," the customer may be willing to expend a few extra pennies to get many extra dollars in case of so-and-so. Assuming away anxiety—and that is a massive assuming away—this course would make sense only if so-and-so were an exceptionally expensive way to die. (It may thus be that radiation-induced deaths are particularly to be avoided and insured at extra value, for the significant chance of large accompanying medical care makes them likely to be expensive. More likely the purchaser has not thought through his decision, at least not like an economist would.)

Net Contribution to Society.   It is frequently proposed that an individual's life or health be valued by the amount of goods that the remainder of society would lose on net, for example through foregone taxes, were that person to die or become ill. There are two basic objections to this standard. First, it fails to take into account the valuation of some very relevant members of society: the individual and his or her family. Second, it looks only at the value that society would attach to the individual's economic contribution, and leaves aside measures such as compassion, bereavement, and the fact that society does not like to see its members die.

It is easy to illustrate the incompleteness of this approach. Would we not pay for some measures that were designed to improve the health and well-being of our elder citizens, even though they are a net drain on society's resources? The conventional answer is: Yes, but that is why we restrict the application of the net contribution measure to individuals in their productive years, or to those whose productive years stretch before them. That answer is unacceptable. For whatever values lead us to have concern for the nonproductive elderly—call them the X term—would apply to our productive individuals as well. The magnitude of this X term should be added to the value of the lost productivity to secure any estimate of the value to the society itself. Perhaps the "net contribution to society" approach is based on some empirical observation that among productive individuals the X term is trivial relative to net contribution. Unfortunately, no evidence is generally given for that claim.

This all implies that net contribution to society should be taken primarily as an indication of a clear lower bound on the value that society in general should place on an individual's life. It should be added to the amount that individuals themselves and their families would pay to avoid the risk. If this does not clearly preclude taking the risk, then it would be worthwhile to assess further society's noneconomic losses.

Valuations of Lives and Risks of Lives in Other Areas of Society. It is frequently asserted that we should observe how much individuals who have high-risk occupations, or who live in high-risk areas, charge for assuming these risks. This "revealed preference," it is expected, will give us some indication as to how society should assess the value of removing such a risk for society in general. The comparison is not fully apt, as long as the first class of risks is voluntarily assumed and compensated. The logical problem is that the people who are assuming the risks are those who value them the least in relation to the benefits they get for risking them. They may be the poor, people who most underestimate risks, people who legitimately have the lowest probability of being injured, people who will die soon anyway, or people who value their own lives the least.

Differential benefits may also account for certain individuals or groups accepting voluntary risks of death. Evel Knievel commands a small fortune for engaging in his dangerous activities. People who would otherwise die or suffer greatly are likely to be willing to undergo life-threatening surgery. Individuals who attach great value to their time might take a plane when a boat would be safer. One conclusion is evident. People who choose to engage in activities that place their lives at greater than usual risk are not representative of society in general. If the benefits and costs of taking such risks are independently distributed across the population, then a valuation of lives based on the assessments of those who voluntarily assume risks would tend to be an underestimate.

Chauncy Starr (1972), operating from the quite different perspective of a physical scientist, has looked at life-saving or life-expending undertakings across a spectrum of activities. Starr draws the important distinction between voluntary and involuntary activities, with the suggestion that free individual choice cannot be expected to yield an efficient outcome when risks are externally imposed, and when individuals cannot inexpensively purchase protection. Starr surveys a potpourri of risks and provides some guidelines for the assessment of alternative categories of risk. The strength of the Starr analysis is that it provides us with useful numerical indicators of the magnitude of present risks and the way these risks may be valued. It stops short, however, of providing us with a coherent methodology that can be employed for setting regulatory standards, or more generally, in forging public policy.

The controversial study directed by Norman Rasmussen of the Massachusetts Institute of Technology (U.S. Atomic Energy Commission 1974), has employed a variant of the Starr approach as one way of conveying the meaning of its assessment of the risks associated with nuclear power generation. The report provides the reader with some comparisons with dangers associated with other sorts of hazards. The implicit assumption running through the analysis is that there is a collection of potential risks of death or illness, of which money and technology are sufficient to eliminate a limited number. By seeing just how much a risk under study contributes to the aggregate risk, we can find out whether that risk is worth accepting.

This brief review makes it clear that there are conceptual and philosophical difficulties inherent in any procedure that attempts to attach a value to life, though conducting assessments with the aid of such procedures may nevertheless be helpful. In many circumstances policy choices may not change substantially if estimates of the value of a life vary by a factor of 10. Getting a valuation that is accurate within a factor of 3 might be very useful.

Clearly, the analyst has a great number of suggestive techniques to provide. By gathering assessments of life valuation from two or three different approaches, the policy decisionmaker can attempt to "triangulate" on a final valuation. If the operation of the policy by itself generates information on the number of lives that are sacrificed, and at what price, then the political process may be well equipped to provide updated decisions about the way and the magnitude at which lives should be valued. A number of useful analyses and surveys of the burgeoning literature have been developed recently. See, in particular, Viscusi (1978) for an estimate, Bailey (1980) for a survey of the field, and Crouch and Wilson (forthcoming) for promising work on comparative risk analysis.

Special Problems in Valuing Lives. Procedures for valuing lives run up against a host of special problems that are unlikely to be encountered with the valuation of traditional commodities. Three of these problems—difficulties in comprehending small risks, anxiety, and risk aversion with respect to total number of lives lost, are addressed here.

Difficulty in Comprehending Small Risks.   Most of the health and safety issues with which regulatory agencies are involved concern low-probability risks, which most people have great difficulty evaluating. Often the probabilities are exceedingly low. A typical individual told that he or she had either an additional 1/10 of 1 percent or 1/100 of 1 percent chance of death over the next year might find it perplexing to distinguish between the two risks. (It would be more perplexing if the numbers were 10^{-10} and 10^{-11}, as they often are in risk analyses.) Fortunately, decision and risk analysis can offer some guidelines. We might ask the individual how much he or she would pay to avoid a 10 percent increased chance of cancer over the same period. Then we might divide this amount by 100 to get an approximate idea of what a 1/10 of 1 percent chance is worth.

Anxiety.   It should be recognized that the procedure above can be misleading, since it fails to consider anxiety. (It also neglects income effects [Zeckhauser 1975].) Once a new element of risk is announced, individuals have something new to think and worry about. It would seem rather unlikely that a 1/10 of 1 percent risk would generate only 1/10 the anxiety of a 1 percent risk of the same loss. In other words, the amount that would be paid to avoid the anxiety associated with a risk would be very nonlinear with the probability of the risk. For smaller risks it would be proportionately greater.

Because the types of risks that arise from most regulated risks are of the low-probability variety, we must expect the anxiety cost to be a fairly substantial proportion of the amount that an individual would pay to avoid the risk. Mere extrapolation from more significant risks in other areas would not seem to be valid. The medical area may provide the best examples of the anxiety-eliminating expenditures that should be borne in mind here. A 40-year-old expectant mother whose future child is at risk from Down's syndrome, a genetic ailment that is detectable by amniocentesis, might welcome that procedure even though she would not have an abortion whatever it reveals. There is a high probability that the results of the test will be negative, and will thereby relieve her anxiety during the course of her pregnancy.

Risk-taking or Risk-averting Behavior on Number of Lives Lost. Should there be risk aversion related to total number of lives lost? The answer seems to depend in part on the scale of the example considered. If there were some threshold, say three lives, below which the general public was not informed of a death, the loss of a single life would not come to the attention of anyone except those immediately involved. Society at large might thus prefer risk aversion on lives lost when a limited number of lives was involved; that is, society should be more willing to take one chance in 1,000 of losing one life rather than one chance in 10,000 of losing 10 lives. However, if the numbers of this hypothetical problem are multiplied one hundredfold to 100 and 1,000, the preference of the uninvolved public might reverse to risk-taking. The loss of either 100 or 1,000 lives would be regarded as a major catastrophe, but the latter would be only 10 percent as likely to occur. The larger loss, using a utility function to define intensities of preference, might not be considered ten times as bad.

Consideration of the valuations of those immediately involved with those who die might strengthen any societal preference for risk-taking. Suppose a happily married childless couple were deciding whether to fly on separate airplanes for a trip. If they thought the matter through, they should almost certainly prefer to take a joint risk of death rather than each taking it separately. Their risks of death would be the same; but all the unfortunate consequences of widowhood would be eliminated.

The spirit of this example can be carried over into the analysis of risks that are of consequence to the general society. If any explosion wipes out a community of 10,000 individuals, most of the people who would have placed a high value on the lives of those killed will have been killed themselves. By contrast, if an additional 10,000 people are killed in auto accidents, most of the major externality sufferers will still be alive. Other things equal, concentrating the lives lost on a geographic basis reduces the externality loss per death. The general lesson is that, at least for those closely connected to individuals with lives at risk, it may be beneficial for society to exhibit risk-preferring behavior.

The Importance of Process

For many societal decisions that affect life-threatening activities, the procedure by which the decision is made may be as important as the outcome. Many analysts dismiss too quickly the significance of having an equitable and widely accepted process. (The criminal justice field is an area in which our convictions about the integrity of process have made it difficult for traditional cost-benefit analysts to have much of an impact. It is no surprise that "process" is a watchword of the legal profession.) When process is important, analysts can take any of three tacks.

First, they can labor earnestly to provide the inputs that are required by the process. They might, for instance, suggest to the Occupational Safety and Health Administration (OSHA) administrator who sets standards for benzene exposure just how many lives the alternative standards will affect, what it will cost to save those lives (at the margin), and what is being spent to save lives in other environmentally affected areas. Second, analysts can investigate the outcomes of the process—has it been producing desirable results? Finally, they can examine the process itself in hope of improving its performance.

All three of these approaches have the virtue of complementing and informing presently accepted procedures for decisionmaking, which is likely to enhance the final outcome of the analysis. Individuals may far prefer an outcome that they believe has been justly derived, to one that rests on unimpeachable but nevertheless distasteful calculations.

This point about the importance of process may find support in elementary economics. (1) Most of the decisions that we are making in the area of environmental and workplace protection, though they may cost or save substantial numbers of absolute lives, can have at most a marginal impact on total life expectancy in the society. (2) The dollars that we will be spending because we tighten standards on various pollutants can run into the billions or even tens of billions of dollars. Still, this expenditure is unlikely to be more than a small percentage of our GNP. (3) The basis for decisions is generally not a continuous variable that ranges between fully acceptable and unacceptable, but a dichotomous choice. Either we are following some procedures that have general adherence, or we are not. The use of an acceptable process for environmental decisionmaking has been described as an "on-off" variable (Zeckhauser 1975). If we can keep this variable "on" without drastically affecting the number of lives or dollars saved, we may gain an extraordinary amount at small cost. (A key question for society, addressed at least implicitly in the Supreme Court's 1980 decision on OSHA's benzene standard, is when do these other costs get too high.)

The more closely a process for making policy choices accords with valued beliefs, the better accepted it will be. One important valued belief is that society will not give up a life to save dollars, even a great many dollars. Rarely is this belief, widely held albeit mistaken, put to a clear test. When it is, it may be desirable for society to spend an inordinate amount on each of a few lives to preserve a comforting myth. Such a myth-preserving action was taken when the federal government assumed the costs of renal dialysis. The specific individuals who would have died in the absence of the government program were known. The lives at stake in this policy context were identified lives. They can be contrasted with the nonpersonalized, statistical lives that are saved, for example, by expenditures to construct highway safety barriers. The valued belief that society will not sacrifice lives for dollars is more strongly maintained when the specific identities of the victims are known. An effort to preserve this valued belief may explain in part the frequently noted difference between the resources expended to save statistical and identified lives. Society, acting collectively, shows itself willing to pay much more to save the latter.

Acceptance of the importance of process in life valuation can have some discomforting implications. We may find that we are spending $100,000 to save a life in one area, but sacrificing lives in others that could be saved for an expenditure of $10,000. The consequence is that with a reallocation of resources we could have both more lives and more money. Yet, if the decisions in the two areas were well accepted by the society, then it might be preferable not to change. Lives and dollars are sacrificed in return for more satisfaction with the ways these decisions have been made. Agreement on process enables society to avoid what might be difficult conflicts involving equity.

In our discussion below under the headings of Prediction, Accounting, and Incentives, we shall have more and harsher words about the problem of misordering (saving expensive years of life, before implementing inexpensive approaches).

Income Distribution. One of the most troubling areas of the life and health evaluation issue is the need to take income distribution into account. Yet it seems that this issue is sometimes introduced as a red herring. One is often told that a certain procedure such as the use of willingness-to-pay as a measure of benefit when establishing safety regulations is unacceptable because it does not concern itself with distributional implications, or because it would value the lives of the poor less than the lives of the rich. These objections could be telling, but only if the objector would accept the particular procedures that would exist if there were a totally egalitarian income distribution. But such acceptance would frequently not be forthcoming, and the distribution-based objection is perhaps merely the most convenient one at hand.

What about the cases in which income distribution or lack of attention to it may be a decisive issue? First, as discussed above, process is important. If the lives or dollars involved, though consequential, are not significant in relation to the total magnitudes for society, then we may strongly object to a scheme that appears to disadvantage the poor, certain ethnic groups, or people who live in particular places, however efficient the scheme may appear. This issue relates to the whole question of efficient and inefficient transfers, whether compensation will be paid for losses incurred, and ex ante versus ex post welfare assessments.

Suppose, for instance, that a poor man would pay up to $5,000 to eliminate a particular risk on his life, and that a rich man would pay up to $50,000. The policy choice is whether to spend $10,000 to eliminate such a risk on either of the two men, or $20,000 to eliminate it on both of them. If income transfers could be made without cost, it would be preferable to leave the life of the poor man at risk while eliminating the risk for the rich man. With the $10,000 saved, we could give the poor man his indifference price for continued exposure to the risk plus a $5,000 bonus. The rich man could be charged part of his $40,000 surplus.

Now income transfer schemes are rarely undertaken to compensate for particular low-level risks that are imposed on individuals, so this sort of transfer cannot be expected to take place. Still there are societal policies that work to some extent in this direction. For example, tax assessments may be revised downward in areas that are newly polluted. If public policymakers really followed the individualistic ethic, they would monitor who gains and who loses on average and at the margin from each policy measure. Then by adjusting policies so that the relative weights placed on different income groups were consistent, a more equitable income distribution could be achieved in an efficient manner. The policies that redistribute the most for a given efficiency loss would carry the heaviest redistributional load. In contrast to the present situation, in which some poorly chosen redistributional efforts incur tremendous efficiency losses, the poor would be substantially better off, and so would the rest of society.

Attention to problems of distribution affects the willingness of many observers to allow the free market to operate. It may well be argued, for instance, that it is unfair to allow individuals to engage in high-risk professions, since the poor will be induced to pursue those professions. But are they not better off to have the opportunity available to them? Provided that they understand the risks they are taking, the answer is yes. What of the objection that we should introduce social policies that reduce their poverty and that would therefore remove their incentive to assume these risks? That objection may be valid, but until those policies are introduced, we should not further reduce the welfare of the poor by denying them occupations just because middle-class individuals would not be willing to accept them. The nineteenth century satirist Anatole France remarked on a variety of prohibitions that discriminate against the poor in this manner: "The law, in its majestic equality, forbids the rich as well as the poor to sleep under bridges, to beg in the streets, and to steal bread."

The whole issue of denying the poor risks that they view as acceptable gets tied up with our perceptions of the income distribution. If we observe that poor people have to sell themselves into potential physical infirmities, we are forced to recognize that the income distribution is much more uneven than we had previously perceived, or that the consequences of that unevenness are more distressing. Prohibiting the poor from taking such risks may be a way of salving the conscience of the middle class at the expense of the welfare of the poor. To the extent that it clouds perceptions about inequalities in the income distribution, it may do the poor a double disservice.

Judging Overall Results.   How people feel about the society in which they are living matters a tremendous amount. Is the government affording them adequate protection? Are large corporations being allowed to foul portions of the environment that by right should be common resources? What sorts of compensation schemes are being carried out? The questions might continue, but the basic point is clear. Because of quite separate factors, a society may prefer a set of policies that produces fewer dollars and fewer lives than would be available through another. That is, depending on how we get there, we may prefer to arrive at point *B* than point *A* in Figure 5−1. Note that the preference for the apparently dominated point is not due to a variation in the lives that are lost; rather, it may relate to the way in which decisions were achieved, the way compensation was carried out, and the like. The omitted dimension is the attractiveness of the processes through which lives were saved and expended.

It is not possible to disentangle completely the attractiveness of a process and the quality of the outcomes that it generates. If a choice procedure usually (though not always) leads to the right results, protects against extremely serious mistakes, and has a logic and internal consistency that supports its integrity, then the procedure itself is likely to be well regarded. If the procedure occasionally selects an inefficient outcome, such as point *B* over point *A* in Figure 5−1, that may turn out to be a cheap price to pay for acceptable process. It would seem unwise to tamper with the procedure on the few occasions when it makes such selections. To do so might well undermine its legitimacy.

Procedures that regularly lead to inferior outcomes, however, are less likely to be respected and cherished, certainly over the long run. This is not to assert that when assessing the attractiveness and legitimacy of a process the members of society are likely to be guided predominantly by the outcomes that they observe or predict it will produce. They will probably also ask, does the procedure pay attention to all lives that are threatened? Does it appear that resource costs are appropriately recognized in its deliberations? Are its meth-

Figure 5-1.   The attractiveness of process in the evaluation of life.

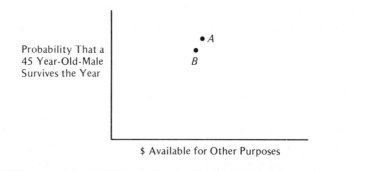

Probability That a
45 Year-Old-Male
Survives the Year

● *A*

●

B

$ Available for Other Purposes

Source: Reprinted with permission from Zeckhauser, Richard and Donald Shepard. 1975. "Procedures for Valuing Lives." *Public Policy* 23, no. 4 (Fall): 460.

ods consistent across choice situations? Using criteria such as these will tend to favor procedures that generally perform effectively. This suggests that attractive procedures can be found that will generate efficient outcomes with a degree of regularity.

Where Should We Go From Here?

We outlined four classes of issues in the beginning of the chapter: valuation, prediction, accounting, and incentives. None of these issues is more important than the others. Like the four legs of a stool, each contributes to a common endeavor. The valuation question, the one that was the most difficult to confront a decade or so ago, has received the greatest attention since then from economists and analysts, certainly when judged in relation to the definitiveness of the answers and the degree of refinement of methods that can be expected. It continues to offer an abundance of intriguing intellectual issues (a number of which are addressed in other chapters in this volume). We believe, however, that future progress in formulating effective policy regarding life-saving activities will require significantly greater attention to questions of prediction, accounting, and incentives. Below, we outline some issues in and approaches to these three areas. The reader is referred to Zeckhauser and Shepard (1976) for further detail.

PREDICTION, INTEGRATED WITH VALUATION

Our interest in improved prediction reflects a desire to pursue issues that can be resolved in preference to those that can merely prolong debate. It is our belief that many policy issues, both broad and narrow, could be effectively resolved if our predictive capabilities were improved.

Many of the important policy issues that affect life-saving are the subject of spirited policy debate. What sort of health system should we have in the United States? How should we generate electricity? We suggest that the most significant disagreements involved in these debates could be resolved if we had the ability to make more accurate predictions about the health, dollar, and other consequences of alternative policies. It is not differences in trade-off rates that lead the proponents and opponents of nuclear power to their conflicting policy conclusions. Rather, those two parties provide quite different estimates of the potential costs of nuclear power, measured in terms of both dollars and the probabilities of loss of health and life. Similarly, the advocates of prepaid health plans (Health Maintenance Organizations) differ from those who support a fee-for-service system in their predictions about the ultimate consequences in terms of costs, efficacy, and acceptability of the care delivered. The arguments of either camp would be refuted, if the predictions of the other could be shown to be accurate.

Milton Friedman, whose views on economic policy frequently diverge from the mainstream, made an equivalent point, "Differences about economic policy among disinterested citizens derive predominantly from different predictions about the economic consequences of taking action—differences that in principle can be eliminated by the progress of positive economics—rather than from fundamental differences in basic values, differences about which men can ultimately only fight," (1953: 5).

There is not space to outline prediction procedures here. The reader is referred to Zeckhauser and Shepard (1976), which provides sample predictions of the benefits from mobile cardiac units and diet control of cholesterol, both designed to reduce deaths due to acute complications of atherosclerosis. It then examines air bags for cars and lower speed limits, interventions designed to reduce motor vehicle fatalities.

Quality-Adjusted Life Years

Significant gains in terms of the effective design of life programs could come from a simple refinement of output measures that would take into account the age of individuals saved, the number of years saved, and the quality of those years. This unit of output will be termed quality-adjusted life year and will be referred to by the acronym QALY. It will be tallied on a year-by-year basis, with QALYs received in year i indicated by q_i and the stream of QALYs as q_1, $q_2, \ldots$. A government policymaker choosing among alternative health-promoting policies should look to their consequences for individuals' QALY streams. We suggest that the appropriate measure for the output of a health-promoting program is the total gain in discounted QALYs it provides to all members of the population. (Discounting imposes severe, but generally not implausible, restrictions on preferences for health at different times.)

Quality levels could be indexed on a variety of arbitrary scales. In order to gain a number of useful properties, we propose they be calibrated using von Neumann–Morgenstern utility, in the manner illustrated by the following example. Assign a year at full function a utility of 1, and a year without life a utility of 0. An individual has a choice between living the rest of his or her life with a specific impairment or having an operation. The operation has a probability x of restoring full function (this will not extend the lifespan, however), and a probability $1-x$ of being immediately fatal. The value of x that would leave the patient indifferent between having and not having the operation is the QALY level for the patient's particular level of impairment. When an alternative will affect different years in different manners, the utility value for each year must be scaled separately.

Let us look at a hypothetical, costless medical procedure using the QALY analysis. (Resource costs to the individual could be included in the calculations by including consumption levels as a determinant of the quality of life, hence the q value, within a period.) An individual has a maximum lifespan of two years. There is a .4 chance of death at the end of the first year whether or not the procedure is performed. The QALY level for death is scaled to be 0. The procedure, which may be conducted at the beginning of any year, entails a mortality rate of .2. If the procedure is a success it will restore the individual to full function, so that $q_1 = 1$ and $q_2 = 1$. In the absence of the procedure, the individual will have a QALY level of .9 the first year and, if still alive, a QALY level of .7 in the second year. Consistent with von Neumann–Morgenstern utility, the QALY value in a period is computed as an expected value. That is, it is a weighted average of the q values for the different outcomes, with the probabilities that the respective outcomes are achieved employed as weights. The individual's alternative lotteries are shown in Table 5–1. The procedure should be undertaken at the beginning of the second year. The QALY stream for that alternative dominates the other two streams.

Table 5-1.   An individual's QALY stream for three hypothetical choices.

Outcomes	No Procedure		Procedure First Year		Procedure Second Year	
	Prob- ability	QALY Stream	Prob- ability	QALY Stream	Prob- ability	QALY Stream
Survive both years	.6	[.9, .7]	.48	[1, 1]	.48	[.9, 1]
Die at end of year	.4	[.9, 0]	.32	[1, 0]	.4	[.9, 0]
Die from procedure first year	—	—	.2	[0, 0]	—	—
Die from procedure second year	—	—	—	—	.12	[.9, 0]
Overall QALY stream		[.9, .42]		[.8, .48]		[.9, .48]

Source: Reprinted with permission from Zeckhauser, Richard, and Donald Shepard. 1976. "Where Now for Saving Lives?" *Law and Contemporary Problems* 40, No. 4 (Autumn): 5–45.

Life-Saving in the Context of Present Policy — A Model that Incorporates Prediction and Valuation

What should we do with our measure once we have it? A simple supply and demand diagram may prove useful in helping us keep our thinking straight on some of the issues to be considered below. The supply curve in Figure 5–2 represents alternative ways to secure one additional QALY. Following the cost-benefit approach, and leaving aside the possibly important question of who receives the years and who pays for them, we would wish to start by purchasing the lives that are cheapest. We would continue purchasing these quality-adjusted life years until the last unit purchased cost us just the amount we were willing to pay for it. If that socially optimal cost per QALY is V_1, then we would purchase up to but not beyond point A.

There has been a great deal of discussion, as we have mentioned, about the way V_1 should be defined. However fascinating the discussion, the diagram shows that it may not be of great operational importance. If the supply curve for lives available is inelastic in the

Figure 5-2.   Supply curve for QALYs.

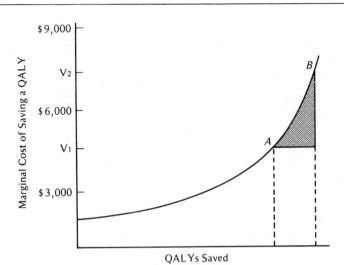

Source: Based on authors' simulation. Reprinted with permission from Zeckhauser, Richard, and Donald Shepard. 1976. "Where Now for Saving Lives?" *Law and Contemporary Problems* 40, no. 4 (Autumn): 5-45.

range of values under consideration, neither the total number of life years nor the total amount spent on preserving life years will vary dramatically if the value placed on a QALY is, say, increased by 70 percent to V_2. Therefore, even if we were to thrash out disagreements on which measures of life valuation are appropriate, or on how they should be estimated, we would not substantially improve performance on our implicit objective function. For example, if our true valuation were V_1, but we mistakenly employed V_2, the shaded area in the diagram would be the cost of our error.

Saving Expensive Life Years Before Those That are Less Costly: Misordering

Even if the relevant portion of the supply curve is inelastic, we might still reap substantial gains through careful and thoughtful attention to decisions for saving lives. The primary difficulty with present decisions, we would argue, is that we are not proceeding smoothly up the supply curve; that is, we are not saving the expected life years that become available to us most cheaply.

The issue of "incorrect" ordering for life-saving has been flagged and flogged in connection with the assertion that we spend much more to save "identified" rather than we do to save "statistical" lives. Whether this out-of-line ordering results in the sacrifice of a great number of life years, of course, depends on whether there are large numbers of identified lives that are saved at high prices. The most frequently cited example is renal dialysis, now estimated to cost around a billion dollars a year. (Though an impressive amount, it is less than 1 percent of our total health expenditures.) There is now speculation that the availability of an artificial heart could make it possible to save a number of identified, salvageable lives through a disastrously uneconomic process. If so, we would expect that a public sacrifice of the belief that we will spare no expense to save a life will be required. At present, it is our impression that the life years lost through undue attention to identified lives do not represent a monumental efficiency problem. The issues of accountability and prediction have played a larger part in creating the misordering problem.

Misordering Due to Differential Accountability.   The problem of differential accountability arises because the penalties and rewards that return to public decisionmakers are far from proportional to the benefits that those decisionmakers generate. This may be true particularly for life-saving decisions, for these are likely to involve the distinctive reward of a free conscience for the decisionmaker. In some life-saving circumstances, the chain of causality will be fuzzy and distended, and accountability will be minimal. In others, particularly where public consciousness has been heightened or identified lives are involved, the consequences of decisions may be highly visible, patterns of causality strongly sketched, and decisionmakers subject to ready penalty if lives are lost in some way that can be tied to their policy choices.

Accountability for expenditures will compete with accountability for lives in either circumstance, but we would expect that the variability in levels of dollar accountability would be somewhat less than that for lives. This suggests that the stronger the emphasis on accountability in life-saving decisions, the greater will be the willingness of public decisionmakers to sacrifice dollars to save quality-adjusted life years. The result will be uneven trade-off rates across life-saving decisions and both fewer QALYs and fewer dollars than would be generated by consistent choice procedures.

The differential accountability problem, alas, does not yield to ready solution. Some progress might be made if we could decentralize decisions and let individuals make their own QALY dollar trade-offs, an approach we shall advocate later. For those decisions that are inevitably subject to centralized control, proposals for beneficial reform seem more pious than promising. Even recognizing this, we suggest that accountability for both dollar expenditures and lives should be strengthened in those areas of life-saving activity where it is presently weak.

Misordering Due to Poor Estimates of Benefits. We may also be led to save expensive QALYs before cheap ones if our predictions of how many QALYs will be saved in different areas for the same level of expenditure are poor. Here, unlike the valuation area, sensitivity to improving estimates could be great. Estimates of benefits per dollar spent can vary by factors of ten or even one thousand. This will be particularly the case when there are many intervening causal steps. (What are the benefits of replacing three Boston teaching hospitals by the new $118 million, 680-bed Brigham and Women's Hospital?) Great variations in estimates of benefit also arise where exceedingly low-level probabilities are involved. (How likely is a core melt accident in a nuclear reactor?)

By changing estimates of these sorts, we can dramatically shift the location of a particular life-saving technology along the supply curve. The problem, we would argue, lies deeper than the persistent difficulty of making informed predictions about how many lives will be saved with particular technologies. Most decisionmaking processes that affect the saving of lives never even attempt to estimate the end product, the expected number of QALYs that are added.

ACCOUNTING

Our discussion of prediction has already provided a limited introduction to one problem of accounting where lives are involved. We have defined appropriate units of measurement. The next step, quite simply, is to add them and subtract them appropriately to compute an accurate total of the benefits and costs of a program. We have not had the opportunity to pursue the important task of developing a complete accounting system. However, we have been able to identify some significant and frequently recurring errors that would be eliminated if such a system were developed. We shall address three of them.

Marginal versus Average Problems

Most policy interventions are proposed as a unit. Thus, we may propose an X million dollar nutrition program, designed to bring all malnourished expectant mothers nutritionally up to an average middle-class American level. An alternative expenditure of the same resources may provide Y home health visits per infant after birth. Sometimes we undertake programs that are defined by a particular level of output, not input. Thus, we may decide to undertake an auto fatalities reduction program to cut traffic fatalities by 10 percent.

A famous early effort of this sort was the Department of Health, Education, and Welfare's Disease Control Memorandum (1966). It outlined a dozen or so interventions, and ranked them in order of the lives saved per dollar expenditure. An advertising program encouraging motorcyclists to wear helmets came out on top.

Unfortunately, the calculations presented in the memorandum do not reveal the information we would like to have. What have we gotten for the last dollars expended on each program? In most cases, though with exceptions, we would expect diminishing returns within each of these alternative programs. That is, the first lives that are saved come cheapest. Maximum efficiency, as is well known, is not achieved by ranking the projects in order of average output per dollar input, but rather by expanding all projects until the output per marginal dollar input is the same. For example, if 98 percent of the benefits of the motorcycle advertising program could be achieved with only half of the proposed expenditure, then it might be undesirable to "waste" the second half of the proposed expenditure. Better to start on a lower average payoff project that may be offering high marginal benefits in the initial range. The principle is a simple one: equate marginal returns across projects.

Worst Case and Best Guess Analyses

Many policy analysts have been indoctrinated in the academic tradition of defending arguments through conservative assumptions. If one is trying to prove a point irrefutably, consideration of the least favorable situation makes sense. This is not, however, an appropriate approach for rational policy analysis. Where policies are being chosen, each possibility should be assigned a probability and an expected performance score should be computed, assuming that we wish to be consistent.

Many variants of worst case analysis are employed frequently in the life valuation area. Two of the most common types are: (a) assume that everything goes wrong and see what the performance will be, and (b) concentrate on the most dangerous aspect of a process. The second variant, being more subtle, is more likely to lead to a misinterpretation. For example, when nuclear-based electricity generation technologies are compared with others, analysis frequently concentrates on the relatively most dangerous aspects of the process: the possibility of reactor accidents, diversion of fissionable material, and disposal of radioactive wastes. Such analyses seldom consider the significant advantage of nuclear over competitive technologies in air pollution (with coal), or danger of military confrontations (with oil).

Worst case analyses generate a variety of biases. First, they lead to distortions in estimates of expected trade-off rates between lives saved and dollars expended. Second, where alternative approaches are being compared, they favor conventional technologies, whose outputs can be estimated with some precision, as opposed to those that are less well understood. Third, they tend to discourage the use of sequential strategies that would enable society to capitalize on learning.

A more purely logical problem, easily overlooked, is associated with using best guesses as the basic parameter estimates in complicated systems. The problems that arise are of two sorts. First, if there are substantial nonlinearities in the system, the use of means, say, rather than entire distributions may lead to misestimates. Second, it is possible that in some situations there will be a correlation of errors, and all parameters will be under- or over-estimated. In engineering reliability studies, interrelated failures are termed "common mode failures." These interrelations increase the probability that an entire system fails (U.S. Atomic Energy Commission, 1974).

Double Counting

An ideal accounting procedure for life valuation would make sure that every valued commodity was included and that no valued commodity was counted twice. In reality, the double counting of compensated risks is a common error.

Consider a hypothetical cost analysis of a coal-based electricity-generator technology. First the dollar costs of producing a unit of electricity are computed to be $100. One input to this calculation is the miners' wages, which reflect their valuation of the risks they run. Let us assume that in deciding what wages to accept they value their lives implicitly at $300,000 apiece, at least where small probabilities are involved. If one miner's life is lost for each hundred thousand units of electricity produced, then $3 of the $100 unit cost of electricity is attributable to risks of miners' lives.

Next we add up other costs, one of which is expected lives lost. What value should society attach to those miners' lives that are lost in the production process? The first step in arriving at an answer is recognition that those lives have already been counted in the $100. That amount is $97 for inputs other than lives, and $3 as a valuation of the lives lost. To attach an additional value because a particular type of input is used would be double counting, no less inappropriate conceptually than listing wear and tear on mine railroad cars separately, then adding the cost (which is also already included in the $100) to the initial dollar total.

Though we should surely wish to avoid double counting, there are some circumstances in which we might want to attach an explicit cost to lives lost. First and important, the miners may not take all the costs associated with their loss of life into account. Other members of society may feel uncomfortable about allowing them to sacrifice their lives; these others might be willing to pay something so that this would not happen. This is a traditional form of uncompensated externality; the miners cannot charge those "concerned others" for loss of income if they indirectly (by pursuing alternative technologies) or directly (say, through legislation) prevent them from working.

It is worth noting that society presently has rather extensive directed transfer programs whose primary function is the promotion of health, suggesting that the right to bodily well-being is perceived to differ significantly from the right to beer and television enjoyment. If we are more concerned about our fellow citizens' health than about other aspects of their consumption, our societal choices should reflect that fact. But given the rather complex nature of societal decision procedures, and the inherent difficulty of calculating levels of health benefits from various programs, we should not assume too quickly that our "revealed preference" as to the magnitude of this externality is an accurate indicator.

The other members of society may also have a self-interested dollars-and-cents concern for a miner's health. Because there are social welfare programs that provide dependency benefits, health coverage, and the like, miners may not take account of the full resource costs of any health risks. The other members of society will share in some of the costs of their losses. We shall explore this matter in greater detail in our subsequent discussion of appropriate incentives.

INCENTIVES AND THE LOCUS OF DECISIONMAKING

Two principles are critical if we are to make appropriate decisions about saving lives. First, we must place decisionmaking authority in the appropriate hands. Second, we must also provide decisionmakers with the incentives and information that will enable them to make appropriate decisions. In the past, most policy discussion on the life-saving issue has taken the locus of decisionmaking as given. It has focused for the most part on the decision problem of the government or other collective organizations. The key question that has been examined, as we stressed earlier, is how lives should be valued for such decisions.

It is now widely asserted that future progress in life-saving will depend largely on the actions of individuals. They will have to drive more safely, eat less, and follow medical regimens more closely than they have to date. In the words of Victor Fuchs (1967), "the greatest potential for improving the health of the American people . . . is to be found in what people do and don't do to and for themselves." Assuming that this is so, we might inquire why this whole area is suitable for policy investigation. Our government, after all, is content to stand by while a citizen becomes a daring golfer, over-indulgent television viewer, or sloppy homemaker.

Suppose careful investigations reveal that the major health gains available per dollar of expenditure could be achieved by changing the actions that individuals take on their own behalf. Then if we assume that individuals should be the primary parties concerned with their own health, and that they have the appropriate incentives to care for themselves, present programs for promoting health would seem clearly overextended.

We might come to a quite different conclusion if we started instead from the premise that the competitive market model may not adequately mirror the type of decision that confronts an individual when making choices that affect his or her health. If so, optimally tailored government policies for saving lives would reflect valuations on those lives different from those implicit in individuals' decisions. If the society would, on the whole, benefit when individuals sacrificed other goods for survival probability or improved health, then the social valuation would appropriately be higher. The desirable direction for policy, of course, would be to make decisions that implicitly placed higher values on these individuals' lives than they themselves had done. This could be accomplished through government regulation. For example, we can make it hard for an individual to drive a car if not wearing seat belts. Alternatively, we might try to provide specific incentives to get individuals to pay more attention to their physical well-being, but leaving the final decision to the individual. For example, a California employer has markedly reduced cigarette smoking through a $7 per week bonus for not smoking on the job (Shepard, 1980). We shall not speculate here on the degree of imperfection in the market for providing health benefits to oneself. We shall argue, however, that if the government does choose to intervene, incentives approaches—as opposed to command-and-control methods—offer numerous advantages.

Why Individuals Might Choose Unhealthy Lifestyles

Before we encourage individuals to pursue more health-promoting lifestyles, we must understand why they might not. We identify four classes of reasons. First, and most important, there are many benefits associated with following unhealthy lifestyles. Most of us eat for recreation as well as for nutrition. We like to drink at parties and then drive home; at times we are in a hurry to get some place, and take liberties with the speed limit. Indeed, we argued earlier that there are relatively few areas where individuals can use money to save their own lives. Most of the trade-offs they make affecting their lifespan relate more to lifestyle than patterns of resource allocation.

Second, there may be externalities among the behaviors of different individuals. Systems of compensation to secure a healthier environment for all may be difficult to establish. It is hard to protect oneself against the drunk driver, the air contaminator, or the person who spreads infection. Moreover, we ourselves may impose some unhealthy externalities on others. The most significant externality is likely to be that between the individual and his or her future self. If one smokes now, one's health is likely to suffer many years later. There is an interesting question, which merits both empirical and philosophical investigation, whether individuals give appropriate weight to their future well-being. To what extent is John Jones at age twenty the same person as John Jones at age forty?

Third, fellow citizens share in the cost of one's illness. This financial relationship probably represents the most significant externality contributing to the divergence between individuals' choices of lifestyles and the pattern of lifestyles that would prove most beneficial for society. Some of this cost sharing arises through private contractual arrangements, whether disability, life, or health insurance plans. Other aspects work indirectly through the market. For example, overall productivity, hence ultimately wages, declines as the absentee rate rises. Finally, government programs that promote health, treat illness, or provide resources to individuals or the families of individuals who are sick, disabled, or dead, create a financial externality through the tax system.

Fourth, individuals who would like to balance health against consumptive pleasure may make suboptimal choices of lifestyle through lack of knowledge. Frequently, the direction of a causal relation is known, but not its magnitude. It is bad to smoke, bad to eat fattening desserts, bad to exceed the speed limit, and bad to eat eggs. For the individual who is willing to give up two of these practices but not all four, it would be nice to know just how bad each is. The trade-offs become much more difficult to estimate when we choose across the spectrum of individual and collective choice. An individual concerned with the risks of nuclear power might be reassured or dismayed to understand that X pounds overweight is equivalent to residence half a mile from a nuclear power plant. This information may help the individual when voting on public issues, as well as when sitting down at the dinner table. Our earlier argument is underscored: substantial gains in life-saving per dollar expended will perhaps be the most readily achieved if we improve our predictions of the benefits from alternative life-promoting interventions.

The Role of Government

There is a role for government in each of the four areas where private behavior may diverge from the optimal behavior for social efficiency. Too many policy analyses, however, leap automatically from diagnosis of an externality or other market imperfection to a prescription for government intervention. Here too, empirical estimation would help. Some of these externalities may be relatively minor. Even if the imperfection is significant, whether the government should intervene or not depends on whether it has effective tools that would enable it to help rather than hurt the matter.

The potential roles for government in encouraging individuals to choose more healthful lifestyles are: establishing incentives to deal with externalities on fellow citizens' health, providing information, and attempting to compensate for the inappropriate incentives created for the most part by private and public compensation programs, such as disability payments for some lower back pains. To the extent that government programs have created these problems, we encounter the problem of creating a pyramid of interventions. Once the government provides compensation for a particular misfortune, it will have an incentive to try to step in to regulate individuals' behaviors so the misfortune is not more likely to occur.

Means to Change Lifestyles

How might government encourage individuals to choose more healthful lifestyles? At the most modest level, the government can merely provide information. If the government can discover, for example, the effects of various diets on health, then it should distribute this information to the general public. Information of this type, except for the costs of dissemination, is a public good. No private entrepreneur would have an incentive to provide this information efficiently, that is, at a price of zero, the marginal cost of making it available. (We distinguish availability costs from dissemination costs.)

Information on the likely consequences of different lifestyles is certainly important; yet we should not overrate its impact. Public education campaigns are rarely evaluated; when they are, often no change in behaviors is observed. A controlled study of television advertisements for wearing seat belts found no increase in the proportion of viewers using them (Robertson et al. 1974). Mandatory warning labels on cigarette packages and ads have apparently had little effect on consumption (U.S. Bureau of the Census 1975).

Often a second type of information is needed: how to change lifestyles if one wants, or has been convinced, to try. In a recent national survey on cigarette smoking, 71 percent of male smokers indicated that they had made some effort to stop, yet other data show that only a small proportion had been successful (Horn 1972). Data on efforts by individuals to lose excessive poundage (except when hospitalized) show similar failures. Only a quarter shed as much as twenty pounds; most of these "successes" eventually return to their former weight (Stunkard 1975). The forces that encourage unhealthy habits in smoking and eating are sturdy; interventions that could empower individuals to control them would be a boon to the national health.

The government can attempt to develop schemes for dealing with externalities among individuals, as might occur with smoking or with driving at excessive speeds. As we have detailed above, the existence of compensatory programs is likely to provide a strong incentive for individuals to allocate less than sufficient resources to the promotion of their own health.

Understanding the possible justifications for government intervention, we should next estimate the magnitudes of the imperfections in any particular circumstances. Finally, we should examine alternative forms of government participation, to see which of them, including the possibility of doing nothing, would prove most desirable.

Basically, the government can choose between active and passive roles. In an active role, the government in effect changes the locus of decisionmaking from the individual to the government. With active role intervention, all individuals will, in effect, have the same decision made for them. Passive role intervention leaves the decision in the hands of the individual, though the government may change the terms of the decision being made.

Active intervention in the health-promotion area is primarily of two types: direct government provision and government regulation. Thus, the government might make available hospitals, nutrition programs, genetic screening programs, and the like. Regulation includes such measures as making air bags mandatory in new cars, and establishing standards that must be met, such as strictures imposed by EPA and OSHA, or setting minimum requirements for the deliverers of different types of medical care.

Passive modes of government intervention primarily include the provision of information and incentives. In some areas, the provision of information could be an alternative to regulation. The government might publicize the benefits of air bags, or establish certification procedures for medical personnel, allowing the customer to decide whether a physician assistant is capable of delivering certain types of care.

The Provision of Incentives

Where externalities are present, the conceptually appropriate means of government intervention is to provide an incentive for efficient behavior. The magnitude of the incentive should be equal to the net social benefits if an individual takes the desired action. Where health and life-saving are concerned, outcomes will be uncertain; estimates of the externality benefit will have to include some probabilistic modeling. If we know what different outcomes are worth, then we should pay differentially for actions according to the probabilities that they lead to different outcomes.

Let us say Jones can smoke or not. If he smokes he has a .20 chance of contracting the less favorable condition. If he does not smoke, that probability falls to .10. The only externality is that it costs society one thousand dollars if he contracts the less favorable condition. It would be worthwhile for society to charge the individual

$$.2(\$1,000) - .1(\$1,000) = \$100 \text{ for smoking.}$$

A few methodological points may suggest the value of a more spirited investigation of various ways of providing appropriate incentives. First, the actual payments that are made as part of an incentive scheme are lump sum transfers. Unlike the use of X-rays or personnel, they do not involve the use of scarce resources. Second, when individuals are allowed to respond to incentives, rather than forced to follow particular regimens, we tend to influence the individuals who attach the least cost to the change in their action. For example, if we were trying to encourage individuals to stop smoking and thereby promote their own health, we would want to get only those individuals whose loss of pleasure from smoking was balanced by health gains. Individuals for whom this pleasure loss is intense—individuals who will incur substantial pains if they stop smoking—should not be required to do so. In the workplace nonsmoking program mentioned above, five of eleven smokers continued their habit, though they agreed the bonus was "a good idea" (Shepard, 1980). Third, incentives can be directed where they do the most good. We can pay fat men to lose weight or change their diets. We do not need to prohibit everyone, thin or chubby, from enjoying fattening foods. Fourth, incentives can convey information. In particular, financial incentives can convey information that otherwise fades into the general background noise of government advice. An individual who is told that five dollars a month will be paid for maintaining his or her weight below a particular level may find that a much more compelling communication of the value of the weight loss than a simple reminder that it is dangerous to be overweight, even if that danger is quantified. Fifth, in addition to their efficiency effects, incentives programs can redistribute the costs of unhealthy behaviors and unfortunate outcomes. Taxing cigarettes, for instance, hurts those who are already disadvantaged, in that they are smokers. If such redistributional consequences are unwelcome, they must be balanced against any efficiency gains an incentives program can expect to achieve.

At present, we have a vast array of public and private programs that reduce individuals' incentives to provide for their own health. Probably the best way to generate countervailing incentives to induce individuals to behave properly would be to restructure some of our "offending" present programs. How this can be done is a challenging subject for research study.

CONCLUSION

Many of the most important issues confronting society directly or indirectly involve the valuation of lives. A number of these issues, such as the choice of technologies for generating electricity, the levels of stringency to be applied in environmental protection, or the promotion of transit modes to compete with the automobile, lie somewhat outside the traditional health-care field. Observing this range of contexts, an economist's first impulse is to attempt to ensure that the values assigned to the preservation of the same life in different areas are constant. This approach may derive from the belief that if risk avoidance could somehow be packaged and sold to individuals, informed consumer sovereigns would reflect such constancy in their own purchases.

Because society does not confront policy issues involving protection against risks on an individual-by-individual basis, results based on hypothetical individual isolated-consumption choices may not apply. This suggests that estimates of the values of lives inferred from market transactions may not be appropriate guides for government decisionmakers. Indeed, this chapter argues that once life valuation is made subject to collective choice, much more than lives and dollars may enter into individuals' valuation functions. Most significantly, the way choices are made may be of vital concern. That is, process may matter. Economists may bemoan this fact, but in view of their professional predilection to take consumers' preferences as given in other contexts, they should not dismiss it.

Procedures for valuing lives must be developed that appropriately reflect not only considerations of process, but also such matters as anxiety, income distribution, and possibilities for compensation. This is a challenging assignment; it should be approached realistically. The search should be for significant insights, useful benchmarks, and helpful guidelines, not unequivocal answers. Present procedures are sufficiently haphazard that even a much qualified analytic approach can provide substantial benefits.

Most analysts would probably agree that we are far from achieving maximum benefit from the resources we are devoting to life-saving activities. With the continued expansion of our expenditures for life-saving, the efficiency loss grows with each passing year.

To curb these losses will require insightful policy reforms. To aid such reforms, we have argued, useful studies might be made: (1) to improve benefit and cost accounting; (2) to refine techniques for predicting the consequences of interventions; and (3) to suggest how incentives should be structured to secure well-considered and efficient life-saving programs.

NOTE TO CHAPTER 5

1. The timing of consumption among years, however, theoretically is optimized. Using a life cycle consumption model, this optimization can be used to infer the relative values of a life at different ages, but not the absolute value.

BIBLIOGRAPHY

Acton, Jan P. 1973. *Evaluating Public Programs to Save Lives: The Case of Heart Attacks.* Research Report R–950–RC. Santa Monica, Ca.: The Rand Corporation.

Bailey, Martin J. 1980. *Reducing Risks to Life; Measurement of the Benefits.* Washington, D.C.: American Enterprise Institute.

Crouch, Edmund, and Richard Wilson. In Press. "Estimate of Risk." *University of British Columbia Journal of Business Administration.*

Friedman, Milton. 1953. *Essays in Positive Economics.* Chicago: University of Chicago Press.

Fuchs, Victor R. 1967. "The Basic Forces Influencing Costs of Medical Care." Address given at the National Conference on Medical Care Costs. Washington, D.C., June 27.

Horn, D. 1972. "Determinants of Change." In *Second World Conference on Smoking and Health,* edited by R.G. Richardson. New York: Pitman, pp. 58–77.

Mishan, Ezra J. 1971. "Evaluation of Life and Limb: A Theoretical Approach." *Journal of Political Economy* 79 (December): 687–705.

Robertson, Lelley, O'Neill, Wixom, Eiswirth, and Haddon. 1974. "A Controlled Study of the Effect of Television Messages on Safety Belt Use." *American Journal Public Health* 64: 1071.

Schelling, Thomas. 1968. "The Life You Save May Be Your Own." In *Problems in Public Expenditure Analysis,* edited by S.B. Chase. Washington, D.C.: Brookings Institution.

Shepard, Donald S. 1980. "Incentives for Not Smoking: Experience at the Speedcall Corporation—A Preliminary Report." Paper presented at the Corporate Commitment to Health, First Executive Conference, Washington, D.C., June 9–10.

Starr, Chauncy. 1972. "Benefit-Cost Studies in Sociotechnical Systems." In *Perspectives on Benefit-Risk Decision Making,* pp. 17–42. Washington, D.C.: National Academy of Engineering, Committee on Public Engineering Policy.

Stunkard, Albert J. 1975. "Presidential Address—1974: From Education to Action in Psychosomatic Medicine: The Case of Obesity." *Psychosomatic Medicine* 37: 195–236.

Thaler, Richard, and Sherwin Rosen. 1974. "The Value of Saving a Life: Evidence from the Labor Market." Discussion Paper 74–2, Department of Economics, University of Rochester.

U.S. Atomic Energy Commission. 1974. "Reactor Safety Study: An Assessment of Accident Risks in U.S. Commercial Nuclear Power Plants." WASH–1400, Washington, D.C.: Government Printing Office, see especially Chapters 6 and 7.

U.S. Bureau of the Census, Department of Commerce. 1975. *Statistical Abstract of the United States 1975*, Washington, D.C.: Government Printing Office, p. 751.

U.S. Department of Health, Education, and Welfare. 1966. "Program Analysis—Selected Disease Control Programs." Washington, D.C., Office of the Assistant Secretary for Program Coordination.

Viscusi, W. Kip. 1978. "Labor Market Valuations of Life and Limb: Empirical Evidence and Policy Implications." *Public Policy* 26: 359–86.

Zeckhauser, Richard J. 1975. "Procedures for Valuing Lives." *Public Policy* 23: 419–464.

Zeckhauser, Richard J., and Donald S. Shepard. 1976. "Where Now For Saving Lives?" *Law and Contemporary Problems* 40, no. 4: 5–45.

DISCUSSION OF PART II

Allen Ferguson: (Moderator) In the absence of Dr. Kneese, because of illness, his colleague Professor Ralph d'Arge of the University of Wyoming will participate in the panel in his stead. We shall begin by hearing the comments of Gus Speth, member of the Council on Environmental Quality.

Gus Speth: I would like to begin with a few comments, based on my personal perceptions from Washington concerning the current regulatory situation. During the past few years, there has been tremendous public concern over various aspects of government activity. Regulation, however, figures only indirectly in this concern. People are most worried about taxes, inefficiencies in government, red tape, and other problems, and not regulation as such. A *Washington Post* poll on what people want from government showed that people really want more for their money—less waste, less inefficiency, and so on. And, of course, everyone wants to reduce taxes. Furthermore, in the environmental area, recent polls asking the question "Would you be willing to pay more for goods and services, in exchange for higher quality of the environment, and less air and water pollution?" revealed that 68 percent of the people answered "yes." When the question was reversed, "Would you want to have somewhat lower prices in exchange for a lower quality of the environment?" only 18 percent of the people in this particular poll answered affirmatively.

The concern has been expressed for many years that regulatory agencies are inefficient and ineffective, yet looking at the people charged with implementing these regulations, there is a sense of dedication to strict and effective enforcement. In response, it is no accident that we are seeing a plethora of studies (one funded by the Business Roundtable[a]), Mobil ads, and many other things attempting, in my judgment, to take the rather unstructured public concern about government interference and turn it into a rigorous antiregulation mood.

I do not think this campaign has been successful yet, and I hope it will not be. Too much depends on maintaining the precious regulatory fabric built up over the past two decades, particularly in the last decade. I think it is more fragile than we imagine, and we must do everything we can to protect it.

One way to make regulation more efficient and less cumbersome is to prevent over-regulation, eliminate red tape, and to do more to quantify the benefits that regulation does bring. But our effort must begin with a restatement of the underlying philosophical and social basis for government regulatory intervention. We must look at the benefits of particular regulatory initiatives that were undertaken in the past. And, in addition, we need to find out the cost of *not* regulating.

For example, one study that could and should be done would be to look at the total cost to society of polychlorinated biphenyls (PCBs).[b] What really happened when PCBs were introduced? What did we lose, in the aggregate? We must be able to come up with better quantitative estimates of the costs of not regulating and the benefits of regulating. As we do this, however, we need to bear in mind the limitations of the quantitative estimates of social benefits. At best, such quantification of the benefits could be used to counter those who are emphasizing the costs of regulation. This might lead to greater recognition on both sides of the issue that we do not have very good data, for either costs or benefits; that is, the quantification problem exists for both costs and benefits. Most environmental and

a. Arthur Andersen Co. 1978. *Cost of Government Regulation.* Washington, D.C.: The Business Roundtable.

b. PCB is an oil that is used in electrical appliances such as transformers and can cause cancer when ingested.

health laws with which I am familiar do require a rough balancing of costs and benefits. There are a few exceptions, but even where the laws prohibit explicit weighing of costs and benefits, I think it will still be most helpful to have these estimates.

Kneese and d'Arge's chapter is an example of what we should be doing more of—that is, developing different methodologies for quantifying the impacts and benefits of regulation. There are two obvious needs. First, as they point out, we could get much better information on the "dose-response" relationships simply by trying to get better health effects data. The second and much more difficult need is deriving dollar values for these impacts on health. Frankly, better quantification of likely health and property effects, in my opinion, is more important than estimating dollar values.

The sixty-city regression analysis cited in the chapter is too aggregated to give conclusive answers. When you lump together doctors, nonwhites, and everyone else as variables, you do not really know what is being measured. The important point is that these analyses are very rudimentary. I think these analyses are unlikely to convince people; they are not quantitatively compelling enough to make people who feel strongly about the issues change their minds. But the difficulty of quantifying benefits should not prevent us from going ahead with the programs that we have in place.

Zeckhauser and Shepard's chapter takes the approach that everything should be rationally analyzed, rationally categorized, and balanced in a numerical or quantitative benefit-cost sense, even to the extent of analyzing different types of deaths. This approach left me cold. If I thought that many of the problems raised in the chapter were relevant to regulatory actions and proceedings, I would be cautious on the entire quantification issue. We must allow for some imperatives that people just simply want, even though they may not be analytically justifiable in some sense.

For example, I think under the Clean Water Act people simply said they wanted clean water as quickly as possible. That was the overwhelming will of Congress and, although you can analyze it to death, it is a fact. There should be room for big political decisions that cut through the analytical structures. People have a right to make such decisions and, fortunately, Congress has made several of them. I am a believer in the Delaney Clause for many of the same reasons. I do not want people putting carcinogens in food, and I have had a difficult time trying to find nitrite-free bacon in the city of

Washington. I do not believe in the market's ability to produce goods simply because people want them.

There are, therefore, some imperatives that stand as useful correctives and counterpoints to some of the severely analytical work that we could be led to in pursuing the quantification of benefits.

Early in the chapter, Zeckhauser and Shepard make a statement that agencies, at least occasionally, are mandated to ignore certain things. That is inconsistent with my understanding of most of the laws. To say, a little later, that the water pollution standards are drawn up with virtually no consideration of the ultimate effects on health and well-being is wrong, in my judgment. Congress made certain of these determinations after extensive hearings, and the agencies certainly pay attention to these things.

There is a feeling in a number of the suggestions that the issue is simply a matter of making adequate information available to people and then they will be able to make up their own minds, in the best way. I find this in error in a number of respects. First, nobody has the kind of information that would permit a perfectly rational choice. Second, people, as people, are entitled to make government-wide decisions on some issues. There is no inherent reason why decisions should be left to the individual. I see no reason why we have to use a word like paternalism to justify a governmental action to protect the public health.

Last, the theory assumes that the information will generate a wide variety of products on the market, which will allow people to make a choice with the information that they have. Yet, I think that there are instances where we really do not have that product choice in effect on the market.

William Nordhaus (Council of Economic Advisors): I would like to say that, although Gus Speth likes botulism, I like nitrites in my bacon.

It seems to me that the roots for reform of the regulatory process are essentially a marriage of better process and better analysis. Today's regulatory process includes three factors. First, we function under singleminded statutes, such as the Delaney Clause. Second, we function with singleminded administrative regulators, who have narrow interests in mind when they view a program. Third, there are a vast number of regulatory decisions. Due to this combination of factors, we essentially have no balance between competing national goals.

On the analytical side of regulation, I think that it is absolutely essential to confront decisionmakers with facts. And the role of benefit analysis is to confront decisionmakers with both the costs and the benefits of certain actions.

Over the last few years, cost analysis has been required for major regulations in the federal government. However, there is still no requirement to do benefit analysis and there is a lot of resistance to this. Two case studies emphasize this point. The first is a proposal by the Department of Transportation (DOT) to provide equal access to transit systems to the handicapped. This is a $2 to $8 billion regulation. It resulted from a tortuous series of legal maneuvers: Congress passed a statute; then the Department of Health, Education, and Welfare (HEW) issued an Executive Order that told everybody else in the government what to do. Now, the DOT is implementing this; it has decided to retrofit a number of subway systems in major cities, as required under the Executive Order.

In some preliminary benefit analysis, which includes the cost to retrofit the subway systems of the major cities divided by the number of rides generated by people who could not otherwise ride (mainly people in wheelchairs), the cost per ride turns out to be about $4,000. This is very expensive and it should indicate that one must go back to the drawing board to come up with a better plan. If benefit analysis had been done here, this regulation might not have been proposed. There is no automatic mechanism that allows you to avoid outrageous examples.

A second example is the performance standard for power plant emissions. Last year, when Congress passed this law, there was a lot of testimony and argument from both sides, but nobody actually did a good analysis of what the costs and benefits of the standard would be. The law is generally regarded as leaning toward a full scrub of sulfur-dioxide emissions. Since its passage, the Environmental Protection Agency (EPA) and a number of others have done a very careful benefit and cost analysis on the effects of the regulation. It shows that this is an expensive regulation and that, if you go the route that Congress and the Administration apparently intended, not only do you end up with higher costs and significantly higher oil imports, but you may end up with more emissions.

Although I do not know what is going to happen in this case, I think that without the later analysis there is no doubt that no one would have questioned the idea of full scrubbing. But when you actually see the analysis done by the agencies that comes out with this kind of a result, you have to sit back and say, "Are we doing the right thing?"

I would like to summarize what I see as the high priorities for use of benefit assessment. First, we lack an overall accounting system. Everybody has his pet risk where either you are going to kill a lot of people here or save a lot of people there. If you added up all the risks that people fear, you probably would kill the population four times. Somehow we have to make sure that the numbers add up.

Second, I think that we have to defuse the human life issue. You cannot avoid it because we deal with an enormous number of health and safety programs. Although we do not want to say that a life is worth one million dollars—or any other figure—we do have to get more consistency of value. Otherwise, we are not going to end up with any more rational numbers than we have now. I think that Zeckhauser and Shepard's chapter does defuse this issue.

Finally, I would like to agree with George Eads on the state of the art. We are never going to know the effects of sulfur, even to an order of magnitude; similarly with most risks. But we do have enough evidence to proceed. We cannot simply say, for example, that we are just not sure that cigarette smoking causes cancer, and therefore, we will issue no regulation. The problem is really the willingness of decisionmakers to use benefit analysis.

Ralph d'Arge: Regarding the sixty-city study, I am in total agreement with Mr. Speth. The specifications, which are quite similar to every famous set of studies by Lester Lave and Eugene Seskin, are highly aggregated so that one wonders whether there is any positive marginal product associated with such a study. What this study does demonstrate, however, is how sensitive these aggregate studies are to the inclusion of just one additional variable. By adding several variables—diet, cigarette smoking, and others—the coefficients on air pollution variables became insignificant, in most cases. What we were trying to demonstrate here was not that such a study could lead to new and fabulously different benefit estimates for the EPA, but rather that there were some significant methodological problems in trying to use cross-city statistical samples.

I am particularly concerned with the estimates of willingness to pay for clean air, which were used in the chapter. In this case, we asked people how much they were willing to pay for air quality, ranging from eleven parts per hundred million of total oxidant down to five parts per hundred million. This commodity was described with pictures and with various descriptive health effects and we tried to remove certain kinds of biases.

We found that what people said they were willing to pay, and what was actually being reflected at the time in the housing market price differentials in Los Angeles were quite similar, after one adjusted for various other components of a market price for housing.

We would rarely question that the price of bread has a direct relationship to how people value it. A statement that a $10,000 price differential for housing exists between areas with eleven and those with five parts per hundred million in total oxidant is similar to saying that the price of bread is roughly 55 cents per loaf. There is an active market for clean air in this community, and although people may have some misperceptions as to what they are actually bidding, they are paying for it.

Richard Zeckhauser: The first issue I will address is whether agencies do or do not look at benefits and costs when formulating their regulations. Bill Nordhaus has provided us with some instructive examples of their failure to do so.

Consider the behavior of the Occupational Safety and Health Administration (OSHA). That agency has made a major point in a number of its proceedings as to what feasibility should mean. (OSHA's statute requires that it take feasibility into account when formulating and enforcing its regulations.) OSHA claims that feasibility should relate solely to technical possibility, not to economic feasibility. Thus, the standard should not depend on any assessment of the costs that accompany it.

Equally disturbing, when promulgating regulation after regulation, OSHA has provided no benefit analysis. The proposed benzene standard had a major supporting assessment developed by the Arthur D. Little Company, but this report included only three pages of benefit analysis, which consisted mainly of one table and one chart. Nowhere were we told how much disease the standard would avoid; not even a high or a low estimate was given.

This standard, incidentally, was overturned by the Fifth District Court last week. The reason it was overturned was that there was no demonstration that its benefits were commensurate with its costs. In the long run, I believe that this defeat will prove beneficial both to OSHA and to occupational health. Leaving aside what should be done with benzene regulation itself, OSHA will be forced to develop more consistent arguments for its interventions. If one thinks, as I do, that there is a political process ultimately limiting society's expenditures in any particular area, then OSHA, by rationalizing its interventions, will be able to achieve more occupational health per dollar it is able to direct to that purpose. A more extreme argument could even be made: If society knew that OSHA's interventions were highly productive, then it might well increase the resources it devotes to occupational health.

The Delaney Clause has also been discussed here. That clause requires the Food and Drug Administration (FDA) to be guided solely by the presence of one benefit: the avoidance of a carcinogen—either observed in humans or, more questionably, when produced in animals fed concentrations of the substance, however high. The prescription is absolute. No further account is to be taken either of the magnitude of the benefit or of the presence of other benefits, for example, protection against botulism.

I do not know how I feel about my hypothetical bacon. I no longer eat the stuff. But if I were a big bacon eater, and if I wanted to decide whether to line up behind Gus or behind Bill at the meat counter, I would want to know how much botulism was being prevented, measured both in terms of probability and severity, versus what risk of cancer I was incurring. I would want to be a well-informed consumer.

Let me clarify what I said about death. A great deal of policy in the United States seems to revolve around the risk of death and particular ways of dying. Cancer is the salient example. Threats of cancer are weighted much more heavily in our policy deliberations than are threats of heart disease. This phenomenon certainly has influenced medical research. Most people feel that over the past five to eight years we have poured too many funds into cancer research relative to other areas.

Although cancer may be the worst way to die, death from heart disease or any other cause is also awful. But why should the worst possibility determine the outcome? In part, it is politics. As some of my friends in the consumer movement say: "Cancer is our issue. If a product has cancer associated with it, then we can stop you—industry, government, whoever you might be—from using it."

Heart disease is not their issue and this may have some unfortunate consequences. Probably not all of you are aware that there has been a dramatic reduction in death due to cardiovascular disease in the last ten years. In this area, many more deaths have been avoided, lives saved, quality of life enhanced, than has been achieved through the whole slew of new health-promoting government regulations. Surprisingly, we do not know why this cardiovascular-death reduction has occurred. Maybe it is just a gratuitous happening, maybe it is jogging, maybe it is better diet—nobody knows. But if we had gathered that information ten years earliei we might have produced this result sooner, or achieved an even greater gain. Perhaps there is an equivalent advance that is available now. If so, we have not been doing the research to find it. This phenomenon was discovered because some people did epidemiological studies, and said, "Amazing, the rate of death through cardiovascular disease is down dramatically." I consider this benefit to be of great importance, and I hate to think that we might so easily have missed it and may be missing equivalent benefits now.

Let me turn to the question of water pollution. One of my students, who is writing her doctoral dissertation, was asked by EPA to look at models of diffusion of pollutants and, in particular, to examine ultimate human health effects. She went around the country and spoke with various EPA laboratories and many individuals. The overwhelming weakness that she diagnosed was that there were no intermedia models of pollution, models that describe how something that gets into the water eventually comes back to hurt human beings. I think that the effect on humans is the central question.

If, disregarding aesthetic consequences, it turns out that water pollution has virtually no health effects, while air pollution has very severe health effects, I would rather tighten up on air pollution and reduce control efforts in the water area. Although I doubt it, the empirical results could, conceivably, come out the opposite way, in which case I would alter standards in the opposite direction. Incidentally, I am delighted that EPA seems to be quite concerned about this range of issues, and is making efforts to identify and rectify possible imbalances.

Finally, I want to make a point about the general health and safety benefits issue. Most discussion centers on particular policy concerns and always increases the tension between the good guys and the bad guys, dollars versus lives—or whatever else it may be. Whether it is the benzene standard or the generic carcinogen standard, it is always posed to sound like a zero-sum game: "What we, the health advocates, are gaining, you, the cost control advocates, are losing." This may be true on an individual issue. But if we have a great number of irrational interventions or noninterventions, with some falling on each side of the fence, then we are spending a fortune to get very little benefit in some domains, while in other areas we are foregoing very significant benefits that would not cost very much to secure. Therefore, if we can start to rationalize and eliminate the outrageous interventions of both overregulation and underregulation, both sides will be better off.

However you measure benefits, there is a curve of possibilities that relates benefits to society's expenditures. Presently we are operating far from the frontier, securing fewer benefits than we could for our expenditures and spending more than necessary to get our present level of benefits. The current political struggle is also away from the curve of possibilities: Should we have more benefits or less costs? If we wish to improve policy dramatically, we must move toward the frontier of feasibility. The critical question for the design of our institutions is how to develop a system that enables us to make beneficial trade-offs across areas and across time. A good start would be to attempt to identify the benefits that would be generated by alternative regulatory interventions. Before we can bargain over costs and benefits in different areas, we must at least know what benefits will be offered.

Nicholas Ashford: I have a question on the Kneese–d'Arge chapter. In trying to correlate the level of air pollution with bronchitis, at what point in time did you choose to measure the air pollution level, and at what point in time did you choose to measure the disease incidence? Were those the same periods of time?

Ralph d'Arge: Yes.

Nicholas Ashford: You must be aware of the long latencies that exist between exposure and effect for chronic disease. I think that you have committed a classic error with the correlation. I would commend you to an article in the *American Journal of Public Health*[c] on the correlation between sulfur-dioxide (SO_2) particulates in 1960

---

c. Weiss. 1978. "Lung Cancer Mortality and Urban Air Pollution." *American Journal of Public Health* 68, no. 8 (August): 773–775.

and lung cancer in the Philadelphia area in 1970. The correlation with increased risk of lung cancer—county-by-county, around Philadelphia—is remarkable.

The second comment that I would like to make is that Dick Zeckhauser asks about how many payoffs we have had from a program of occupational cancer prevention. I only want to remind you that the payoff from regulating the problem of occupational cancer will only come twenty or more years from now because of the long latency of cancer. It is a mistake to look for the payoff now.

Richard Zeckhauser: I did not say anything about that. I simply said that there were many diseases to be concerned about, and we should not enshrine cancer and forget all others.

Nicholas Ashford: The point is, you cannot find the benefits of the payoff at this time, which brings up an interesting question about how you discount benefits. By the way, the Fifth District Court case concerning the benzene standard did not say that the controls that were imposed on industry were not reasonably related to the benefits. And that is a very different issue, one that asks whether the imposed controls can be shown to *have* a payoff. We must not confuse the issue of whether costs are worth the benefits with the burden of proof that goes to show substantial evidence of benefit efficiency.

Ralph d'Arge: I would like to respond to the issue of latency. There are all kinds of lag structures for every one of the different kinds of diseases. We are aware of that problem. However, the studies that have been done by economists using epidemiology have traditionally ignored these lag structures, so we did the same.

There is a second problem: If you do not die from disease "A," you are going to die from disease "B" or "C." So there is a natural interdependence of all of the dependent variables that we have in these statistical relationships. This statistical dependency is not pulled out, which is a problem.

Rhea Cohen: In response to Mr. Nordhaus's comment on transit systems, I would like to point out that the study on the cost to improve the system was based on present users of the transit system. However, you do not know who would use it after improvement. You do not know how many handicapped there are, for instance, who have been discouraged over the years by their own experiences, or by what society has taught them, who do not use the public facilities. They are not counted in the study.

It is very difficult, then, for anyone to believe the price tag of $4,000 to serve a single passenger. I think that such numbers are meaningless. I would rather see the cost, not in terms of dollars, but in terms of benefits. A physically handicapped woman with children, for example, would well understand the benefit of being able to use public transportation to take her children somewhere.

If economists are unable to write benefit analyses this way, other people can. The agencies trying to investigate methods of tallying benefits should look to other kinds of input. Somebody has to analyze a proposed decision in terms of the benefits to people's lives — not simply in terms of dollar costs. Government agencies, so far, have lacked the capability, or impetus, to develop this kind of analysis.

William Nordhaus: The point that disturbs me in your comment is that you say the number is irrelevant. Although I was oversimplifying, I think the number does indicate that cities should try to develop alternative transportation modes that handicapped people would be much more likely to use — and that are much less expensive.

In fact, you are absolutely right that many handicapped people will not ride the subway because it is inconvenient. It is a lot more convenient to have personalized services. As it turns out, you can lower the cost and get more benefits by using some careful analysis that asks what things cost and what the consequences are. It goes back to the Kleindorfer–Kunreuther paper, discussed in Part I, where you have to ask how consumers are going to respond to a certain set of rules.

This dialogue does highlight one difficulty that I perceive in reaching more rational solutions. A conflict arises between the hard-hearted people, on one side, who insist on looking at the numbers and who do not proceed if something does not make sense, and, on the other side, the people who have a heart and say that the numbers are irrelevant. Without numbers, I doubt that they will have the effect of really swaying people due to the many assumptions that go into the analysis, the fallibility of them, and the preliminary nature of the major conclusions.

On the issue of whether benefit analysis is now being done, I think it is obvious that work is not being done. Although when agencies, the ones that I follow most closely, do issue regulations, the question of weighing costs and benefits and cost effectiveness do come into the picture—not in a strict quantitative sense, however.

One issue on which I agree with Dick Zeckhauser is that we are overemphasizing cancer relative to other health hazards. I do not think that we have paid nearly enough attention to teratogensis, mutagenic consequences other than cancer, and all of our other chronic health hazards. There has been not too much focus on cancer, in my judgment, but too little focus on these other hazards.

Mark Silbergeld: I am surprised that Bill Nordhaus did not mention that the real issue about putting the elevators in the subways is actually the mainstream issue. There is a much more cost-effective process, which is minibusing; but the handicapped want to feel that they are part of the mainstream. They are insisting on being able to use the subway like everyone else. It is a "quality of life" issue.

Robert Rauch: First, in response to Mr. Nordhaus's contention that partial scrubbing of sulfur-dioxide emissions from power plants will result in a greater reduction in such emissions than full scrubbing, I think that, looking back at that analysis, you would find that full scrubbing does give a greater reduction.

But, aside from that point, what troubles me about the analysis that Nordhaus has referred to is that it is so incomplete, so simplistic, on the benefit side that it is of very little utility. There is absolutely nothing in the Clean Air Act that hangs on the total SO_2 emissions nationwide. The benefits, such as there are, of that particular set of regulations depend on much more microanalysis of the impact of the emissions on certain regions of the country. I think that this type of analysis, if offered as an example of the direction in which we should be going, at least on the benefit side, is extremely inadequate.

Let me discuss several points regarding the very difficult and emotional issue of determining what value we should put on an individual life. It has been suggested that there are many different ways to save lives, which is certainly true.

Once a risk—from a chemical plant or some other source of danger—has been identified for a certain group of people, it is very difficult for this society, which puts a great deal of emphasis on individual lives, to simply, callously say, "I am sorry, it costs too much money to protect you." As a society we simply do not do that. This is similar to telling a hospitalized patient, "You have a very serious disease. We think that there are ways of curing you, but, quite honestly, it costs too much money. You have had your quotient of health care." It would not be cost effective to save this patient since the high cost of providing additional treatment would reduce what could be spent to save someone else. It is very difficult for people to make this sort of judgment.

However, one cannot simply trade-off lives against each other. If the life at stake is your own, it is not easy to say, "Well, I will sacrifice my life because it is cheaper to save the other fellow's life." Once we, as a society, identify a risk, we do try, within limits, to prevent that risk. I think this is a correct approach.

An assumption that is made on this issue is that there are other people who can be saved at less cost. Although this may be true, many times it is difficult to identify these other people. And often, once identified, it is politically difficult, or impossible, to protect them.

Let me give you an illustration. At the Environmental Defense Fund we are constantly asking ourselves if we are going after the chemicals that really offer the most serious hazards—are we getting the most bang for the dollars that we are spending? One issue that has come up repeatedly within our own group is why are we not doing more about smoking? As a group, we are very concerned about the health effects of toxic chemicals. Why are we devoting so much time to some of these chemicals, which, admittedly, threaten a smaller number of people than the number exposed to cigarette smoke?

The answer is really quite clear. The political obstacles to banning cigarettes, or to stopping people from doing something that is harmful to them, are virtually insurmountable. As a result, although it is more cost effective to get people to give up cigarettes than to regulate these other chemicals, politically it is very difficult.

This brings us back to the point that you have to do the best that you can with the hazards that you can identify and are able to control. It is not always a question of selecting the "best" alternative, because frequently you do not know what the alternatives are and, even if you do know them, you may not be able to do anything.

William Nordhaus: May I make just one point about the identified versus statistical lives issue. I agree with your discussion of what happens, but I do not agree with your comment that the Environmental Defense Fund deals mostly with identified lives. Generally, there are no very significant probabilities for death associated with having, for example, a higher level of pollution. Everyone who lives in a polluted city thinks that he or she is not going to be the one to die from the pollution. Therefore, most of the decisions that we are dealing with do not get into the charged atmosphere that you talk about.

The National Institutes of Health (NIH) made a conscious decision not to support an artificial heart; this would probably be more expensive than renal dialysis, on a yearly basis. They did not want to devote the resources to what they knew would be an identified life problem. This was their political prediction. What I am saying is that there are technologies like the artificial heart, which, seven years from now, may be developed in some other country, and this is when we will have to confront the issue head-on.

Robert Rauch: I would also like to make one quick comment on the identified versus unidentified lives issue. There are many, many times where we can, with a fair amount of certainty, identify a group within which a risk will occur. I offer one example. The EPA is now grappling with the issue of regulating airborne arsenic. Since arsenic comes from relatively few sources in this country, it is fairly easy to identify who is at risk. Although you cannot determine which individuals within this group are going to get cancer, you do know the group. In my judgment, it is very hard for the EPA to simply say, it costs too much to regulate arsenic, so we are going to turn to something else and forget about you. This troubles me. I do not think that Congress, if the issue was stated this way, would take such a course of action.

Unidentified Speaker: Many comments have been made on the adequacy or inadequacy of analyses on particularly tough issues. Some information was offered on how to attack them on an emotional ground. It seems to me that this is not the issue, though, because analyses always take place within the agencies, among the decision-making staffs.

I think an aspect that we have ignored is how to debunk, or at least air, bad analyses. These probably have as much, or more, effect on decisionmaking processes than good analyses. Those of us who have been with regulatory agencies have ample examples. I offer one that deals with a five-year-old decision of the FCC to monitor the mobile spectrums to make more efficient use of them. A basis for this decision was a study that showed that the cost of eliminating mobile spectrum use for offshore oil rigs would exceed the GNP, every year. Certainly, this study resulted in one more mobile unit surviving than might have otherwise. But there was no rebuttal—no good analysis of the study was ever done.

I do not think that decisionmakers are well served by incomplete analysis, and incomplete information, as much as they are poorly served by blatantly bad analysis or blatantly biased analysis.

Mark Silbergeld: The question of handicapped access to the subway provides a very interesting model of a situation in which, for reasons other than the economic analysis, it is difficult to apply benefit-cost analysis. Therefore, in this case, the decision should not rely substantially on benefit-cost analysis.

In contrast, suppose the FDA discovers that a particular drug on the market has very serious side effects that were not disclosed in the original research, on the basis of which the new drug application was approved. Here, a benefit-cost analysis to measure the benefits of the drug versus the risks of the side effects might be a reliable decision tool.

The subway problem, as I see it, is a very different model since there are some very practical problems aside from the question of whether the subway is a good way to develop transportation for the handicapped. First, at the planning and design stages, the decisionmakers had to face the general issue of mass transportation. They had no authority to make decisions specific to transportation of the handicapped.

Then there are many other problems. For instance, the money is available for the subway, even though, in truth, there are other more cost-effective means of providing transportation to the handicapped, such as personalized services. So, even if the decisionmakers conclude that the best thing to do is to pay handicapped people's taxicab fares, or to drive a bus around the neighborhoods, the subway appropriations cannot be spent on these alternatives.

Rationally, perhaps, this is the time to go back and get money for another program. However, more specific, narrower programs to provide effective transportation for the handicapped may not be politically achievable. To say that some other theoretical possibilities are more cost effective does not mean that they can be achieved politically.

Finally, if you talk about a more specific case, the political constituency for handicapped use of the Washington subway is very strong. A great number of people are interested in using that transportation medium while there is not a big political constituency for other means of ground transportation. In this particular model, therefore, it is too late to use the cost-benefit measurement to decide how the handicapped should be transported because the political and financial decisions on allocation of transportation resources already have been made.

Richard Zeckhauser: No interest group that fares well on a particular issue is then going to want to give up what it has gained. I do not blame any of them. I was just allocated a very good office in our new building. Although I would have allocated the office differently, I did not go back to the Dean and say, "You made a mistake. I would like to have a handicapped person here."

George Eads: I think that the political process is a highly imperfect one. Many constituencies with political clout get benefits that are out of line with social benefits and cost calculations because the process does not follow "effectiveness calculations." The question is how we can improve this, so that particular groups with good data and different ideas do not dramatically distort what society, as a whole, would like to do.

Unidentified Speaker: For the record, the way that the subway decision was reached was that Secretary Califano, shortly after taking office, found his house surrounded every day by wheelchairs. And they would not go away until he issued this regulation. His wife got rather upset about the whole situation, which helped get the regulation out pretty fast. It did not matter whether benefit analysis was done or not.

The point is that if a reasonable number for the cost per passenger had been reached, then people would have said, "That is reasonable; let's proceed." However, with the result we reached, people tended to sit back and ask themselves, "Can we do something better? Is there a way that we can move down toward the frontier?"

Richard Zeckhauser: I want to offer a different idea about benefits. Should we do a micro- or more macroanalysis of what the benefits of regulations are? The issue of setting standards may have far more importance in that they provide legal norms that produce liability suits, which we know are causing industries a tremendous problem at this point. Regulations are having a tremendous effect on chemical process technology and product redesign. The whole purpose seems to be to try to institutionalize changed behavior of the chemical- and materials-related industries in the health areas, so that they can readjust their technology. Can we have economic growth that is consistent with these kinds of policies?

Norman Waitzman: In our discussion today, especially with the panel of economists, we have concentrated on imperfections in the market mechanism for allocating health and safety. And it has been suggested that if only various imperfections of the market could be corrected, we would eliminate the need for health, safety, and environmental regulation.

First is the information problem. If consumers and workers had perfect information and if all of the risks associated with environmental hazards were known, we would somehow arrive at rational prices for injury and disease. Second is what economists call the externality problem. If only the social "costs" of contamination of natural resources and deterioration of health due to pollution, which are not presently reflected in the producers' prices for products, were somehow "internalized" by firms, we would get the right price for pollution. Third is the problem of a discount rate. Unfortunately, the effects of health and safety hazards are not as fleeting as a market exchange. If we only knew the right discount rate, if only the intergenerational burden posed by certain drugs and particulates could be reflected in the present account, we would pay our share for the next generation's inheritance of a deteriorated environment.

But I think that the issue demands more than a concern for market imperfection. Let us step back for a moment and take a look at market theory, and its basis in a peculiar definition of rationality. I think that the two axes on Zeckhauser's Figure 5–2, comparing costs to benefits, are incommensurate. Only by embracing a neoclassical definition of rationality can these axes appear on the same graph.

A lot of comments have suggested that quantity and quality are being compared here—medicine weighed against cosmetics—and there is a sense that something is wrong. The market definition of rationality is just maximizing income. But, is that what really constitutes rational behavior? After all, dollars are a means to limited ends. Do we sacrifice our ultimate goals to obtain them? This definition of rationality suffers, then, because there is no consideration of ordering of preferences. As rational beings with long-term goals, we consider certain things more important than others, certain goods more important than others. Furthermore, certain decisions set a framework for other decisions.

For example, when I buy a camera, I assume that film will be both available and affordable. I do not have much of a preference for film unless I like photography. More important, I depend on an environment conducive to picture-taking as well as my own physical well-being. Yet, the market takes all preferences—first-order, second-order, and so on—and throws them into a common pot: cameras, film, environment, safety. There is a point where the cost of satisfying an additional first-order preference will be greater than satisfying an additional second-order preference. At this juncture, some people will not have their first-order preferences fulfilled because the price of second-order preferences precludes the meeting of those preferences.

Some of the first-order preferences in our lives are health, safety, food, and some of the basic necessities. If some of us realized when we went into the market and bought a cigarette, which we felt to be a second-order preference, that we were hurting some other person's ability to reach his or her first preference, and somebody came up and asked, "Would you give up smoking to allow somebody to have health, or to allow more people to have their first-order preferences?" many of us would say, "You bet I would." This is not just out of "equity" considerations or sheer compassion, but because it is rational. This is the second discrepancy with the neoclassical definition of rationality. Is it not reasonable that in a community where the extent to which personal preferences can be met depends on large institutions and widespread social production, that each participant have a chance to satisfy his first-order preferences? It is rational, because the satisfaction of each of our preferences is dependent on the cooperation of everyone else.

Sure, there are going to be decisions where we are trading lives for lives, first-order preferences for first-order preferences, and we as a community will have to make decisions as to where and how to do it. But when we are producing second- and third-order preferences to the detriment of first-order preferences, and this is what the neo-classical market would have us do with its basis in a peculiar definition of rationality, then I think we ought to sit back and wonder what is in the cost-benefit calculations. On Zeckhauser's figure, the benefit axis seems to embody first-order preferences while the cost axis seems to be jumbled with lesser preferences.

Ralph d'Arge: Just a very quick point. In terms of economic theory, there have been some developments in the past fifteen years that adequately take care of first-order and second-order preferences. In fact, some of the calculations that we make in our chapter are based on these. There is no contradiction.

Richard Zeckhauser: I would like to cite an article by Torbet and Nordhaus that I think is useful since it relates to some of these issues. They looked at the question of what the GNP does and does not include and developed an alternative measure. I do not know if this has been implemented since Bill has gotten to Washington, but it will be shortly. The measure is called MEW and I think it is a very useful concept for people who are worried about such things as environmental quality and health and ways of incorporating them into our measures of aggregate welfare to society.

Kathleen Sheekey: I want to comment briefly on the freedom of choice argument, which has been advocated as a viable alternative to regulation. Consumers, even the most well informed, do *not* have true freedom of choice. There are several examples that come to mind, but I am going to use Dr. Nordhaus's admitted preference for nitrite bacon versus Mr. Speth's fruitless search for nitrite-free bacon in the Washington area.

The reason Mr. Speth cannot find this bacon is that, under current U.S. Department of Agriculture (USDA) regulations, manufacturers of nitrite-free meat products are prevented from selling them under their traditional names. Bacon, by definition, must contain nitrite. So Gus is having to spend a lot of time finding nitrite-free bacon be-

cause it is sold under such names as "fresh pork breakfast strips."
Now, how many of you think Gus has *real* freedom of choice?

Allen Ferguson: One thing that has not gotten the attention that I
had expected is precisely this question of the role of misinformation
and biased information in the whole decision process. I think it is
worthwhile to try to bring this into future discussions.

I suspect that everyone would agree that incompetent benefit-cost
analysis is not likely to advance any cause very far. I put into that
category a lot of purposefully biased benefit-cost analysis generated
by parties at interest. This is an important part of the underbrush
that has to be cut away before one can address seriously the role of
benefit analysis in the evaluation of prospective regulations. There
has been an amazing amount of dismally bad benefit-cost analysis
and to characterize benefit-cost analysis on the basis of this bad history does not address the question of the relevance of good analysis.

The role of analysis is to try to identify consequences, not to
make an effort to guess at what the political outcomes of the decision process will be. Its purpose is to throw out to people, both those
who have political power and those who do not, the romantic notion
that the truth is somehow relevant. I sense no disagreement with the
notion that there should be serious concern with the efficacy of proposed regulations.

There also seems to be little disagreement that wherever possible,
health to health relationships should be balanced out. Although there
are obviously political, and frequently statutory, prohibitions against
making health to health comparisons, I sense very little disagreement
that there should be such comparisons made and that the cancer versus botulism trade-off is a legitimate one to be considered.

The question of dominance seems again to be clearly accepted.
If it is possible to find regulatory actions that will both decrease
the resource cost and increase the social benefits, these actions are
clearly justified. I think that most of us would agree that this deter-
mination cannot be made without some kind of assessment of benefits. There is no way to decide that a regulatory move will decrease
costs and increase benefits without at least a quick, but unbiased,
appraisal of the benefits.

Finally, there seems to be little disagreement with the proposition
that there is no justification for adopting policies that are grossly

different, in terms of the expenditure per expected life saved or per quality-adjusted life year saved, on a statistical basis. I am not talking about the case where we know whose life is at risk and whose life is to be saved. I sense that there would be no strong argument that it is socially beneficial to spend two or three orders of magnitude more resources on reducing one specified risk of death from one cause, than is spent on reducing the same risk of death from another cause.

DISTRIBUTIVE CONSIDERATIONS IN BENEFIT ASSESSMENT

6 DISTRIBUTIVE IMPLICATIONS OF ECONOMIC CONTROLS*

*Ezra Mishan***

FOUNDATIONS OF THE CONCEPT OF ECONOMIC EFFICIENCY

The distributional effects of measures designed to reduce pollution levels, in particular over generations, will be the primary subject of this chapter. Such effects cannot be appraised properly, however, without some understanding of the rationale by which changes are ranked by economists on the scale of "economic efficiency." In order to promote this understanding a somewhat fundamentalist approach is necessary. Therefore, the following exposition will be initially restricted to what is described by economists as "comparative statics"—a comparison of one possible equilibrium situation with one or more others. The simple but crucial ideas that emerge from this comparison will be then used to illuminate the distributional implications of the basic economic criterion adopted to rank alternative projects, each of which produces a sequence of net social gains and losses over chronological time.

---

*Some of the material in this chapter is not, as yet, standard doctrine, and draws upon unpublished material of which only some is submitted to the professional journals. Anyone wishing to quote passages from this chapter should bear this fact in mind.

**Formerly with the London School of Economics, Professor Mishan is now at the City University of London.

We may begin, therefore, with an existing equilibrium, situation I, with the option of reorganizing the economy in some particulars so as to reach a new equilibrium, situation II. The change contemplated may be small (for example, an additional yard of cloth x is to be produced in situation II accompanied by a little less of other things), or it may be large (for example, a bridge is to be built or aerosols to be banned, as a result of which the consumption of other things is to be diminished or increased respectively). In general, such changes affect the welfare of a number of people in the community for better or for worse. Manifestly, then, such changes have distributional effects. Yet, whatever the pattern of these distributional changes, the economist vaunts a criterion by which he or she can pronounce on the economic efficiency alone of the movement from I to II.

At first glance, this criterion appears to be the soul of simplicity. It is supposed that the change in welfare experienced by each person in the community (which is often taken to be coterminous with the national state), can be reduced to a money equivalent, v. For example, if the change from I to II makes person A better off to such an extent that A is willing, at most, to pay $20 for it, the v in this case is equal to $20.[1] If this same change from I to II makes another person B worse off but is reconcilable for a sum of $15, the value of B's loss is reckoned as $15. A third person C can be wholly indifferent to the change, his or her v being, therefore, equal to zero. And so we could go on assessing the vs of every person in the community.

Thus, if there are but three persons in the community, A, B, and C, as above, the algebraic sum of their individual vs (using a plus sign for gain and a minus sign for loss) would be +$20, −$15, and 0, or an algebraic total of +$5. This algebraic total of individual vs can be represented by a capital V, and interjected as the "net social benefit" accruing from a change from I to II. If this V is positive, as it is in the above example, the economist affirms that situation II is economically more efficient than I. In the absence of all other considerations, the economist would prescribe a movement from I to II. On the other hand, if this V were negative, a movement from I to II would be regarded as one inflicting a "net social loss" on the community of $5.

In essence, this algebraic total V is the allocative measure used by the economist in ranking two or more alternative situations or projects.[2] The art of the economist consists of discovering ways of capturing the data comprised in V, by direct and indirect methods.

In a comparison of situations I and II, the magnitude of net social benefit V might be regarded as no more than an input into the political decisionmaking process. Yet the fact is that economists as a whole attach to V more significance than that. For if a project confidentially calculated by economists to confer a large positive V on the community were rejected by the legislature, they would feel justified in asserting that, notwithstanding political opinion on the matter, the project does confer a net social benefit. Again, if a situation II were judged by economists to be valued aggregatively by the community as higher than I, they would affirm II to be economically more efficient than I—however much the public preferred I to II.

My allegation that economists as a whole regard the value of V as more than just an input into the decisionmaking process is borne out *inter alia* by the fact that the enormous postwar literature dealing with the effects of pollutants on health, safety, and amenity is couched in terms of "efficient" solutions, or of solutions having "desirable optimality proportions," or of synonyms for these normative terms. Such conclusions are in no way made contingent upon the state of public opinion, but are conceived as entirely independent of it.

Let us take this a stage further. Consider a very small change, say, an increase in the current output of electronic watches by a single watch. Someone, we shall imagine, is willing to pay $25 for this additional watch. On the other hand, the resources that have to be diverted from producing other goods in order to produce this extra watch entail a minimal loss of value to consumers of $15. The V of this small change is, of course, +$10 (+$25, −$15). On economic grounds alone, then, this extra watch ought to be produced.

But how many more of these electronic watches ought to be produced? The answer is no less apparent: We should continue producing additional watches as long as the V in each case is positive—in other words, as long as the value of each additional watch exceeds its "opportunity cost."

Now the economist assumes that, *ceteris paribus*, the value of an additional watch declines as more watches are sold. In consequence, whether the unit cost of an additional watch remains constant, rises, or falls, an output of watches will be reached at which the value of one more watch, the "marginal" watch, will be no greater than the additional, or "marginal," opportunity cost of its production. A further extension of the output beyond this point entails a negative V;

the marginal value of a watch being then below its marginal opportunity cost. From these simple reflections, it would seem that the "optimal" output of electronic watches is that for which all possible net benefits are captured; the output in fact for which the marginal value of these electronic watches (say, their market price) is equal to the marginal opportunity cost. For a somewhat smaller output than this optimal output some positive V is foregone; for a somewhat larger output than this optimal output, some negative V is entailed.

Extending this concept to all market goods, an ideal composition of the output of the economy would be one for which, in the production of each good, price is equal to marginal cost. At all events, we have a rationale for the economist's standard allocative rule: Choose for each good that output for which price is equal to marginal opportunity cost.[3]

It is popularly believed by economists that a perfectly competitive economy tends to produce optimal outputs of all goods—provided that the welfare effects on individuals fully register in the price mechanism. This proviso is critical since there are generally many effects on people's welfare that are "external" to the price mechanism. For example, the effects on people's health or on their amenity, which are associated with the output of spillovers or pollutants accompanying the production or consumption of certain goods, do not enter the pricing system. It is, then, left to the economist to determine a value of the loss suffered by the community from the release of pollutants. A schedule of marginal losses may be added by the economist to the existing schedule of marginal commercial cost shown by the market, the sum of these schedules being designated the schedule of marginal social cost.

In general, therefore, the schedule of marginal cost of a good producing noxious spillover effects lies above that of marginal commercial cost. And since the marginal social cost schedule is the "true" schedule, the resulting optimal, or ideal, output—that for which price is equal to marginal social cost—will generally be smaller than the equilibrium output toward which the market tends.

The economist seeks both to estimate this optimal output that is, generally, smaller than the competitive equilibrium output and, also, to suggest least-cost ways—for instance an "optimal tax"—of inducing private industry to produce the optimal output.

Although in the extensive literature on spillovers there are a number of counter examples to the proposition that in a competitive economy the outputs of goods having adverse spillovers tend to exceed their optimal outputs, they are all somewhat contrived and lack plausibility.[4]

RATIONALE OF THE CONCEPT OF ECONOMIC EFFICIENCY

Since it will be central to my examination of intergenerational distribution later in the chapter, it is necessary to determine what rationale can be attributed to the standard norm of economic efficiency before going further. In other words, on what grounds, if any, can the economist justify the use of V, the algebraic aggregate of individual valuations, as a guiding criterion that is independent of political decisions?

The singularity of the economic method consists in the adoption of what may be referred to as the basic economic maxim—that the objective data for the economist are the subjective valuations of the individual members of society, and nothing more. What is more, these valuations are accepted by the economist as relevant data irrespective of the tastes of the individual or the current state of his or her information. There is, for the economist, no abstraction such as "the general good," and no such entity as "the state," to be considered in addition to the welfare of the individuals who comprise society—a view that accords with the philosophic position sometimes referred to as methodological individualism, and associated with the rise of libertarianism.

Since a large number of people are usually affected by an economic change, a further criterion is necessary in ranking alternative economic situations. One criterion that would attract widespread support would be that of an actual "Pareto improvement," defined as a change for which each member of society is made no worse off and one member, at least, is made better off.

But changes that meet such a criterion are not likely to be common in the world we live in. If the economist adopted an actual Pareto improvement as his or her criterion, very few economic changes would be countenanced by the economist. Bearing in mind that nearly all of the economic changes that are contemplated raise the welfare of some persons while lowering the welfare of others, the criterion chosen by economists can properly be described as a *poten-*

tial Pareto improvement. Thus, a situation II is ranked above a situation I on economic grounds if, in a *costless* movement from I to II, the aggregate value of individual gains exceeds the aggregate value of individual losses. As indicated earlier, the excess value of aggregate gains over losses arising from this change is commonly referred to as the net social benefit V of the change, and its magnitude taken to be the economic measure of this net social benefit.

Assuming this net social benefit to be positive, the recommended change from I to II may be rationalized by the proposition that a costless redistribution of the net gains contemplated can be imagined that, were it implemented, would make every individual in society better off than he or she was in the original situation I.

Clearly, the economist's criterion, this *potential* Pareto improvement, which is sometimes referred to as the *Pareto criterion*, can be met by a change that makes the rich still richer, and the poor, poorer. For this reason, among others, there have been objections to its adoption. Others have suggested provisos in order to guard against such a contingency. However, notwithstanding misgivings and proposals for distributional safeguards, the standard allocative criterion employed today by economists is no more than this Pareto criterion. A change that is said to increase "economic efficiency" is nothing more than a change that meets the Pareto improvement.

Inasmuch as the sanction for any norm of economic efficiency has to rest ultimately on its acceptability to the society in question, it cannot be grounded in any group or individual value judgment. And since, as indicated, it cannot be grounded in the political will of that society either, the norm of economic efficiency has to rest on an ethical consensus, in a "virtual constitution" that is impervious to the vicissitudes of political office. Moreover, inasmuch as society's ethics transcend its politics, the outcome resulting from application of the norm of economic efficiency transcends the outcome reached by the political mechanism. The crucial question is then, can we assume that this Pareto criterion, upon which all allocative propositions are in fact raised, is ethically acceptable?

Although at first glance the Pareto criterion looks far from compelling, a belief that society as a whole, in its ethical capacity, would agree to abide by it in all ordinary circumstances can draw upon a number of considerations that arise from notions about the actual operation of the economy: (1) such changes that are, in fact, potential Pareto improvements do not usually have regressive distributional effects; (2) a progressive tax system, in any case, provides a safeguard against pronounced distributional consequences of any economic change; (3) a succession of economic changes, over time, that is countenanced by the Pareto criterion will not have markedly regressive distributional effects and will, therefore, tend to bring about an actual Pareto improvement; and, (4) a succession of economic changes that meet the Pareto criterion has a better chance of raising the general level of welfare than a succession of changes that meet any other criterion.

An acceptance of a clear distinction between a political and an economic criterion does have the merit, at least, of assigning a role to the economist that is entirely independent of the political process. Yet if economists appear to give primacy to "economic efficiency" over considerations of distribution, it is not necessarily because they believe that economic efficiency should take precedence over equity and distribution. It is simply that, provided economists are guided by the Pareto criterion, their craft enables them often enough to come up with specific numbers or, at least, unambiguous results. Concern with distributional changes, on the other hand, enable the economist to come up only with very general statements or abstract theorems about political orderings.

PERSONAL DOUBTS ABOUT THE CURRENT VALIDITY OF THE CRITERION OF ECONOMIC EFFICIENCY

Reflection on recent developments suggests that the consensus necessary for a normative allocation economics is disintegrating. First, there appears to be a growing reluctance among economists, lawyers, sociologists, and others, to accept without reservation the judgment of the market (even in the absence of spillovers), in the face of substantial expenditures on commercial advertising designed to influence the valuations placed on goods by the buying public, and to create a "need" for new goods. Second, there is the question of the proper rates of depletion of a large number of fuels and materials. Although prior to World War II the question was one of limited concern to society at large, and of limited importance in economics, the current scale of resource consumption has made it a topic of growing concern to the public at the same time that it has become one of controversy among economists.

There is no doubt that there is currently a deep division of opinion among informed members of the public, including economists, about the wisdom of current and proposed economic policies on resource consumption—which amounts, also, to a division of opinion about whether the valuations currently attributed to "finite" resources (either under existing economic arrangements or under "ideal" competitive arrangements) have any normative significance. Certainly, a number of reputable economists have argued that the existing valuations of fuels and minerals and their current rates of consumption cannot be justified without criteria that include the viewpoint of future generations.

Finally, there is a growing realization that as the consequences of consumer innovation (for example, involving food additives, chemical drugs, pesticides, synthetic materials, and a variety of new gadgets) tend to unfold slowly over time, their valuation at any point in time by the buying public (as determined by their market prices, to which individual purchases adjust) may bear no relation whatever to the net benefits, if any, conferred over time. Indeed, it can be convincingly argued that the very pace of change today with respect to new models of goods, or new goods themselves, is such that it is no longer possible for the buying public to learn from its own experience how to assess the relative merits of a large proportion of the goods coming onto the market. As a result, society can have no confidence that individual valuations of these goods at the time of purchase have any ex post correspondence with people's subjective wants (whether socially approved or not) to justify them, on the standard argument, as indicators of claims on society's resources.

Assuming that this latter belief becomes so widely accepted as virtually to become unanimous, it follows that for a growing proportion of market goods, the individual subjective valuations upon which the allocation economist has to depend will no longer be indicative of the subjective experience of benefits by the buyers. But even if this belief is not widely accepted, the continuance of a division of belief about the extent and importance of this development must also act to prevent the allocation economist from invoking an ethical sanction for this use of individual valuations taken, in the first instance, from market prices.

Of course, on particular issues, allocation economists may be able to speak with greater confidence than on others. They may, for instance, have less hesitation in calculating the net benefits of a better food distribution in one of the poorer countries of the world (at least if they were willing to disregard the long-run effects of population growth). But for many of the public projects of the affluent society, even where they are designed to provide the population with lower costs of inputs of different forms of energy or basic materials, conscientious economists can no longer speak with authority. For they are amply aware that the value to be placed on such basic inputs is part of a highly controversial topic and, that such inputs are used in a wide range of items and gadgets about whose social justification the community may be divided in opinion.

GENERAL REMARKS UPON THE ALLOCATIVE AND DISTRIBUTIONAL EFFECTS OF CORRECTING SPILLOVERS

For heuristic reasons we have concentrated until now on a reduction of the output of the good itself, the production or use of which creates noxious spillover, as the sole means of reducing the spillover. If that is the only means of reducing the spillover, the reduction of the unchecked competitive equilibrium output to an optimal output entails the lowest cost reduction of the unchecked spillover level to its optimal level.

More generally, however, there are a number of different ways of diminishing the effects of any particular spillover—for instance, the relocating of industrial plants away from urban centers, or the introduction of new antipollution technologies. In the attempt to reduce any given amount of spillover at least cost, a good manager will experiment to discover the "optimal" combination of various spillover-reducing methods available. Indeed, the manager will have an incentive to encourage innovation in these respects. At all events, the notion of seeking an optimal combination of spillover-reducing methods in order to minimize the cost of any required spillover-reduction is analogous to the familiar assumption of economic theory that the entrepreneur seeks to combine productive resources in those proportions that minimize the cost of the good being produced. And just as it would be more expensive to produce any particular good if one were allowed to use only one productive resource, or only two, or three, and so on, it generally is more expensive to reduce a given amount of pollution by only one method, say output reduction, than if one had access to all the different ways of doing so.

It is for this reason, among others, that the economist favors the so-called effluent tax—a tax levied on each unit of pollution or efflu- ent emitted at a given locality—since it provides an immediate incen- tive for managers, not only to reduce their level of effluent to the point at which the price of their product covers both its marginal commercial cost *plus* the tax, but to minimize the cost of reducing the chosen amount of effluent by employing an optimal combination of methods.

Nevertheless, ways other than an effluent tax have to be consid- ered. In some particular cases, reduction of the output of the associ- ated good is the only method currently available, in which case the choice to be faced is that of an excise tax, a rationing scheme, direct regulation of the industry, or doing nothing at all. In an emergency, however, direct regulation can be extended to a ban on the produc- tion or the sale of the good in question.

In ordinary circumstances, however, each method of curtailing adverse spillovers is judged by reference both to its allocative and equity effects. Concerning the latter, in particular the distributional components, it is evident that without a mass of empirical evidence the question of whether the use of any given combination of spill- over-reducing methods has, on balance, a regressive or progressive distributional impact cannot be answered. Of course, in seeking to curb a particular group of spillovers, say the alleged harmful effects on health of food additives, by means of a tax on such additives, it is plausible to believe that the distributional effects will tend to be regressive. But crudely, the poor spend a larger proportion of their incomes on foods than do the rich. Hence, a tax that falls on foods is likely to prove a greater burden, proportionally, on the income of the poor. (I say "likely to" because the particular foods that will rise in price as a result of the taxes may have close substitutes that re- main untaxed, so by shifting to the substitutes the burden of the tax can largely be escaped).

If, on the other hand, environmental spillovers are at issue, the introduction of open air amenities to curb the industrial effluent in residential areas occupied by the poor would seem to have progressive distributional effects if the revenues are to be raised by progressive taxes.[5]

Before ending this section there are three considerations to bear in mind regarding spillovers and the possibility of their correction, especially in connection with the sort of spillovers that have been growing since the end of World War II.

First, there is a caution against being influenced by ideological presuppositions. Civil servants can be expected to rationalize a preference for government regulation. In contrast, many economists, especially those of the "Chicago School," tend to rationalize their preference for a market solution. Although I usually go along with them in this respect, since I also am alarmed at the extent of bureaucratic intervention in all countries of the West, I do not subscribe to their eccentric view that concern with the environment is an "elitist" preoccupation and that all environmental measures seek to militate against the interests of the working man. Indeed, such a view is not easy to reconcile with their frequent statements about the "distorting" effects of government tariffs or farm subsidies. If, for example, the government proposed a subsidy on coffee or meat, on the grounds that the poor would benefit most from such subsidies, Chicago economists, among others, would lay stress on the resulting malallocation of resources involved. They would argue that if helping the poor were the objective, it could be better accomplished by direct transfers of income to the poor, in this way allowing them the choice of buying what they wished at prices that reflected their true costs. Their position would then require that the poor pay the true, or "social" costs of goods that use up scarce environmental resources (in other words, the full social costs of goods whose production or use damages the environment) in the interest of avoiding a malallocation of resources, the possible regressive distributional effects being dealt with by a direct transfer of income to the poor.

We may concede always that the costs, both pecuniary and bureaucratic, of administering a tax must enter the calculus. But this is a pragmatic, not a dogmatic, issue. And in any case, if the anti-environmentalist sentiment of some members of the Chicago School turns on this latter point (the dislike of any extension of government powers), it would reduce controversy if they made it explicit rather than giving the appearance of seeking populist sympathy by referring to environmental economists as "elitists" who deliberately ignore the consequence of their pro-environmental measures on the interests of the working man.

Second, economists should and generally do take into account the "transactions costs" of their proposals, that is, all the incidental costs involved in each of these proposals for dealing with any particular range of spillovers. These include the costs of extending bureaucracies, including the costs of monitoring and policing effluent; possible changes of infrastructure; and the incurring of capital and maintenance costs. It is possible, therefore, that the best solution after all might be to bear with the existing spillovers rather than incur heavy transactions costs in a bid to reduce them to some optimal or politically agreed level.

However, what economists do not always recognize, or do not emphasize sufficiently, is that in the world we live in, the closest attention to economic considerations of spillovers does not, of itself, warrant a conclusion that social welfare must rise over time. This is simply because, as indicated earlier, it takes time for society to realize the range of nonmarket consequences generated by the production and consumption of a new good. And by the time the consequences are widely recognized, it may be more economic to continue to bear with them, no matter how insufferable, than to incur the seemingly appalling costs of dismantling the associated infrastructure to return to the *status quo ante*. Perhaps not all economists would agree that the introduction of the private automobile is a wonderful case in point. But reflections on its far-reaching consequences—its adoption as a major means of transport, its effect on the size and shape of our cities, and its effect on the national character and way of life—are very sobering; as, indeed, are reflections on the cost of a changeover to a nonautomobile society. In this connection, the assumption of "given tastes" obviously is suspect. There is ample evidence that people have limited imaginations and that they are averse to bearing with some initial hardship or tedium in order to attain what might prove to be a more satisfactory way of life.

Third, we are impelled to recognize the character of the new kind of spillover effects that have grown rapidly since World War II. They are, for the most part, the side effects of recent technological innovation and have in common particular features that separate them from the more conventional spillover effects (effluent, noise, fume, congestion, aesthetic decline, and general disamenity) that are typical of so much of the postwar literature on externalities. There are three chief distinguishing features of this new category of spillovers that seem intractable to familiar economic methods:

1. Since the industrial processes, or their products, are new to this planet, there is limited experience of the nature or incidence of their side effects. The consequences for humanity of the continuance and spread of these new industrial activities and their products are, therefore, as yet under a gigantic question mark. Specific consequences are sometimes suspected, and give rise to speculation and controversy. It is both expected and feared that other side effects will emerge with the passage of time.

2. There is, in these cases, an intelligent apprehension that the spillovers associated with these new activities may well take the form of large-scale disasters having, possibly, global dimensions. In particular, the damage caused may be irreversible and possibly fatal to humanity, and perhaps also to other or all forms of life on earth.

3. Some part or all of the as yet imperfectly understood hazards of continuing these new activities are likely to fall on future generations. And there can be no reasonable presumption that safe, technical methods for dealing with them will be discovered in the future.

The question is, then, whether the economist or any scientist can produce meaningful figures purporting to be an economic contribution to the decisionmaking process when the problem under consideration is one involving spillovers of this new kind, having the singular features mentioned above. In pursuance of my main theme, however, I shall concentrate only on the third feature mentioned, drawing attention in particular to the bias of the distribution of benefits and costs over generational time that arise from adopting the economist's traditional discounted present value (DPV) criteria for ranking of alternative investment projects.

CONDITIONS UNDER WHICH DPV IN RANKING INVESTMENT IS VALID

Once the aggregate benefits and losses resulting from an economic change are no longer conceived in terms of a new perpetual equilibrium flow (valued, say in dollars per annum) but, instead, from a particular pattern of benefits and losses over chronological time, a device is necessary to compare alternative "streams" of benefits and losses. The device conventionally used is a discount rate that, when properly calculated and employed, may be rationalized as meeting the Pareto criterion.

In order to appreciate this we have to assume that each person affected by the project anticipates a stream of benefits—which term, henceforth, is to include not only positive benefits but also "disbenefits" or losses over the future. Abiding by the basic maxim, each person can be supposed indifferent to the difference between the receipt of a particular sum this year, and the particular benefits and losses that can be anticipated (with certainty) over a lifetime as a result of the project in question. If the person is indifferent, say, to the difference between the receipt (or loss) of $1.00 in a given year and the receipt (or loss) of $1.05 in the following year, the economist would say, that over this period of time at least, the "rate of time preference" is equal to 5 percent per annum. If this rate of time preference remained constant over the person's life time, the DPV of the anticipated stream of benefits amounts to a sum that he or she would accept today as equivalent in welfare to this anticipated stream of benefits over time.

Letting each person affected by the project have the same rate of time preference, r (which we can, in this case, suppose to be equal exactly to the current yield on all investment, private and public), the aggregate of the individual's DPVs is equal exactly to the DPV, at rate r, of the stream of aggregate benefits for society. It follows that if the DPV at rate r of a project A is larger than the DPV at rate r of a project B, a Pareto criterion is met by choosing the A project over the B. (To illustrate, if the DPV of project A comes to $100 million and that of project B to $70 million, the community of all affected individuals can, by costless redistribution, be made better off by an aggregate amount equal to a DPV of $30 million by adopting project A rather than project B).

Adopting now the further assumption that this time-rate of preference r is common to all members of succeeding generations also, the condition under which it is Pareto-valid to use DPV, or for that matter compounded terminal value (CTV), is the existence of a common point of overlap—a common point of time, that is, at which each person affected by the project is alive.

This can be illustrated in the simplest possible case of two persons taken from two different generations, each one being supposed capable of making rational decisions, for sixty years of his or her life. Their rational lives are assumed to overlap by 20 years. Thus we imagine person A to be alive in this sense from year 0 to year 60, and to receive a stream of benefits that on balance raises his or her welfare. Person B, on the other hand, is alive from year 40 to year 100, and receives a stream of benefits from the project that on balance reduces his or her welfare.

Since r is the time-rate of preference common to both, A's benefit stream can be transformed into an aggregate value of, let us suppose, exactly $100 at year 0, or into an equivalent welfare value of $100 $(1+r)^t$ for any year t up to 60. Inasmuch as A is indifferent to the difference between all such sums $100 $(1+r)^t$ for t equal to 0, 1, . . . , 60, such sums can be represented by a continuous line sloping upward from year 0 to 60. Such a continuous line, with the value measured vertically on a logarithmic scale, and time measured horizontally on an ordinary scale, is depicted in Figure 6-1 and can be interpreted as a "time-indifference" curve.

Person B's time-indifference curve is constructed on the same principle and under the supposition that it is exactly equivalent to a loss of $300 in year 40. If r is now taken, for convenience, to be such that $1 today is worth $2 in twenty year's time, person B's loss of $300 in year 40 is equivalent to a loss of $600 in year 60 or a loss of $1,000 in year 100. Similarly, A's net benefit of $100 in year 0 is

Figure 6-1. Time indifference curve for persons from different generations.

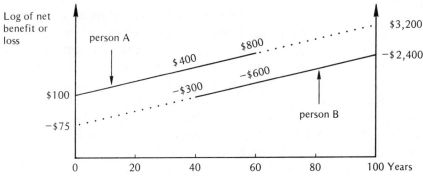
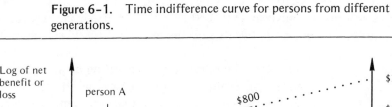

equivalent in welfare to a benefit of $400 in year 40 and a benefit of $800 in year 60.

As depicted in Figure 6-1, at any point of time between their years of overlap (between years 40 and 60) the values placed by persons A and B on their respective streams are such that the benefit-loss ratio is 4 to 3 — A gains 4 for every 3 that B loses. This benefit-loss ratio, being greater than unity, meets a Pareto criterion without violating the basic maxim, for A's gain is such that, via costless redistribution, both persons could be made better off. Adopting this benefit-loss (or benefit-cost) ratio as a criterion, either discounting the values to year 0, or alternatively compounding them at r to year 100, simply multiplies both numerator and denominator by a common scalar. It does not, therefore, alter the benefit-loss ratio of 4 to 3. It follows that if a common point of overlap exists among all individuals of successive generations, the use of DPV or CTV in obtaining a benefit-cost ratio greater than unity can be justified as meeting a Pareto criterion.

As a corollary to the preceding argument, if a common point of overlap does *not* exist for successive generations then, since the basic maxim is no longer met, neither is the Pareto criterion for a benefit-cost ratio above unity. If, for example, a third person, C, beginning his or her rational life in year 100, values the benefit stream of the project at $1,000 in year 100, then C is certainly *not* indifferent to the difference between receiving $1,000 in year 100 and receiving $250 in year 60 since C was not alive in year 60. Nor, for that matter, will person A be indifferent to the difference between a net receipt of $800 in year 60 and a net receipt of $3,200 in year 100 since A will not be alive in year 100. A valid comparison, at a common point of time, as between persons A and B is, therefore, not possible.

Hence, in a time context, the basic maxim requiring economists to accept as data people's own evaluations only of the goods and bads resulting from any economic change, poses a real problem whenever the time span of the project covers a number of successive generations. For each person's valuation is now dated only over his or her own rational lifetime. And there may no longer be a common year during which the valuations of all persons affected by the project can be directly compared, and the algebraic sum of such valuations be determined, or cast into benefit-cost form.

THE PROBLEM OF EVALUATING
LONG-LIVED PROJECTS

Three ways of getting around this difficulty have been proposed: (1) a belief that over time, wealth (or per capita income) will continue to rise so that there is no cause for alarm if a project happens to inflict some losses on future generations; (2) the introduction of such "externalities" as altruism, or a concern for generations yet to be born; and (3) the notion of intergeneration interventions, either directly or through institutional mechanisms.

With respect to the first point, this once common belief is controversial today in view of rapid destruction of environmental goods and the creation of environmental hazards. It is all too possible that future generations, if they survive, will on balance enjoy a much lower level of welfare than the existing generation. Nevertheless, even if we were convinced that real per capita income, or real welfare, were to grow over generational time, there is no warrant for using a DPV benefit-cost criterion in the belief that it is a reflection of the Pareto criterion.

The second point is barely worthy of mention, since resort to such devices have not been found necessary in the conventional cost-benefit analysis. Even if they are allowable, however, such externalities cannot be supposed to take a form that justifies extending the time rate of preference r for each person to cover all time prior to birth and after death. In any case, this recourse to externalities to justify the use of rate r over many generations reveals the weakness of the argument since such externalities are not necessary in the intrageneration case. In the latter case it can be assumed that each person is a wholly selfish being. Even though this assumption is not quite true, evaluation of a project over time should be able to deal with such a case.

The third way round the difficulty is worth extended comment, if only because the conditions drawn have been misinterpreted. What is involved can be brought out starkly by adopting the somewhat extreme example used by Myrick Freeman (1977) in order to illustrate his assertion that, in project evaluation, it makes economic sense to discount to the present the value of damages expected to be borne by generations who will be alive many thousands of years from today. Thus a colossal amount of damage, equal in value to $D, to be experienced in 100,000 years time should, according to Freeman, be discounted to the present to equal, say, $80 today. If all the immediate benefits of such a project are equal to $100, and the benefit-cost ratio, therefore, exceeds unity, the project is to be regarded as economically efficient.

Freeman argues that the justification for this conclusion resides in the fact that if $80 were invested today, and continuously reinvested at the discount rate r for 100,000 years, it would compound exactly to this sum $D. The beneficiaries from this sum $D would, in 100,000 years time then be able to compensate those destined to suffer the loss of $D, leaving a net gain of $20 for today's generation. According to Freeman, a potential Pareto improvement is thereby met as required by the economist.

Now with respect to the hypothetical time stream devised by Freeman, a potential Pareto improvement would indeed be met. But clearly this time stream is not the original stream that conferred a benefit on today's generation of $100 and inflicted damage equal to $D on generations living 100,000 years from today. What Freeman's argument amounts to, therefore, is the sanctioning of an actual intergeneration project, which by recourse to investment opportunity, could be changed into a different intergeneration project, that could then meet the conventional potential Pareto improvement. Since in his example both a hypothetical project and a hypothetical compensation test are involved, Freeman is in effect ascribing allocative virtue to an economic change that meets a *potential* potential Pareto improvement.[6]

Of course, a *potential* potential Pareto improvement is of no consequence in itself. The economist might prefer to envisage instead a more complex form of hypothetical intervention over time, one involving both transfers between generations (via investment opportunities) and transfers between members of each generation at select moments of time. Yet the same conclusion holds, for a consensus on the acceptability of the conventional Pareto improvement among members of a given generation, at a given point in time, may be presumed to exist for the reasons given earlier. In contrast, a consensus among members of all generations involved in the long-lived investment project may *not* be presumed to exist. For among other things, there are no mechanisms that can be counted on to diffuse net benefits among all members of this intergenerational community; nothing, in fact, to prevent later generations having to shoulder heavy burdens while earlier generations reap benefits. In these circumstances, the economist is impelled to face directly the intergenerational distribution implications of long-lived projects.

Once economists face this, they will find no good reason to expect that projects ranked on a DPV criterion will result in anything like random interpretation distributional effects—say, about a half of the total value of the projects undertaken by the existing generation having, on balance, a beneficial effect on some later generation, the remainder having offsetting damaging effects on the nth generation.

Bearing in mind that a rate of discount as low as 3 percent—and many economists have proposed using rates of 10 percent or more within an intergeneration context—reduces a gain or loss of $1 million incurred in 500 years' time to less than $1 today, it should be manifest that a DPV criterion will select projects that discriminate markedly against future generations in favor of the present.[7] Projects that are expected to produce immense benefits for future generations at a modest cost to the present generation are easily rejected on this criterion, whereas projects that are expected to inflict immense damage on future generations and confer small benefits on the present generation are easily accepted by it.

Bearing in mind that for the first time in history, we have begun to make decisions on the extent of our intervention in the biosphere, which could have momentous consequences for the future of this planet, and possibly subject future generations to irremediable resource shortages or irreversible disasters, the continued use of DPV criterion by economists engaged in project evaluation involving future generations can no longer be justified.[8]

NOTES TO CHAPTER 6

1. The professional economist will recognize that there are at least two ways of measuring the individual vs corresponding to the change—a compensation variation and an equivalent variation—which is the source of familiar paradoxes. In the absence of a consensus, or a law reflecting such a consensus, requiring the use of one of these measures to the exclusion of the other in the relevant circumstances, good practice would seem to require the economist to evaluate projects in terms of each and to recommend on allocative grounds only when the results of such evaluation are consistent with respect to ranking.

2. Some economists have of late been flirting with the older Neoclassical tradition, which would seek to "refine" these data by multiplying the v attributable to the change by each person by a "util" weight, one that varies in some arbitrary way with the income of each person—the lower the income the greater the weight. By this device, some economists believe they can somehow integrate distributional and allocative considerations.

3. The professional economist will notice that I am ignoring the problem of "second best." Since I am to reveal additional weakness in the current methods of project evaluation, it serves no purpose here to discuss the implications of the second best theory for benefit-cost analysis.

4. A brief description of some of these "perverse" cases are given in my survey article, "The Postwar Literature on Externalities," *Journal of Economic Literature*, 1971.

5. Some economists who habitually frown on government intervention in the economy, argue that any success in improving the environment of the poor in the cities will eventually result in rents rising, as wealthy suburbanites will then be attracted back to the city by these environmental improvements. Assuming the poor do not own their homes, this is conceivably an outcome. Whether or not there have been many, or any, such cases, I do not know.

6. Since the DPV procedure being recommended by Freeman in this intergeneration context is not conceived as being in any way contingent upon actual agreements between governments of all generations involved, specifically to invest the receipts of earlier generations continuously with the object of presenting to this ultimate generation the sum D calculated to offset the losses it will then suffer, this transfer between generations via institutional mechanisms is clearly as hypothetical as the subsequent redistribution among members of that last generation that ensures that none of them is made worse off.

7. A CTV criterion carries exactly the same direction of distributional bias, since it magnifies \$1 of gain or loss to the present generation to more than \$1 million of gain or loss in 500 years' time.

8. This interpretation of the conventional DPV criterion when applied to intergeneration projects does not change, nor can it be justified, even if it were the case—as some economists allege—that public investment necessarily displaces private investment yielding, say, r in perpetuity, which r (in the absence of externalities) ought therefore to be regarded as the opportunity yield whenever public projects are being contemplated. For public projects that over time yield on average more than r, and which, therefore, pass a conventional DPV criterion, are quite capable of having patterns of benefits and losses over time that are distinctly unfavorable to future generations.

BIBLIOGRAPHY

Freeman, Myrick. 1977. "A Short Argument in Favor of Discounting Intergenerational Effects." *Futures* (October).

Mishan, Ezra J. 1975. *Cost-Benefit Analysis*, second edition. Reading, Mass.: Allen and Unwin.

_____ . Forthcoming. "A Difficulty in Using the Discount Rate in Long-Term Projects." *Zeitschift Für Nationalokonomie.*

_____ . Forthcoming. "On the Present Status of Allocative Propositions." *Journal of Economic Issues.*

_____ . 1971. "The Postwar Literature on Externalities." *Journal of Economic Literature.*

7 DISTRIBUTIONAL OBJECTIVES IN HEALTH AND SAFETY REGULATION*

*David Harrison, Jr.***

Most health and safety regulations are designed to help particular groups. Workers should be spared the traumas of injury or chronic disease from their work. Drivers should be able to rely upon the basic safety of their cars. Drug users should be spared the risks of serious side effects. Those who live near factories or power plants should not have to breathe polluted air. Those who live near disposal sites should not have their water supply contaminated. Distributional considerations are thus an important motivation for many of the government's efforts to improve health and safety through regulation of private behavior. Of course the groups targeted vary greatly in size. Most of us are (or will be) drivers while very few of us are likely to live next door to a Love Canal.

The distributional analysis that lies behind this desire to help particular groups may be simplistic and incomplete. The most common failings are either to ignore the costs of regulation or to assume that the firms whose behavior is regulated will pay the costs. Indeed, part of the enthusiasm for regulating major industries such as chemicals

* This chapter is a revised version of the one used as the basis for discussion at the conference. One of the major changes, in response to conference comments, is the addition of an example.

** David Harrison is currently Associate Professor in the John F. Kennedy School of Government at Harvard University. He served as senior staff economist for regulation in the President's Council of Economic Advisers from 1979 to 1980.

177

or automobiles may be due to the implicit assumption that these companies pay for the controls. Similarly, many proponents of worker safety regulations believe the company should pay to ensure a safe workplace. But costs for these programs are much more likely to be borne ultimately by consumers or workers rather than stockholders or managers. A more complete analysis thus may reveal that other deserving groups—low income consumers, for example—may be worse off with the regulation in place. Moreover, even the benefit distribution may be more complicated than first appears. For example, landlords may obtain some of the benefits of cleaner air if property values increase when air quality is improved. Or others in an insurance risk pool may gain from increasing product or workplace safety because they save the cost of subsidizing the medical care of victims.

Providing a more complete and sophisticated distributional analysis for health and safety regulations is clearly a large task. Indeed, the difficulty of performing a distributional analysis is one rationale for ignoring distributional considerations in setting health and safety regulations. For those who question the quality of the analyses of the *overall* costs and benefits that are actually performed by regulatory agencies, the further task of estimating the differential impacts of the regulation on various subgroups may seem silly. Moreover, distributional considerations may obstruct sensible choices; since almost every regulatory change harms some group, concern for equity may paralyze the policy-making process. In addition, many believe that distributional objectives should not be pursued by changing individual policies since equity can be achieved more efficiently by direct cash transfers. It is preferable, so this argument goes, to ignore effects on individual groups; regulations should be set only if overall benefits exceed costs.

It is tempting to take these inadequacies and difficulties as evidence that distributional considerations should play no role in health and safety regulation. My own view is that distributional analysis can provide an important complement to analysis of overall costs and benefits. But I do not want to overstate the case. Since much of health and safety regulation is in its infancy, there is no doubt that large gains can be made by lowering the costs of achieving health and safety objectives and focusing on cost-effective regulation. The original mandates of agencies like the Environmental Protection Agency (EPA), the Consumer Product Safety Commission (CPSC), the National Highway Transportation Safety Administration (NHTSA), and the Occupational Safety and Health Administration (OSHA) were very broad. These agencies had to cope with problems ignored for many years and for which information was scarce. The original efforts are bound to have failings in efficiency.

Distributional considerations can be incorporated as health and safety regulation matures. Careful distributional analysis can complement efficiency analysis in several important ways. Some regulations may simply be rejected because of their distributional implications. Efficiency is clearly not society's only objective, and society may well decide not to make all changes in which gains outweigh losses if losers are not compensated. Similarly, one might provide benefits to deserving groups even though a lump sum cash transfer would, in theory, be more efficient. As Okun (1975) points out in his widely read set of lectures, there are many places where society deliberately opts for equality in ways that compromise efficiency.

Another function of careful distributional analysis is to clarify the true winners and losers from controversial health and safety regulations. The solution to regulatory paralysis due to complaints by losers is not to assume that such complaints are irrelevant but rather to subject them to careful analysis. Opponents of a regulation may argue that it harms low income consumers, only benefits one region, or leads to plant shut-downs. Analyzing the magnitude of such losses puts them in perspective, sets the stage for an informed comparison of efficiency and equity, and may lead to a compensation scheme that increases the chances for adoption of regulations desirable on overall efficiency grounds.

Distributional analysis may also assist the agency in identifying promising regulatory areas. As mentioned, the agencies that regulate health and safety are often given very general statutory mandates. While much of the storm and stress surrounding these agencies concerns their decisions in particular cases, their contribution to overall welfare may depend more upon the areas in which they choose to regulate than on the specific choices they make in each case. One way for the agency to focus its regulatory efforts would be to consider regulations designed to help particular groups. For example, it may be useful for the CPSC to focus on improving the safety of products that are used by children, and thus their research efforts could be targeted toward identifying the major causes of childhood accidents and the effectiveness of their regulatory tools in reducing accident rates.

Having provided a case for including distributional considerations in setting health and safety regulations, the remainder of this chapter considers some methodological issues. The next section lists the groups that might be relevant for a distributional analysis and provides my preferences for the most appropriate groupings. I then note some methodological difficulties in identifying distributional effects and provide an example from air pollution control. I conclude with a discussion of a question that is relevant for overall evaluations but which is particularly important in an equity analysis—to what extent should regulations be set by using *societal* judgments on unacceptable risks rather than by summing individual values?

GROUPS FOR DISTRIBUTIVE ANALYSIS

Regulating health and safety invariably imposes costs on some group —consumers, workers, or stockholders—and thus any regulation is inequitable by some criteria. Moreover, there is invariably some pattern to the regulation's benefits, particularly for programs targeted to particular groups; mine workers clearly receive the benefits from mine safety regulations. In the abstract, we may want to help or indemnify every group. But when choices must be made among various regulations or compensation schemes, what groupings should be used to judge equity effects?

I have identified seven groupings that might be used in a distributional analysis of the benefits of health and safety regulations:

1. Income
2. Race
3. Ability to protect oneself from harm
4. Existing health risk
5. Identifiability of the victim
6. Number of dependents
7. Geographic area

To many, a major function of government is to reduce inequality. According to this view, government regulations and policies should systematically favor those in lower income groups. Perhaps the most detailed and extreme arguments are those of Kantian philosophers such as John Rawls (1970) who contends that principles of justice require that any changes made by government favor the poor. Rawls argues that such a rule would be chosen by people if they had a "veil of ignorance" about their own status and thus chose rules on a disinterested basis. Economists typically view inequality as a necessary result of an efficient economy, although most would consider reducing inequality a desirable goal of public policy.

Eliminating racial inequality is also often considered an important goal of public policy in the U.S., although it is not usually considered in the context of health and safety regulation.[1] Preference for Blacks in particular can be justified as compensation either for past injustices or for current discrimination. Although the magnitude of the harm caused by racial discrimination is the subject of considerable dispute, as are the offsetting gains to Blacks from existing affirmative action programs, there seems little doubt that Blacks still suffer from discrimination in labor and housing markets (Ashenfelter and Rees 1974; Yinger 1979).

Several groups are not able to protect themselves from health or safety hazards and thus might be special targets of government programs.[2] Children represent one such group, since they are not likely to have the judgment and maturity that protects older persons from risks. Of course, infants and toddlers are particularly vulnerable, and regulations on crib safety or child-proof tops for medicine bottles are clearly designed to protect them from harm. Indeed, some believe that small children should receive even more protection, for example by requiring that they ride in car seats. Other groups that may fall in this category are adults with physical or psychological handicaps and workers with little real choice but to engage in hazardous occupations. One possible rationale for the Food and Drug Administration's (FDA) review of new drugs is that potential users may often be in such pain or facing such dim hopes for recovery that they lose the ability to make rational trade-offs involving drugs that promise relief.

Some economists argue that regulating worker health and safety is unnecessary and undesirable since those in risky occupations are compensated by wage differentials that represent "hazardous duty pay." (Smith 1976). Indeed, these wage differentials provide the basis for the empirical estimates of workers' willingness-to-pay to avoid health or safety risks. It is likely, however, that many hazardous jobs are performed by workers who for reasons of ignorance, immobility, or perceived or real lack of alternatives have little ability to avoid the risks. For example, many occupational risks are subtle — such as those from exposure to carcinogenic substances—and workers may well be unaware of the true risks. Society may therefore be justified in treating the hazards faced by these workers specially.

Another means of categorizing beneficiaries is by the level of their overall health risk. This classification is a variant of the concern for inequality, in this case measured by health rather than income. Using this criterion, government regulators would seek to reduce the disparity between health risks and thus favor regulations that protect high risk individuals. Programs would focus on reducing risks for groups like the elderly and the chronically ill in the health area or mine workers in the safety area. Of course, such programs may be justified on efficiency grounds regardless of these distributional effects, since reducing dangers to high-risk persons may well be cost-effective. But a concern for those with the greatest risks may in some cases compromise overall effectiveness. Reducing risks for the elderly poses this dilemma most acutely. While the elderly face greater risks of death or serious illness, the benefits to them measured in years of prolonged life or reduced illness are less than if the same death or illness rate changes applied to younger people. (Zeckhauser and Shepard 1975).

Victims that are clearly identifiable are compelling beneficiaries. Consider the different public reactions to fifty workers trapped in a coal mine compared to fifty persons killed in auto accidents. Of course, government regulatory programs are designed to prevent accidents like mine disasters and this criterion may differentiate direct expenditure programs (to save trapped miners or provide cancer treatment) from regulatory programs that reduce the risks of mine cave-ins or cancer. But even regulatory programs may be favored when the beneficiaries are very specific, as in the case of mine safety regulations, rather than quite general, as in the case of auto safety or air pollution programs. Identifiability, of course, represents a continuum, since even for general auto safety or air pollution programs it is possible to identify persons that are most likely to benefit.

One might also "break ties" by providing health and safety benefits to those with a large number of dependents. Our greater apparent concern with occupational health and safety—rather than safety and health in nonwork circumstances—may be due in part to a notion that workers have more dependents. Injuries to those with dependents affect more people both because dependents anguish over the loss and because of the economic loss to spouses and children left without a breadwinner. Of course, part of this economic loss is transferred to the rest of society through social security, workmen's compensation and private insurance.

The final categorization is for geographic areas, which can be many classifications—central city versus suburb, urban versus rural, sunbelt versus snowbelt. The location of beneficiaries clearly affects congressional decisions on health and safety legislation—as it does other government programs—although it may be difficult to predict the coalitions that might determine any particular issue. For example, members of Congress from West Virginia and Kentucky represent both mine workers and mine owners. Nevertheless, the political will to initiate change often depends upon the location of specific interest groups. These geographic criteria imply that groups with the most powerful congressional representatives will be the ones for whom priorities in health and safety regulation are set.

Which of these various criteria should be used in setting health and safety regulations? There is no correct answer to this question, although it is useful to think through one's own choices. The first three categorizations seem particularly compelling. Favoring those with low incomes accords with straightforward notions of equity and justice, while preference for Blacks still seems necessary to offset other discrimination. Although better equalizing mechanisms may be available, until alternatives are actually implemented it seems appropriate to promote health and safety regulations favoring the poor and Blacks and to avoid regulations that directly or indirectly (through the costs they impose) decrease their welfare substantially.

Using health and safety regulations to protect those who cannot help themselves suggests, for example, that the CPSC concentrate its safety regulations on products used by children and that OSHA target its regulations to protect workers with little real choice than to bear the risks of their employment. These regulations, however, should also be subject to efficiency tests; agencies should seek the most cost-effective means of providing protection, and the benefits should be roughly commensurate with the costs.

Performing additional distributional analyses may be useful, if only to quantify claims that are made by opponents or supporters. Opponents of a particular regulation may claim that the regulation is unfair to urban residents or to residents of the Northeast. I see no equity reason for a federal agency to distinguish among people on the basis of where they live. Nevertheless, geography clearly plays a role in the general political process in which all the regulatory agencies operate. Moreover, geography may serve as a proxy for income or racial effects that are either not quantifiable or not easily introduced into the decisionmaking process. Geographic assessments, however, should at least be based on correct information to avoid a regulation that is both bad for the country as a whole (i.e., inefficient or inequitable) and of little real benefit to its geographically based supporters.

ESTIMATING DISTRIBUTIONAL IMPACTS

This section highlights two major difficulties in performing a distributional analysis of benefits. The first issue involves identifying all persons who gain from the regulation, including those who gain from a process I refer to as benefit shifting. The second issue involves accounting for differences in the values that groups place on reductions of health and safety risks. These issues are largely additions to those required to estimate overall benefits, since overall analysis need not consider whether some benefits are transferred, and uses an average figure to value benefits. One common assumption, however, is that benefit assessment should determine the values that *individuals* place on their own health and safety improvement. The last section steps back and examines the issue of whether—and when—*society* may wish to substitute its own values in health and safety regulation. Since it is important to consider these two additional methodological issues against a background of the general issues, this section begins with an overview of the procedures for estimating overall benefits.[3]

Estimating Overall Benefits. Health and safety regulations respond to risks of illness, death, and injury, and thus the first step for the analyst is to determine how much the regulation will reduce these risks. Will significantly fewer persons get cancer because a drug is not marketed? What deaths will be prevented by requiring passive restraints in cars rather than relying upon lap belts? What deaths or illnesses would be prevented by reducing a standard for worker exposure to benzene from ten parts per million to one part per million?

Preparing these estimates often requires considerable ingenuity and heroic assumptions. The results are invariably unsatisfactory to the purist. Nevertheless, this analysis can clarify the general magnitudes of the risks that may be reduced, since the case for taking the action to ban a product or limit some emission is usually based upon evidence of its dangerous effects. It may even be possible to express the uncertainty about the size of the overall risk in formal terms by listing the range of possible values and the probability that the analyst attaches to each one.[4]

Even if one had accurate and universally accepted estimates of the benefits of a regulation, there would still be difficulties in using the information to make decisions. Many of these difficulties center on the issues of aggregating benefits—over time, over type of health effect, and over level of the health risk.[5] Consider the example of a health regulation that reduces the concentration of a pollutant believed to cause respiratory illness at low doses. Suppose that one had reliable estimates of the various illness rates (asthma, bronchitis, and pneumonia, for example) and death rates resulting from various concentrations, and estimates of exposure levels with and without the program. How should this information be combined? One possibility is to add up the illness data to obtain the total days of illness that are avoided under the regulation. But should asthma and pneumonia simply be added? Should reduced illness this year and reduced illness in twenty years time be added, or should health benefits in the future be discounted? Does it matter whether a given total number of illness days or years of reduced life are generated by reducing small risks for a large number of persons or by reducing large risks for a small number of persons? The situation is even more complicated when illness and death rates must be compared. How should one summarize the health benefits of a program that reduces both illness rates and death rates?

These aggregation dilemmas have led Zeckhauser and Shepard (1976) to propose that health effects be summarized by a single measure, which they term the quality-adjusted life year (or QALY). This measure would take into account the number of years of reduced illness or premature death generated under a regulation as well as the quality of the years affected. For example, saving the (statistical) life of a healthy 40-year-old may have a value of 1.0 QALY, while providing a year of relief from asthma for the same person may have a value of 0.1 QALY. While the consensus required to implement such an aggregation procedure may not yet exist, the framework allows one to address aggregation issues directly and thereby avoid the regulatory paralysis or inconsistency that may result from emphasizing the uniqueness of the benefits from each regulatory program.

The concept of quality-adjusted life years leads naturally to the final logical step—at least to economists—in calculating the overall benefits of health or safety regulation: estimation of the willingness to pay for the health benefits. The different weights used to estimate QALY represent trade-offs among various health or safety risks, while willingness to pay measures the trade-off between health benefits and other goods and services. Of course for some purposes, assessing this final trade-off may not be necessary. Once the aggregation issues discussed above are resolved, cost-effectiveness analysis can be a powerful tool for evaluating the overall effects of health and safety programs (Raiffa *et al.* 1977). Indeed, if one incorporated distributional weights to account for effects on different population groups, cost-effectiveness analysis could encompass equity considerations as well. Appropriately weighted aggregates of benefits and costs could then be compared both to eliminate clear outliers—regulations that provide very little health benefits for the costs they impose—and to provide incentives to proceed further in areas where regulation is very cost-effective. But ultimate decisions on how much health and safety to provide often require that we assess—explicitly or implicitly—the value placed on health benefits.

To many, placing a monetary value on health and safety improvements is misguided or even immoral. This criticism seems based upon a misperception of the objective of valuing health benefits in money terms. The analyst does not attempt to quantify the value of a human life; rather he attempts to estimate the individual's willingness to pay for the reduced risk of premature death. The confusion is probably due in part to the early efforts to determine an economic value for a human life by estimating the resources lost to society from premature death (Rice 1967; Rice and Cooper 1967). These estimates were based primarily on medical expenses (doctor's bills, hospital charges, medication costs, and the like) and the individual's earnings had his or her life been prolonged. The value for an individual life saved using this approach was typically in the range of $150,000 to $250,000. One issue of debate is whether the present value of the decedent's future consumption should be subtracted from the foregone earnings to obtain a net benefit to society. The logic of calculating society's interest in the individual's longevity implies that net earnings are relevant, but the implications of this measure—that the individual's welfare should not count—seem counterintuitive at best. This entire approach, moreover, rests on shaky economic and philosophical grounds. Using earnings to measure the value of reducing death rates implies that society does not wish to prolong the lives of retired persons or those unable to work; indeed, in their extreme, these calculations imply that society would be better off if we hastened their death. The economic objection to gross earnings as a measure of the benefits of prolonged life is that it does not relate to the demand of individuals for survival. As Schelling (1968) and Mishan (1971) have pointed out, the appropriate measure for programs that prolong life is a measure of the individual's willingness to pay for reduced risk of death.

Despite its theoretical appeal, however, willingness to pay is difficult to estimate empirically. The handful of studies in this area use two basic approaches. The first approach uses a questionnaire to elicit estimates of willingness to pay. For example, Acton (1973) estimates a value for a life saved of between $28,000 to $43,000 based on responses to a questionnaire eliciting valuations of ambulance programs that would decrease the risk of death by 1/500 and 1/1000. The second approach to valuing risk reductions is to use information from the labor market on the assumption that wage differentials between safe and risky occupations provide an indirect measure of the value individuals place on reducing risks. Thaler and Rosen (1976) estimated that workers were on average compensated an extra $200 per year for an increased death rate of 0.001 per year, implying a value of a statistical life of $200,000. Other studies using these two approaches have yielded varying empirical results.

It is not difficult to criticize these empirical studies since the task of eliciting estimates of such a nonmarket item as the risk of death is a formidable one. Questionnaire studies presuppose that the respondents understood the questions and gave meaningful answers. These may be unwarranted assumptions, given the difficulty most people have in comprehending small changes in risk and the possibility that respondents would act differently if they actually had to pay for the reduced risk. The labor market studies depend upon the workers knowing the risks they face and being representative of the population as a whole in terms of their attitudes toward risk. Variations in the worker sample, as well as in statistical procedures, have led to vast differences in results for these wage studies. Nevertheless, despite their inevitable limitations, these empirical studies can help regulators cope with the difficult issue of drawing a line for health and safety regulation. For example, regulators can use the range of values from these studies to test the sensitivity of their choices to beneficiaries' valuations of reduced risk.

The basic methodology of a distributional analysis is the same as that of an overall analysis, except that the population is broken into subgroups. The task is to estimate the effect of the particular regulation on each group's health and, perhaps, willingness to pay. Survey results and other data used to determine overall benefits often include information to estimate benefits to particular subgroups, although it may be necessary—as in the example given in the next section—to collect other data. But a distributional analysis may introduce methodological complications as well. Two additional complications are discussed below.

Identifying All the Beneficiaries. The principal beneficiaries of a specific health or safety regulation are typically easy to identify because, as noted in the beginning of the paper, most regulations are designed to help a particular group. Common beneficiary groups are workers in particular plants, users of particular products, residents in particular polluted areas, or occupants of particular vehicles. Thus, in order to determine the income profile of beneficiaries, one would first consider the income profile of the primary beneficiaries. But a full analysis of beneficiaries would take into account the possibility that others receive benefits as well, either as net additions to the primary beneficiaries or as beneficiaries of market operations that shift some of the primary benefits.

Providing a complete inventory of beneficiaries may be most important for environmental improvement programs, since the benefits vary by location and people spend their days in different areas. For example, most empirical studies of air pollution control only estimate benefits to people where they live. But many gain from air quality improvements at work and, as shown below in the example, these workplace benefits may seriously change the results of a distributional analysis. At a broader level, the issue of completeness raises the question of who gains when a given individual's risk of death or illness is reduced. Certainly the individual gains; but so do his family and friends. Should an analysis include these benefits as well? The person's employer gains from a worker's greater health or lessened risk of death.[6] I expect, however, that including these broader beneficiaries would not change a distributional result substantially.

The process of benefit shifting is analogous to the shifting that transfers control costs from producers of regulated products to consumers or employees, although benefit shifting is less prevalent and certainly less widely acknowledged. The clearest example of benefit shifting occurs when tenants receive improvements in some environmental amenity. Part of these improvements will be shifted to landlords in the form of higher rents. Other benefit shifting occurs because of insurance arrangements. If the direct beneficiaries of a health or safety program have insurance, part of the benefits of reducing illness or accidents eventually accrues to the group as a whole in the form of reduced payments. Note, however, that it may be possible for the primary beneficiaries to retain all benefits if they can obtain lower premiums as a group. For example, owners of cars with airbags may be able to retain the full benefits of lower accident costs if insurance companies provide discounts for airbag-equipped cars.

Valuation of Health Benefits.   As discussed above, one of the thorniest issues in the analysis of health and safety regulatory programs involves placing a dollar value on health benefits. From an overall perspective it may not be necessary to calculate dollar costs if sufficient agreement existed on procedures for aggregating various types of health benefits; cost-effectiveness analysis could then be used to choose among programs. But a distributional analysis would be seriously incomplete if valuations were not included. The poor may place a lower value on health benefits than the rich and thus the benefits to the poor would be overestimated if physical benefits—reductions in illness rates or death rates—were used to measure distributional effects.

High income households probably value relief from illness more highly than the poor because health is very likely a good whose value increases with income. Those with higher incomes should place a greater dollar value on illness benefits for four principal reasons: treatment costs would be easier to bear; relief from pain and suffering is probably a superior good for which the rich would pay more; earnings are greater and thus wage losses from an illness would be greater; and the value of leisure time lost would be greater.

Analyzing differential willingness to pay for reduction in death rates is more problematical, but the pattern is almost certainly the same as that for illness benefits: low income households are probably less concerned about risk than high income households and thus less willing to pay for reduced risk of death. Moreover, there are more older persons in the low income group who, having less time to live and fewer dependents, may value decreases in the risk of death less highly than the young.[7] Acton (1973) provides empirical support for these a priori views; his regression results imply an income elasticity of willingness to pay for reductions in the risk of death that lies between 0.5 and 1.

AN EXAMPLE: AIR POLLUTION CONTROL [8]

The 1970 Clean Air Act amendments established ambitious goals for improving air quality. While there were other objectives, the major purpose of the amendments was to protect public health. Section 109 of the Clean Air Act required EPA to set national primary ambient air quality standards for major pollutants "the attainment and maintenance of which . . . allowing an adequate margin of safety, are requisite to protect the public health." The amendments also mandated a number of regulatory means to achieve the air quality goals. The set of limitations on automotive emissions is one of the largest and most controversial programs under the amendments and represents a major effort to improve public health through regulation. (See Harrison [1975] for a summary of the specific requirements on automotive emissions established under the 1970 amendments.)

This section presents information on the distribution of benefits of the automotive emission control program for the Boston metropolitan area to provide an example of how a distributional analysis of a major health or safety regulation might be performed. The example is not a complete distributional analysis since it is limited to residents of one urban area and it does not consider costs. (See Harrison [1975] for an analysis of the national cost and benefit distribution.) This example was chosen primarily to illustrate the importance of providing a complete accounting of beneficiaries and permitting the value of a given air quality improvement to vary by income group. The example includes workers and landlords as additional beneficiaries from the control program and uses two techniques to estimate willingness to pay by income group—a property value technique and a health effects example. The results for Boston corroborate the general impression that the urban poor obtain greater air quality benefits than other income groups. But when workplace benefits and differences in the valuation of physical benefits by income group are considered, the results are much less favorable to the poor: the absolute level of benefits, measured in dollars, in fact rises consistently and substantially with income.[9]

Housing Value Results.   Table 7−1 summarizes the steps in estimating average air quality benefits for seven income groups in the Boston metropolitan area. The first row lists the physical air quality benefits that Bostonians receive at home. These estimates are based upon a meteorological model that predicts air quality with and without the auto emission standards and on U.S. Census estimates of households by income group in each Boston area census tract. Physical benefits are distributed in a favorable manner to the poor, reflecting the greater concentration of the poor in central areas that receive the largest air quality improvements. Households in the lowest income group, on average, receive almost 50 percent greater benefits from the auto emission control program than households in the highest income group.

The next two rows in Table 7−1 transform benefit estimates into dollars based upon a relationship between households' willingness to pay and the level of air quality and income. This relationship was derived in a earlier study of housing prices. (Harrison and Rubinfeld, 1978b). For our purposes, the most important result is that people's valuation of a given air quality improvement increases with income.[10] The first row of dollar benefit estimates in Table 7−1 shows a baseline case dependent upon the assumption that rents do not rise as a result of the air quality improvements. The second estimate assumes rents increase and thereby shift benefits from renters to owners. The distributional patterns in these two cases are very different. Dollar benefits are mildly favorable to the poor when renters are assumed to retain all their air quality benefits. But if rents increase to shift air quality benefits to owners, dollar benefits markedly favor the rich; per household benefits range from $92 for those in the lowest income group to $252 for those in the highest income group.

Cleaner air around one's home accounts for only part of the benefits from improved air quality. Household members will also benefit

Table 7–1. Annual air quality benefits by income group in Boston SMSA.

	Income Group (000's)						
	$0–6	$6–10	$10–14	$14–20	$20–30	$30–50	$50+
Physical benefits[a] at home	6.74	6.65	6.48	5.97	5.36	4.91	4.60
Dollar benefits[b] no rent increase	182	180	180	166	152	146	162
Dollar benefits[b] rent increase	92	100	110	150	192	222	252
Physical benefits[a] at work	6.16	6.17	6.14	6.13	6.13	6.16	6.32
Dollar benefits at work[b][c]	12	22	34	44	70	112	174
Dollar benefits at home and work[b][d]	104	122	144	194	262	334	426
Percentage of income	2.9	1.5	1.2	1.1	1.0	0.84	0.71

a. Expressed as NOX concentration improvements (24 hour annual average in parts per billion).

b. Income groups and dollar benefits in 1980 dollars. The figures were obtained by multiplying the 1970 dollar results in Harrison and Rubinfeld (1978b) by two, approximately the multiple of the consumer price index from 1970 to mid–1980.

c. Assumes workplace benefits are valued at one-third of residence benefits.

d. Assumes workplace benefits are valued at one-third of residence benefits and renters' benefits are shifted to landlords.

from better air quality where they work, go to school, shop, and visit friends. Workplace benefits probably constitute the only other important category since shops, friends, and schools are usually close to home. Table 7–1 shows estimates of average air quality benefits by income group for workers in the Boston area. Workplace benefits are approximately the same for all groups, and thus the distribution of the combined work and residence benefits is less favorable to the poor than the residence benefits taken alone. The next row translates the proposed benefits into dollars, assuming that workplace benefits are valued at only one-third of residence benefits because more family time is spent at home than at work. Unlike residence benefits, air quality improvements at the workplace favor higher income households; benefits range from $12 per year for the lowest income group to $174 per year in the highest income group.

The final two rows in Table 7–1 summarize dollar benefits, taking into account both the additional benefits to workers and benefit shifting to landlords. Under these assumptions, dollar benefits increase substantially with income; average benefits are $104 for the lowest income group and $426 for the highest income group. This pattern is much different than the baseline case—ignoring these two complications—in which dollar benefits were mildly favorable to the poor.

Valuing Health Benefits Directly. A second method of estimating distributional effects is to perform a two-step procedure of first estimating changes in disease and death rates due to the air pollution regulations and then translating these figures into dollar values. This procedure is more likely to isolate the *health* benefits of improved air quality, since the housing value method undoubtedly takes into account other benefits of cleaner air, such as smaller cleaning and maintenance costs, less odor, and better visibility. Automobile pollutants have been associated with increased mortality rates, various respiratory and heart diseases, and minor but pervasive maladies such as headaches and eye irritation (Harrison 1975, Appendix A; Lave and Seskin 1977). According to a recent National Academy of Sciences (1974) study, the current set of automotive emission controls generates approximately $1.7 billion per year in health benefits for American households, and thus per capita benefits of approximately $8 per year or $24 per household. Do these health benefits differ systematically by income group? If so, are they distributed in favor of the rich or the poor? While there is not enough data to answer these questions with confidence, it is possible to outline the factors that determine whether health benefits will favor the poor or the rich, and to use available health information to provide illustrative examples.

The National Academy of Sciences (1974) study estimated the average change in the death rate following a 10 percent decrease in nitrogen oxides (NOX) concentrations (the average NOX decreases in the Boston area from the automotive emission control program) to be approximately 2.3 deaths per 100,000 population. Recent re-analysis suggests a somewhat greater impact: Lave and Seskin (1977) obtained estimates of 6.1 deaths per 100,000 for the unadjusted total mortality rate and 4.0 deaths per 100,000 for the age–sex–race adjusted total mortality rate. Table 7–2 shows a set of sample calculations that translate the estimate of 4.0 deaths per 100,000 population into average dollars by income group. In the first row are average rates of chronic bronchitis (a respiratory ailment linked to auto emission concentrations) for households in each income group, based on data collected by the Public Health Service. The second row presents the mortality benefits accruing to each income group, calculated by multiplying 4.0 deaths per 100,000 by the ratio of each income group's bronchitis rate to the average illness rate for the seven groups (33.1). Because the incidence of bronchitis is higher among low income persons, the resulting mortality benefits favor the poor. The estimated mortality rate improvements range from 3.72 deaths per 100,000 for the two highest income groups to 4.77 deaths per 100,000 for the lowest income group. Note that these figures may understate the degree to which distribution of mortality benefits favor the poor, because they ignore the greater improvements in air quality received by the poor.

The third row of Table 7–2 lists hypothetical dollar values for a one-unit (1 death per 100,000) change in the risk of death based upon the scant empirical evidence that was summarized above. A household earning of $17,000 per year (1980 dollars) is assumed to value the reduction at $4.00, which implies a statistical value of life of $400,000, a figure obtained by modifying the results of Thaler and Rosen (1976) for changes in the price level. Results are presented for values of the income elasticity of willingness to pay of unity (i.e., a household with an income of $8,000 is assumed to value a one-unit change only 8/17 as much as a household earning $17,000, or at

Table 7-2. Sample calculations of dollar health benefits by income group.

	Income Group (000's)						
	$0–6	$6–10	$10–14	$14–20	$20–30	$30–50	$50+
(1) Bronchitis rate (illness per 1000)	39.50	35.00	31.00	32.30	32.60	30.80	30.80
(2) Estimated mortality benefit (deaths per 100,000)	4.77	4.23	3.75	3.90	3.94	3.72	3.72
(3) Value of one unit change ($)							
E = 1.0[a]	0.82	1.88	2.84	4.50	5.88	9.40	14.12
E = 0.5	2.44	2.96	3.40	4.50	4.96	6.72	9.08
(4) Mortality benefits ($ per year)							
E = 1.0	4.00	7.96	10.66	15.60	23.16	34.96	52.52
E = 0.5	11.64	12.52	12.76	15.60	19.54	25.00	33.78
(5) Benefits as percentage of income							
E = 1.0	0.11	0.10	0.09	0.09	0.09	0.09	0.09
E = 0.5	0.32	0.16	0.11	0.09	0.08	0.06	0.06

a. E = elasticity of willingness to pay for mortality decreases with respect to income.

Source: derived from Harrison and Rubinfeld (1978b).

$1.88 rather than $4.00) and 0.5, approximately the range found by Acton (1973) in his study of the willingness to pay for reductions in the risk of death from heart attack. The estimated dollar value of mortality benefits using these average valuation figures are given in the fourth row. Assuming an elasticity of 1.0, the dollar values range from around $4 for the lowest income group to $52 for the highest income group. Benefits do not favor the rich as much if the income elasticity is 0.5, ranging only from $12 to $34.

Reduced illness benefits are probably more favorable to the rich than death risk benefits. Acute respiratory diseases, such as the colds and sore throats that are often associated with pollution exposure, are less skewed to the poor than are the chronic diseases used to proxy increased risk of death. Moreover, high income persons probably value minor incapacities more highly than low income persons. If person-days are approximately equal for all income groups and if income elasticity of the valuation of such days is substantially greater than unity, illness benefits would markedly favor the rich.

SOCIETAL JUDGMENTS ON HEALTH AND SAFETY

The methodology outlined above presumes that society's welfare depends solely on individuals' own valuations of their interests. Yet there are many cases in which we impose rules that could not be supported on the basis of individual valuations. For example, both the 55 mile per hour speed limit and the requirement that motorcyclists wear helmets would probably be rejected by motorists and motorcyclists if a vote were taken. More extreme examples of the imposition of a societal judgment are prohibitions against suicide and mercy killings.[11] Society makes a judgment in these cases that is different from the individual's.

Should such societal judgments be used in the case of health or safety regulation? Put differently, should occupational safety regulations be set on the basis of workers' evaluations of the costs and benefits, or according to the evaluation of society expressed through statutes or agency rulemaking? This is not merely a theoretical squabble. Consider the case of a regulation that will create a safer work environment but will also result in either a 25 percent decline in the industry's workforce or a 25 percent decrease in wages. Suppose that if the workers were to vote on the regulation, they would overwhelmingly defeat the measure, preferring physical hazards to the threat of a layoff or lower wages. Should the public override the workers' judgment and adopt the safety regulation?

A similar dilemma arises in assessing the equity impacts of a regulation. Suppose one is considering a regulation that provides fewer overall benefits than an alternative, but provides benefits to low income blacks. Should one use the group's own valuation of their benefits or some societal judgment of what is good for them? These valuations may be quite different if the group places a much lower value on reducing risks of illness or death than does society in general. Take the air pollution example given above. Since low income households do not place great value upon the health benefits of air pollution reduction, using their valuations may indicate that the net benefits (benefits minus costs) to the poor are actually negative. Should the program be considered inequitable even though it provides more health benefits to the poor than the rich, and many think that the poor ought to value better health more highly?

While there are no clearcut criteria for deciding these cases, I propose that the decision hinge on the magnitude of the harm to be prevented; major risks of injury, death, or illness should be society's judgments rather than individual valuations. This criterion would, I believe, cover regulations on motorcycle helmets and major regulations on mine safety; it might also cover a ban on skateboarding in the street to protect children from serious injuries. These and similar regulations represent minimum standards of health and safety below which individual judgments would not apply. For example, as a matter of societal policy, mine workers would not be allowed to sell their right to minimum safety for higher pay or greater job security.

Beyond these minimum standards, however, it seems appropriate to evaluate costs and benefits on the basis of individual preferences. Relatively minor health and safety dangers should be treated like ordinary "goods and services" where individual values are respected. Just as we allow persons to smoke, become overweight, and forego exercise—all of which have significant impacts on health—we should allow individual judgments about public efforts to improve health. If mine workers place a low value on a safety proposal that would reduce somewhat the risk of a broken bone, that low valuation should be used in deciding the program's desirability.

Applying this criterion, of course, requires categorizing health and safety risks as minor or major. While most would agree that common upper-respiratory infections and reversible injuries such as sprains are minor health risks and that substantial risks of death or more serious irreversible illness are major risks, there is a large middle ground. Although it is not possible to be precise about the boundary, the problem of drawing lines of this sort is a common one. For example, judges and juries often must determine whether a doctor acted reasonably in performing a certain operation. I expect that analogous rules of thumb about major and minor health and safety risks would evolve as agencies and legislative bodies develop precedents.

Distinguishing between major and minor risks can be viewed as one means of interjecting considerations of *process* into an evaluation of health and safety regulation. Zeckhauser (1975) has emphasized that society is interested in process—that is, the ways in which decisions are made—as well as outcomes of regulatory interventions. It is desirable that people accept the procedures for decisionmaking, even if the resulting decisions do not generate the greatest health benefits per dollar expended. He gives an example of the federal government assuming the costs of renal dialysis machines—at an enormous cost per life saved—as a decision justified as a means of preserving the myth that society will not give up a life to save dollars. In this context, making the distinction between minor and major risks to separate the cases where society preempts individual judgments is presumed to be an acceptable process. The logical next step would be to test whether such a distinction has general adherence.

Most discussion of equity issues assumes that goals of efficiency and equity will conflict. For example, Okun (1975) titles his set of lectures, *Efficiency and Equality: The Big Trade-off.* The basic dilemma is seen as choosing between programs that benefit deserving groups and those that provide larger total benefits. It may, however, be possible to modify health and safety regulations to make them both more efficient and more equitable. I have argued elsewhere (Harrison 1977), for example, that permitting automotive standards to vary according to the severity of the air pollution problem will make the program both more cost-effective and more beneficial to the poor. Thus, while trade-offs between efficiency and equity objectives will occur in health and safety regulation, one should not ignore the possibility that these goals will coincide.

NOTES TO CHAPTER 7

1. For example, I know of no study that estimates the distribution by race of the costs or benefits of a health or safety regulation. Freeman (1972), however, does provide information on air pollution exposure by race.

2. Future generations represent one such group with no ability to protect itself from this generation's environmental legacy. Professor Mishan considers intergenerational issues in detail in Chapter 6.

3. These issues are explored in much more detail in other papers in this volume. Since this conference is on benefits, I ignore the equally important issues of estimating the overall costs of regulations. These costs include the *increased* health or safety risks (greater heart disease from banning a diet control drug, for example) that are the focus of the technique known as risk-benefit analysis.

4. Raiffa *et al.* (1975) argue that uncertainty in risk estimates should be described explicitly whenever possible.

5. The distributional considerations that are the subject of this chapter can be viewed as another aggregation issue, in this case over people.

6. The potential benefits to companies of healthier employees was highlighted in a recent *Boston Globe* series of articles. See "The People Investment," *Boston Globe*, September 22, 1980, p. 24.

7. Freeman (1977) obtains the opposite result in his theoretical model—that older people would value decreases in the risk of death *more* highly than the young. Freeman's model distinguished controllable and uncontrollable causes of death. Since the probability of dying from an uncontrollable cause increases with age, the marginal willingness to pay for a decrease in a controllable cause of death increases with age, other things equal, in his model.

8. This example is based on Harrison and Rubinfeld (1978b), which provides the details of the estimation procedures. Other distributional studies include Freeman (1972), Harrison (1975), Gianessi, *et al.* (1977), Peskin (1978), Seneca and Asch (1978), and Zupan (1973).

9. When expressed as a percentage of income, however, air quality benefits generally favor the poor even when the complications are added. See Harrison and Rubinfeld (1978b).

10. The income elasticity of willingness to pay for air quality improvements is 1.2. The estimated relationship also implies that air quality improvements are valued more highly in more polluted rather than less polluted areas.

11. Some might argue that these regulations can be explained on the basis of the external effects of the private behavior. For example, you or I may bear some of the medical costs of a motorcyclist's injury or a suicide's

death because of government or private insurance arrangements. I expect, however, that those external effects provide little explanation for the various rules.

REFERENCES

Acton, Jan. 1973. *Evaluating Public Programs to Save Lives: The Case of Heart Attacks*. Research Report R—73—02. Santa Monica, Ca.: The Rand Corporation.

Ashfelter, Orley, and Albert Rees. 1974. *Discrimination in Labor Markets*. Princeton, N.J.: Princeton University Press.

Freeman, A. Myrick. 1972. "The Distribution of Environmental Quality." In *Environmental Quality Analysis*, edited by Allen V. Kneese and Blair T. Bower, pp. 243—278. Baltimore: Johns Hopkins University Press.

Freeman, A. Myrick. 1977. "Some Extensions of a Simple Value of Life Saving Model." Discussion Paper D—19. Washington, D.C.: Resources for the Future.

Gianessi, Leonard P.; Henry M. Peskin; and Edward Wolff. 1977. "The Distributional Implications of National Air Pollution Damage Estimates." In *Distribution of Economic Well-Being*, edited by F. Thomas Juster, pp. 201—227. Cambridge, Mass.: Ballinger Publishing Company.

Harrison, David, Jr. 1975. *Who Pays for Clean Air*. Cambridge, Mass.:Ballinger Publishing Company.

Harrison, David, Jr. 1977. "Controlling Automotive Emissions: How to Save More Than $1 Billion per Year and Help the Poor Too." *Public Policy* 25: 527—553.

Harrison, David, Jr., and Daniel L. Rubinfeld. 1978a. "Hedonic Housing Prices and the Demand for Clean Air." *Journal of Environmental Economics and Management* 5: 81—102.

Harrison, David, Jr., and Daniel L. Rubinfeld. 1978b. "The Distribution Benefits from Improvements in Urban Air Quality." *Journal of Environmental Economics and Management* 5: 313—332.

Lave, Lester B., and Eugene P. Seskin. 1977. *Air Pollution and Human Health*. Baltimore: Johns Hopkins University Press.

Mishan, Ezra J. 1971. "Evaluation of Life and Limb: A Theoretical Approach." *Journal of Political Economy* 79: 687—705.

National Academy of Sciences. 1974. *The Costs and Benefits of Automobile Emission Control*. Vol. 4 of *Air Quality and Automobile Control*. Washington, D.C.: U.S. Government Printing Office.

Okun, Arthur M. 1975. *Equality and Efficiency: The Big Tradeoff*. Washington, D.C.: The Brookings Institution.

Peskin, Henry M. 1978. "Environmental Policy and the Distribution of Benefits and Costs." In *Current Issues in U.S. Environmental Policy*. Edited by Paul R. Portney, pp. 144—163. Baltimore: Johns Hopkins University Press.

Raiffa, Howard; William B. Schwartz; and Milton C. Weinstein. 1977. "Evaluating Health Effects of Societal Decisions and Programs." In *Decision Making in the Environmental Agency.* Volume IIb. Prepared for the Committee on Natural Resources, National Research Council. Washington, D.C.: National Academy of Sciences.

Rawls, John. 1971. *A Theory of Justice.* Cambridge, Mass.: Harvard University Press.

Schelling, Thomas C. 1968. "The Life You Save May be Your Own." In *Problems in Public Expenditure Analysis*, edited by S.B. Chase, pp. 127–162. Washington, D.C.: The Brookings Institution.

Seneca, Joseph, and Peter Asch. 1978. "Some Evidence on the Distribution of Air Quality." *Land Economics* 54: 278–297.

Smith, Richard S. 1976. *The Occupational Safety and Health Act: Its Goals and Its Achievements.* Washington, D.C.: American Enterprise Institute.

Thaler, Richard S., and Sherwin Rosen. 1976. "The Value of Saving a Life: Evidence from the Labor Market." In *Household Production and Consumption*, edited by N. Terlecky, pp. 265–302. New York: Columbia University Press.

Yinger, John M. 1979. "Prejudice and Discrimination in Urban Housing Markets." In *Current Issues in Urban Economics*, edited by Peter Mieskowsky and Mahlon Straszheim, pp. 430–468. Baltimore: Johns Hopkins University Press.

Zeckhauser, Richard. 1978. "Procedures for Valuing Lives." *Public Policy* 23: 419–464.

Zeckhauser, Richard, and Donald Shepard. 1976. "Where Now for Saving Lives?" *Law and Contemporary Problems* 40: 5–45.

Zupan, Jeffrey M. 1973. *The Distribution of Air Quality in the New York Region.* Baltimore: Johns Hopkins University Press.

DISCUSSION OF PART III

Paul Weaver (Moderator): Joan Claybrook, the Administrator of the National Highway Traffic Safety Administration, will begin.

Joan Claybrook: I am delighted to be at a conference to discuss benefits. I spend most of each day worrying about costs because most of the people who comment to the Department of Transportation on auto safety and fuel economy matters are discussing costs; and the benefits are usually ignored. I make a practice of reading speeches of the auto industry executives, searching in vain for any discussion of benefits, and I have decided that my new project in this job is to try to bring the benefits to their attention.

Second, I would like to say that if bureaucratization is a problem, so is academic jargon. I had a terrible time getting through these chapters, and I realized in that course of events that there is a vast gulf between those of us who deal in the day-to-day world of regulations, and those who comment, analyze, and write papers about this activity.

Third, I would like to comment on one thing that hampers my ability to deal with the issue of this particular panel, and that is that I think product regulation, which Susan King (Chairman of the Consumer Product Safety Commission) and I are primarily involved in, is least amenable to distributive analysis. Our activities tend to deal

203

with a manufacturing concern, and one of the reasons that there is such a thing as federal regulation, rather than state regulation or other ways of affecting the design and performance of products, is that this constitutes an attempt to make regulations pertain to all people. This is just the opposite of what we are talking about here, as I understand it.

Fourth, one of the things that I find most difficult in the concept of benefit analysis is that there is a challenge in the level of specificity of benefits to be described, analyzed, and assessed, that is in excess of the information that we have to work with. This is a very basic and difficult problem. We can do analyses in a much more general way, but, at least in most areas, it is very hard to get accurate enough and supportable enough detailed information to do any kind of specific economic analyses. Certainly this is true of the health and safety areas, although we are in the process of trying to develop data through accident investigation and other techniques for gathering information.

Fifth, one of the things that Mishan's and Harrison's chapters specifically eliminated from discussion was the issue of the political relationship of economic analysis to the real world. By eliminating that issue, I concluded that the authors were saying that economic analysis is a tool for management. It is a tool—a tool for choosing priorities, for deciding what is the right, or good, thing to do. However, it certainly is not the only element in the decisionmaking process. I feel this very strongly because, among other reasons, the standards that we set in the product area are performance standards and when you set a performance standard, you work very hard to avoid delimiting the options for design. A manufacturer, in conformance with such standards, can choose a design that is either enormously cost beneficial or not enormously cost beneficial. Therefore, before you can make the assessment of the cost or, indeed, the benefit, you have to know what design is being used to carry out the regulation.

A good example of this is the car bumper regulation, issued by our agency some years ago, which is a performance regulation. The original bumpers put on cars were very heavy—far heavier than they had to be. Therefore, when people went to replace them after an accident, they found that they were much more costly than they previously had been. When fuel economy became a problem, additional regulations were issued. A very successful attempt by manufacturers resulted to reduce enormously the weight of bumpers, thereby reducing their cost, in order to comply with this new element of regulation.

Therefore, another issue that is very pertinent to any discussion of benefits is the interrelationship of standards for regulation. Very often this is looked upon as a trade-off. That is, if you have fuel economy that is going to harm safety, and indeed this is a possibility, not a necessity; you very often can find other technologies or methods for achieving both aims. We have certainly done this with our experimental safety vehicles. In other examples, such as fuel economy and bumper regulation, one has been very consonant with the other. I think this has been the key that made the bumper regulation more effective. It is also the key that made it more difficult for some types of bumpers to be used. With the fuel economy regulation added on, the manufacturers decided to manufacture different kinds of bumpers, for a different economic goal.

Henry Aaron (Assistant Secretary, Department of Health, Education, and Welfare): I would like to make some comments about three approaches to regulation. The first approach I would characterize as the engineering-professional mentality. It rests on the knowledge— the expertise—of the professionally qualified. It requires the general application of standard or best practice, and mandates such practice on everybody; sometimes it takes the form of licensing requirements that limit entry into a particular activity. It leads to health and safety standards that may have little or no relationship to the actual benefits, in terms of reduced injuries or reduced mortality. In the case of organizations such as the Professional Standards Review Organizations (PSROs), which deal with health utilization, the approach sometimes leads to agonizingly slow, and sometimes completely imperceptible, progress toward the achievement of stated objectives.

The second approach I would characterize as the legalistic mentality—not legal, but legalistic. Some of the severest critics of this approach are lawyers. This approach typically, although not invariably, is characterized by stipulating in great detail particular methods of achieving particular outcomes. Such extreme detail has brought adverse publicity to the Occupational Safety and Health Administration (OSHA) in a number of its regulations and has brought a good deal of red tape into regulations that the Department of Health, Education, and Welfare (HEW), is responsible for.

It also leads to emphasis on rules that may be contrary to very strong incentives that people face. For example, certificate-of-need requirements have run in the face of very strong contrary incentives to invest in health equipment and buildings. Such regulations have not yet demonstrated their effectiveness, and I think that is putting it very gently. The risk of this approach, of course, is that in stipulating detailed means of achieving goals, one may exclude more effective ways of achieving them. Indeed, one may end up making goals out of things that really should be means or instruments.

The third approach is the economic mentality. True to my disciplinary training, I think on balance it is under-represented among regulation writers. But, in some cases, it can lead to fairly silly results. In general, this approach tries to regulate incentives to achieve desired outcomes. Where incentives are not at hand, it stipulates outcomes—genuine outcomes—and permits the subjects of regulation to choose the method of achieving such outcomes. In so doing, however, I think economists sometimes forget that one of the basic motivations for regulation is the collective decision that certain things are going to be decided outside the marketplace and not by economic incentives. We determine that we are going to require certain outcomes and treat them, in effect, as a kind of right that individuals should not be denied.

The possibility of carrying the economic approach to extremes, I think, was demonstrated most clearly in one of our leading economic journals, by one author who argued that the market produces the optimal amount of housing discrimination. People who are discriminated against have the option to bribe the discriminators not to engage in such behavior. By failing to do so, they demonstrate that the value to them of not being discriminated against is less than the value to the discriminators of engaging in that behavior.

However, I also feel that the advantage of the economic approach is that it makes us think twice about classifying things as rights that on more consideration we might not wish to. For example, it warns us against defining as inalienable rights such things as double insulation in homes or identifying as infinite the value of human life, or primeval air cleanliness.

The chapters by Mishan and Harrison are very different from one another and neither clearly expresses any of the three approaches that I just described. My main conclusion after reading them is that I would have gotten a good deal more from both, if they had devoted more space to more specific applications, and then followed those applications with an attempt to deduce general principles or broader ideas from them.

I would like to have seen some attention paid to one or more topics that are very important from a regulatory standpoint at HEW: how PSROs operate; how certificate-of-need legislation should be applied; licensing standards in the health professions; whether they should be extended or drawn back; what the distributive implications or the administrative problems would be from hospital cost containment; capital investment limitations; grants for closure and conversion of hospital beds. I pick HEW areas because these are the ones that I see every day. I would urge that conferences such as this should deal, to the maximum extent possible, with specific problems about which we can find real data.

I had a basic problem with Mishan's chapter. He rejects the central axiom of the economist's approach to regulation; namely, that information is available to undergird calculations on costs and benefits of achieving specific regulatory goals. I feel that he went even further and argued that we also lack the information to apply either the professional or the legal approach to regulation. In particular, he writes that the industrial process and products that have been developed pose "a gigantic question mark." They threatened "large-scale disasters . . . possibly fatal to humanity, and perhaps also to other or all forms of life on earth." I refer to these passages not because I disagree with them, but because I do not know what to do about them. And I do not think that the chapter gives any guidance about what to do about them.

These threats are so serious that, again going back to the economic model, there are literally no informed consumers or producers. However, informed consumers and producers are necessary, normally, if we want to rely on markets for the allocation of resources. Not only that, there are no informed regulators either. The dangers seem to me so extreme and so unspecified, that we are really helpless before a kind of threat that I call omnicide. I do not know how to handle this and Mishan does not help.

A second issue concerns discounting of risks and benefits that accrue to later generations—generations that are not connected with our own, in the sense that none of us will be alive in that generation, and none of the people alive in that generation are alive now. It is suggested that the application of even modest discount rates rapidly leads one to disregard benefits or costs accruing to future generations. The implication is that we should not apply discount rates in looking at the impacts of current decisions on future generations. If we were to apply this to investments, it would suggest that any perpetuity, however small the payout and however large the present cost, should be undertaken simply because any infinite stream of small benefits will exceed any finite current cost. This is not a tenable position and, therefore, it seems that one has to use discounting in looking at future benefits and costs.

Harrison's chapter is, I think, more modest in tone than Mishan's, but raises basic questions as well. Harrison argues that it is appropriate and important to take distributional considerations into account when making regulatory policy, and that, in particular, one should show special solicitude for the poor and the defenseless; for those who are not able to get out of the way of threats, due to their age, infirmity, or lack of options. He also suggests that, to the extent that regulation deals with risks, it should focus on major risks, not with minor risks that are better left to the marketplace. Put in other terms, public judgment should only be used for major risks, and should not override private valuations of minor risks.

I read much of the chapter as an attempt to justify the inclusion of distributional considerations, which strikes me—based, again, on HEW experience—as worrying about the wrong problem. I see no problem with bringing distributional considerations into deliberations when data are available. Rather, when data are available, the contrary problem arises; it is how to get efficiency considerations into deliberations. There is a kind of Gresham's law that if distributional information is available, it drives out any consideration of efficiency. I am not sure whether this applies equally to all fields, but it is certainly the case in the policy issues that arise in the HEW area.

The suggestion that special attention should be paid to the risks faced by the poor and the defenseless is nothing more than a value judgment, which I share, that inequality in the current income distribution is excessive and should be reduced. However, somebody who is undisturbed about the distribution of income, who likes it the way it is, or even feels that we are doing too much in the way of income redistribution, might disagree both with Mr. Harrison and with me on this score.

I also agree with the suggestion that we steer clear of minor risks and stick to major ones. The implication of the chapter is that we too often ignore this stricture.

I am still left with the question of where do we go from here. And I am not sure, having read both chapters, what we should do differently about particular regulatory problems that we face. I think it would be most useful in the discussion that follows, to attempt to pick out some particular problems and try to apply the principles that were developed in these two chapters.

Susan King (Chairman of the Consumer Product Safety Commission):   I want to respond to these chapters from the perspective of one who is involved in the implementation of policy as the chairman of the Consumer Product Safety Commission (CPSC). We at the Commission are very much concerned with questions of unreasonable risk of injury associated with consumer products. The Commission must deal with reality and part of this reality is specific statutory requirements that require us to make economic analyses of the impacts of pending legislation as part of the rule-making process. Other laws require that we show a causal relationship between the product and the hazard, and between the proposed regulation and the hazard. Therefore, we have evolved as good a capability for doing cost-benefit analysis as any agency concerned with health and safety regulation.

At CPSC we have tried to focus on criteria for decisionmaking to decide why we are regulating, and then, to decide how we are going to regulate. This involves, obviously, a number of value judgments and a number of balancing and weighing considerations. The elements of these decisions include at least the following things: the number of injuries involved, the severity of the injury, and the vulnerability of the population—a point that David Harrison made in his chapter.

Presently, we are placing a new and important emphasis on the question of the unforeseeability of the risk, such as with potential fire hazards when using cellulose home insulation and aluminum wiring, and the avoidability of the risk where innocent bystanders are involved.

Our experience with cost-benefit analysis has left us with many questions as to its utility.

I agree with David Harrison's conclusion that equity considerations must be an important part of the decisionmaking process; they are in the Consumer Product Safety Commission. Our experience in delineating groups for special consideration suggests that we have a difficult time developing the necessary data to make distributional analyses based on income. Therefore, we have focused on children, the elderly, and the handicapped—groups that either cannot foresee, or avoid certain kinds of risks or problems.

The difficulties in developing the necessary data on the net effects of regulation on particular individuals or households raises an important issue that Harrison fails to mention. The cost of obtaining such data, upon which distributional analysis depends, is high. The policy issue is, therefore, whether this data-gathering process is worth the effort and cost. I see no simple answer to this question.

The data gathering and analysis process is further complicated by the fact that business exaggerates the costs, and we must depend on business to provide us the information on costs. A second problem is that often the victim of a particular hazard is not the product's purchaser, but someone else.

I think these very practical problems are of great importance to those of us who must do the day-to-day analysis. Most of the chapters in this book deal with a much higher level of generality and abstraction. They do not deal with the concrete realities within which we operate, including the political constraints as well as the details of obtaining the necessary information, as described above. If these mundane issues were given more serious consideration, the chapters would be much more worthwhile to those of us who do the actual regulation.

For instance, in a real decisionmaking situation, the questions posed in Mishan's work simply do not occur. We are involved in a highly dynamic process and it is extraordinarily difficult to draw from his chapter how we might take pictures in time and make value judgments concerning one state of affairs as opposed to another. Obviously, in rulemaking, we do assess the state of the market and the state of the regulation, prior to and after rulemaking. However, once the process begins, the process itself has a very important impact on the considerations of what the ultimate evaluation of a regulation will be.

Furthermore, I do not think we can trust the judgment of the marketplace in producing a desirable level of product safety, because consumers cannot learn how to assess the relative merits of safe products and because the manufacturer has no incentive to produce a safer product. Unless someone becomes very aggressive and attempts to define safety as a desirable product attribute, the choice of product safety will, more often than not, be available to the consumer.

I think, as all three of us have said, we regulators need from the economists a much greater awareness of the limitations and enormous uncertainty of the arena within which we work. All of us are working together under severe budgetary constraints. How we set priorities and make decisions is frequently dictated by the Office of Management and Budget (OMB), often with the stroke of a pen, and not by months of sitting down with theoretical models and attempting to decide which is the most economically efficient way to regulate, or where equity will have to be realized. There is not an adequate understanding of the immediacy of the problems with which we deal and the daily pressures that are on us. The political considerations are enormous and in the last two or three months this entire question of the regulatory budget has become a very important topic. It is quite clear to us that elements of the private sector are seeking to exploit a public uncertainty and a political need to respond to public anger, by attacking the regulatory process.

We must make our choices within these constraints and do our best to be cost effective. The question of whether product safety is something the government should be involved in will ultimately be decided not by the economist, but by Congress and the White House. It is terribly important that people who are concerned about rational decisionmaking inject some sanity into this current regulatory debate so that choices are not made as a result of irrational political response to an uninformed dialogue.

Paul Weaver: One point on which all three agency heads agree is that it would have been useful had the two chapters tried to show the implications of the principles of distributive justice in terms of some particular empirical cases.

We will begin the authors' rebuttals with David Harrison of Harvard University.

David Harrison: I would like to make three points that relate to the panelists' comments. Since we are being encouraged to apply our analyses to particular examples of health and safety regulation, I will try to use some examples.

The first point I would like to address is the use and possible abuse of information on distributive considerations in public policymaking in the health and safety areas. Henry Aaron alluded to a "Gresham's Law" in which distributional information drives out information on efficiency. Since the original Gresham's Law stated that "bad money drives out good," I gather the implication is that bad distributional information drives out good efficiency analysis. I agree that the possibility exists for distributional information to be abused, but I expect that the abuses are very similar to those associated with the use of benefit-cost studies in some cases. Using benefit-cost studies to justify decisions already made seems roughly equivalent to arguing that a project will help or hurt the poor as a way of obtaining support for a position based on one's own self interest or prior beliefs. I think the more general issue is what role *any* analysis plays in the decisionmaking process. True skeptics would argue that explicit analyses seldom provide a good guide to the true basis for policy decisions.

This leads me to my second point, which relates to the quality of distributive analysis used as the basis for policy recommendations. My impression is that most so-called equity analyses are quite primitive and may even be misleading. Take automotive emission control, the case with which I am most familiar. Most distributive analyses consist of arguments that require the automobile manufacturers to "clean up their cars." This is equitable since automobile control costs would be borne by the automobile companies while benefits would accrue to current victims of high air pollution concentrations. Naturally that distributive argument makes the case for strict automotive standards quite compelling. But if one goes further to consider the ultimate incidence of automotive emission control costs, it is obvious that most of the costs will be borne by automobile users rather than by auto company executives or stock holders. A more detailed distributive analysis reveals considerable variations in cost and benefit incidence by income group and geographic area. When one goes even further to consider the relative importance that people in different socioeconomic groups place on air quality improvements, the possibility arises that the poor, particularly the rural poor, will actually be net losers. The distributive considerations imply a much more skeptical position on strict controls than that based on the simple assertion that automobile companies pay the costs and urban residents get the benefits. Indeed, I have argued that both efficiency and equity considerations favor a two-car strategy in which strict standards apply to heavily polluted urban areas and lenient standards apply to less polluted urban areas and rural areas. My general recommendation is that more detailed distributional analyses be made part of the benefit-cost analysis done on major policy matters. With better information we would be able to avoid the possibility of recommending actions that are both inefficient and inequitable.

My third, and final, point is that looking at regulations from the distributive standpoint provides an additional advantage to the regulator by identifying areas in which to target limited resources. Both Susan King and Joan Claybrook pointed out the large gaps in information that exist in the regulatory areas in which they deal. How unsafe are various products? What will be the reduction in automobile accidents if various changes are made in the car's design? What road hazards can be reduced by regulatory means? Typically, there is very little information on the identity of possible regulations, let alone their full costs and benefits. The regulator is thus faced with the question of how to begin to find promising areas that would be appropriate given their Congressional mandate.

One way of providing focus would be to ask what groups you are attempting to help. For example, I gather from Susan King's comments that the Consumer Product Safety Commission attempts to identify product injuries that occur to the vulnerable population—the young, the old, and the handicapped. I consider these efforts to be in the spirit of my recommendation that particular attention be paid to those with relatively little ability to protect themselves from hazards. I would classify efforts to deal with unknown hazards, such as the fire hazards of home insulation, in the same category. While it is crucial that the regulator carry the analysis further and ask how much any proposed regulation would actually reduce risks to these vulnerable groups and what the costs would be, considering distributive considerations in this way strikes me as a helpful first step in selecting regulatory areas to pursue given the enormous number of potential opportunities.

Ezra Mishan: I want to emphasize the point made by Joan Claybrook that benefit-cost analysis is a tool, which can be used in the decisionmaking process. I hope all of you will bear in mind, however, that it is just one of the tools—a modest one—and one must not expect more from the economist than that. But to be a tool, it must have a criterion that is distinct from the criterion that would be used in the political process. It must have a rationale, and therefore, I was concerned at a fundamental level to make that rationale quite clear, and to show how shaky it is. This is not what you really wanted—you wanted to come out with a decision criterion. But the fact is that the economic input into decisiomaking is rather shaky.

In my chapter, I start off with statics. So, you may wonder, what is this academic doing playing around with static analysis, when we need dynamics? I use it only as an expositional device. The complaint was also made that the economists use jargon. Here is a particular attempt to eschew jargon; to make things fairly simple, because only by using this initial static equilibrium could I make the principle clear. Later in the chapter, I did put it in what you might call a dynamic context, in a limited way. Suffice it to say, I was concerned with the chronological flow over time of costs and benefits.

Henry Aaron also faulted me for not writing what he wanted — more specific applications of benefit-cost analysis, in particular, those in which he is interested. I have a similar grudge against novelist Graham Greene. His novels always leave me depressed because they end on a sad note. But economists do believe that there is division of labor in this and I, as a theorist, cannot help writing theory. It is up to you to make use of this in specific cases.

I assume the uncertainty you have been talking about is political uncertainty. Economists have no prescription to give. They do have a theory of politics in which they are supposed to be able to predict the actions of the bureaucrats and politicians, but they do not have any prescriptive advice to give on the same level as they believe they can give in economics.

Aaron also felt dissatisfied about my new kind of spillover, which is marked by three particular features: the uncertainty of the damage, the possible irreversibility of the damage, and the effects it might have on future generations. I simply pointed out that the usual literature in economics has not as yet come to terms with these difficulties — I doubt whether it can. We must understand that it is now possible that there are no technical solutions to certain problems, and this new kind of spillover may well be one of them. We are in a world in which there can be no clearcut technical solution resting on a broad consensus. In these circumstances, the honest thing to do is to describe the possibilities clearly and to come to a political decision, no matter how painful it is.

Regarding the discount rate, perhaps he misunderstood me. The implication is not that we should not use discount rates. The chapter simply states that there are certain conditions to be met if we are to continue to use discount rates. Those conditions I laid down fairly clearly. One is that future generations are not involved. If they are involved, the discount rate does not meet the usual kind of criteria;

that is to say, we can only justify the use of a discount rate if an unchanged population exists over the time period in question.

The problem of the many generation case has only recently been uncovered, but the intergeneration distributional consequences certainly will now have to be faced. Let us say that the standard efficiency criterion does have distributional consequences that can be ignored, not within a static context, but within a context in which the population remains constant. Then we can somehow get around ignoring the distributional implication by a number of arguments. You can call them plausible or specious, if you wish, but there they are. However, when you come to an intergeneration context, these arguments are no longer valid and we have to treat the problem somewhat differently. The ethical appeal of the implied criterion is then much weaker.

Richard Zeckhauser: I want to ask the members of the panel a fairly difficult question. I would like you to assume that we have all the information in the world. Assume that we have two unsafe models of the same product—one of which is cheaper but less safe. And assume that 90 percent of the poor will, even given the perfect information, buy the cheaper, less safe model. What should CPSC do? How should we go about dealing with that?

Joan Claybrook: I would like to comment on that. First of all, as David Harrison pointed out, we must start by determining whether it is a major risk or a minor risk. If it is a major risk, then I think there is a responsibility to install preventive design because there are tremendous costs of repair of damage as it occurs. There are plenty of examples where, although you could have very good information available to the public, people with less income would certainly buy the cheaper product, even though it is less safe. My reaction to this is that if we are dealing with a major risk, then we set some kind of a minimal basic standard, below which no one is exposed to the risks. From there, you make information available, as best you can, so that those who have some value systems, which they want to apply to the purchase of products, know that they can buy a more expensive—and safer—item.

I think that the major problem with the operation of the marketplace in a technological society is that nobody has the technological capability and knowledge to buy the safer product. Therefore, there is an assumption that you cannot sell safety. I challenge anyone to tell me the crash characteristics of different automobiles, comparatively. This information simply does not exist. We have been asked to develop it by the Congress, and we are now working to do that.

It is an enormously difficult task because you have to set a test procedure against which all similar products are tested. The procedure must have no bias effect, regardless of the differences between the product.

This has never been done by the manufacturers, and they certainly have a better capability, at least in the beginning, to do it than a government agency. The problem is that each manufacturer would want its own test procedure that would be apt to include a bias for its product. So, for products that Susan King and I are concerned with, you never have the perfect world where all information is available.

Richard Zeckhauser: People frequently say that they cannot say what they would do because the information is not available. You cannot decide what you would do if you had all the information in the world; therefore, how are you going to make regulatory decisions?

Joan Claybrook: In our agency, we make regulatory decisions based on the risk. Both Susan and I are charged by statute with trying to reduce unreasonable risk. To do this, we make calculations based on accident investigation, death certificates that we collect from all states, and so on. Accidents, by the way, are very complex entities, and there is no one, single cause of most of them. You have to look at them in a different analytical way, in order to decide what remedy you are going to apply.

For example, we look at an accident in two different forms. First, we look at the cause—tires, brakes, alcoholic drivers—of the accident itself and how we can reduce that. Second, we look at what causes the injury to see what preventative measures—collapsible steering assemblies, laminated windshields, head restraints—can be taken.

Where we are most concerned about the lack of information is when we get down to the question of how to actually measure the value of the remedy. It is a very predictive, that is uncertain, activity to prove to you that a laminated windshield that protects your face in a crash has X dollars worth of benefits, based on the number of accidents expected. Although this is very hard to do prior to a regulation's taking effect, it is what makes the standard particularly valuable.

Susan King: Smoke detectors make a good example of a case where we have some information, but not perfect information. It is quite clear that in the purchase of smoke detectors it is very much those who are better educated and better able to afford smoke detectors who are installing them in their homes. It is the lower quality housing, the older housing, the inner-city housing, the ghetto housing, and the rental housing that does not have the benefit of smoke detector protection. The problem here, however, is a building code question rather than one over which we would have jurisdiction.

We deal with questions like this, as Joan said, first by looking at the severity of the risk and the injury information that we have available, and second, by finding the cost of the fix and the different options that are available for fixing. There will be instances in which the decision will be made by the regulator, regardless of the fact that the lower income consumer would not choose the fix. The regulatory agency will make a value judgment of whether some sort of standard, or ban, or requirement should be injected into the process.

Unidentified Speaker: I would like to pursue this question a little further to focus, not on whether a regulatory action should be taken, but on the results of an action that is taken. To what extent do you try to take into account not the individual benefit that a person might get if he or she buys this product, and does not tamper with it as specified under the regulation, but the overall statistical probability of reducing accidents?

Joan Claybrook: A wonderful example of this is child restraints. Child restraints are enormously important to use because children are very lightweight and in a crash they fly all over the interior of the car. We know absolutely that virtually any child restraint that is used is better than none. We also know that issuing a requirement for improved performance of child restraints will increase the price. What we do not know is whether a small increase in the price of a child restraint is going to cause fewer people to use them, than use them today. My own "seat of the pants" view is that the biggest deficiency is that we have never told the public how terribly important it is to use child restraints. I think that if people knew the importance of restraints, they would be much more likely to buy them regardless of a ten or fifteen dollar difference in price. People value their children more than this. However, this is a good example of a case where we really do not know the answer.

George Eads: How do we proceed beyond the risk identification issue? I would like to have some discussion of how we should take the intermediate step; namely, having identified the risk, how we determine what the change in the risk is going to be and how and when people are going to use this change. Then I will worry about whether the change is worth the cost. Child restraints, air brakes, and swimming pool slides are all very good examples.

Having identified both a real hazard and its various possible fixes, what sort of things are done to make sure that the imposed remedy will, in fact, have an effect on the hazard? I see this as a major weak link in such work.

Joan Claybrook: We try to address this question in the issue of safety belts versus passive restraints. Safety belts are fantastic. They work as well as just about anything you could ever put in a car. If you have a small car and you wear your safety belt, you are as well-off as you are without a seat belt in the largest, most wonderful vehicle you could possibly buy to protect yourself in a crash. But virtually no one uses them, so what is the best method of trying to reduce the deaths and injuries (47,000 deaths a year and millions of injuries) that occur in automobile accidents? This is where the concept of passive restraints is important. Therefore, we issued a requirement that manufacturers build into a car a passive type of restraint that operates when the crash occurs regardless of whether you have been smart enough in advance to figure out that this is what will protect you in the crash.

The controversy that arises over this issue is that many people say, "Well, I ought to be able to die if I want to, and not have to use restraints," or "Everybody should not have to pay the increased price of building passive restraints into vehicles; they ought to have a choice." This is the dogma that we are faced with, and the very issue that you raised.

George Eads: To address your example, is there not some controversy over whether, given the kinds of accidents that occur, passive restraints will, in fact, produce the results claimed for them? What I have found in looking at agencies such as CPSC, is that there is a reluctance to ask this question, or to really try to test these things out in the real world.

There is a large amount of work done on test tracks and with crash sleds, where consumer products are presented in an idealized situation to see what happens. However, many tested products fail when people actually use them in a real world situation. If more work were done on what really happens out in the field with these products, you would have a more credible product for the consumer, and they would be more likely to believe you.

I am perfectly willing to believe that people will not use seat belts, and, therefore, it is reasonable to consider another type of restraint. What I want to be sure of as a person who does use seat belts is that when you mandate the passive devices, I will not be exposed to greater risk; and I am not convinced of that now.

Joan Claybrook: Let me comment on several points. First, the way that we measure the benefits of a device such as this is by looking at the modes of the crash in which it works best, and then asking if it works well or not. We also look at where those crashes occur.

Fifty-five percent of the fatalities occur in frontal crashes. For this reason, the agency tried to address the issue of restraint systems because they provide the best benefit in frontal crashes. There is also some benefit in other crash modes, but they work best in frontal crashes.

The two passive restraint systems that have been developed in the marketplace thus far are the air bag and the passive belt. The air bag works in frontal crashes; it does not work in side, rear, or roll-over crashes. In rear crashes, no restraint system is really valuable. Here, your seat structure and head rest are the parts of the vehicle that are of value and a very small portion of the deaths occur in rear crashes. In side crashes, the major benefit to you is the structure of the door and its padding. Occasionally, a restraint system works in an off-angular crash—the air bag works in crashes 30 degrees either side of frontal. But to qualify as a side hit, we use almost a direct side hit. The lap belt is the most important thing in a roll-over crash.

Our standard requires passive protection sufficient to prevent serious injury or death to a passenger in a car that has been smashed into a wall at 30 miles per hour. Our measurement tool for this is an instrumented dummy. We also require that there be a restraint system, of sorts, to protect you in side and roll-over crashes and we give the manufacturer the option of using different restraint systems for different types of crashes.

Therefore, the manufacturers are going to use air bags and/or lap belts. We estimate that the use of lap belts will be approximately what it is today. This is a conservative estimate because more people are willing to use lap belts than they are to use today's shoulder harness or shoulder harness–lap combination. Many people do not like the shoulder harnesses because they are not very well designed.

This is the analysis of how we wrote one standard that tries to protect you, not just in the frontal crash, but in the other modes of crash also. People who have been surveyed among the public have never really had a choice of restraint systems. Today there is only one restraint system, and, since many people do not like it, they do not use it. What this new standard will do is to allow manufacturers to put any variety of restraint systems in a car that they can divine, as long as these systems meet the requirements of the standard.

The way that we estimated the payoff of this standard was by looking at the number of deaths that occur in front angular crashes. We studied 15 thousand tow-away accidents to assess the value that safety belts provide today, given both their capability and their usage. From this study, we derived an estimate of the number of people who today do not use restraint systems but would be protected by a passive type of restraint system. I acknowledge to you that this is a very difficult kind of assessment to make. However, because the problem is so enormous, the payoff is going to more than outweigh any cost. On a pure economic basis, we estimate it to be $286,000 per life, which I think is awful.

Ezra Mishan: I am sorry that Professor Milton Friedman is not at these proceedings. He would be frightfully restless because I think his thoughts would be as follows. Suppose that we could isolate all products that carry some element of risk. It is very hard to think of some that do not carry an element of risk. After all, the roof here might collapse suddenly. Therefore, we should probably have a regulation for keeping the roof up, or some protection if it falls down.

I just want to ask these people who have become so articulate in telling us what method they are taking to protect the public, what are the sorts of choices in which they would not intervene? Where would they say that, even though a benefit-cost analysis might be positive, and might even warrant intervention, they should not intervene? Where should one have free choice in taking his or her own risk?

Susan King: I think we are faced with that problem right now with skateboards. Norway has banned skateboards; other European countries have moved to restrict their use. The Americans for Democratic Action (ADA) has decided that CPSC is severely derelict in its duty for not banning skateboards. They are the most rapidly rising incidence of child injury and, of late, many more deaths are occurring due to skateboard accidents.

This is a public pressure decision, since people feel that it is foolish for government to become involved in an effort to ban skateboards. The choice left to the regulatory agency here is an informational one. If we can convince skateboarders to wear safety equipment, we will probably have done the most that we can in this country right now to deal with severe injuries and accidents involving small children.

Ezra Mishan: You have given me an answer by a single example. I want to know if you have a principle by which to distinguish those instances in which you would not intervene from those in which you would where a risk is involved.

Joan Claybrook: I think, one, is where information is sufficient to help people make informed decisions. Two, is where the hazard is relatively small. And if you are going to ask me what relatively means, I am not going to tell you. And, three, is when we do not know what the best remedy is.

The one thing that we are most concerned about is that we do not want a set of regulations that produces a worse result than the present circumstances. And we want to be sure of the effect of a regulation on injury and death levels. As far as I am concerned, the real question is are you going to reduce injuries or are you not going to reduce injuries.

Stephen Breyer: I would like to know how you determine this.

Joan Claybrook: Let me state some alternatives to the required installation of air bags. One is a tax on automobiles of some fraction of the cost of the air bag, which would be earmarked for the government for an advertising campaign. I can imaginatively conceive of distributing that information nationwide. An air bag is a superior product—if you have a very high speed crash it performs better than a seat belt. It distributes the forces better.

The present safety belts work well except in certain circumstances. They do not work well for pregnant women, for small children, for oversized people, and sometimes for older people who either cannot reach them or are so enormously uncomfortable in them that they simply will not use them under any circumstance.

Stephen Breyer: We are not a paternalistic society. Why should government be able to say that I cannot run the risk of something if I want to? For example, many people who ride motorcycles do not want to wear helmets. Why should they have to? Do you feel guilty about this?

Joan Claybrook: No, I do not. It depends on who else may have to bear the cost.

Stephen Breyer: You say that you are trying to get out information so that people can make intelligent choices. But when you use a benefit-cost analysis to see if you are getting at the problem, you do not put "improved information" on the benefit side. Rather, you put something that you can measure—usually called, "lives saved."

Then the next step is that you try to do those things that will save lives because now you are aiming simply at saving lives. You have tossed out the window the question of whether or not people are going to have a choice, whatever the cost. You seem to be pushed toward looking at the objective totally in terms of life-saving, which you can get a hold on, and leave aside what your basic rationale was in the first place.

My uninformed reaction to seat belts is that if people do not wear them, why should we force them to? If some people are not going to wear seat belts on their own, why tell everybody that they have to use this air bag?

Joan Claybrook: We do not tell them that. We have a performance standard, which is what I tried to say in the beginning. They can use anything that they want to as long as it is passive.

Stephen Breyer: The only reason you have a performance standard in this area is because, in fact, the thing was delayed so long that the standard could not be written initially. The standards that are written or proposed have ruled out the passive belts.

Joan Claybrook: That is not true. There was no such thing as a passive belt in existence in the ingenuity of the American or the foreign manufacturers until 1974. The original rule was proposed in 1969. It went into effect in 1972.

The standards that we issue do attempt to offer a choice of technology. Sometimes they do not, that is correct. But the original standard that was written is virtually identical to the one that exists today. What the standard really did was to give the manufacturers the incentive to go and find some alternative to air bags to meet the standard. And the standard does allow a passive belt as well as an air bag.

I would like to comment on forcing people to wear seat belts. I think that is much more intrusive regulation than requiring a product to be manufactured to meet some minimum safety requirement.

Stephen Breyer: However, you still have a performance standard that says that you cannot sell a car without, say, a seat belt that comes over you without the car costing three hundred dollars extra.

I have instincts, too, and they tell me that these things that pop out at you will not work. Perhaps they will work today and maybe tomorrow, but are they going to work ten years from now? When you have millions of anything complicated, all kinds of things go wrong.

Joan Claybrook: That is your fear of technology.

Stephen Breyer: But these are reactions of the uninformed consumer and you are in the position of actually having to tell these people what to do. How will you do it?

For example, we bought a $50 car seat for our child. Even though I consider myself well-off, this was a big expense for me. Therefore, I really do not think that people who have a lot less money are going to go out and spend $50 for this seat. How do you deal with the question of whether or not the seat will be purchased?

Joan Claybrook: On the baby seat, if I had my druthers—and I have not had them yet—what I would do is to design the back seats of cars so that a child would be safe there without a restraint system. The biggest problem of child restraints is getting the child to sit in the restraint. The second biggest problem is getting the parents to be disciplined enough to put the child in it.

Stephen Breyer: But, you do not want more children to be killed as a result of what you do. An important thing to know is whether these restrictions will, in fact, be useful. How do you find out the answer to that? What have you actually done?

Joan Claybrook: Tennessee has issued a requirement that every child under four has to be in a child restraint. We are doing an evaluation of this law where you have an absolute requirement, which may give us some information.

Stephen Breyer: Have you started a study or even looked at the question of whether the increased price of the child seat, in states without the Tennessee law, will mean that fewer people will buy the seats?

Joan Claybrook: To the best of my knowledge, it has increased them. With our priority of promoting child restraints, manufacturers have found that there is a better market for them. Therefore, more people are marketing them and the child restraints have become more available rather than less so.

Stephen Breyer: No, that is not an answer. You have not shown that raising the price has no effect on their sale.

Joan Claybrook: Well, the price has not been raised much by our present standard. It will be raised by a new standard.

Howard Kunreuther: It seems to me that one of the real challenges for agencies, such as the Consumer Product Safety Commission, would be to begin to undertake surveys and studies to understand what the consumer really thinks.

For example, in the smoke detector case, do people really know the risk of what would happen should a fire break out? How do they value the smoke detector? What is their knowledge compared to that of the regulatory agencies? We think that we understand where consumers fit in. Yet there is a lack of knowledge in terms of how they would respond to this kind of situation.

Susan King: We have done a considerable number of studies to try to determine what the impact is when there is full information available. However, we should also discuss what the impact is of adequate information and education. The changing of human behavior is a very complex and long-term operation. It may be that it is multigenerational before you can begin to measure any success in terms of reduction of injuries and deaths.

A good example is the child-proof caps on drugs. There are some fourteen or fifteen products that are now mandatorily covered with the child-proof caps. The cost estimate is a penny or less per package of drugs. The choice is available to the consumer who has children in the house whether or not to keep the cap secured so that the children cannot get the bottle opened.

Studies that we have done to evaluate the effectiveness of the standard indicate that we have dramatically reduced poisoning and accidental ingestion of toxic drugs by children. There are now half the number of deaths from drug poisoning.

Making an evaluation of a regulatory action is, to us, a fairly positive response. But we are always making judgments after the fact because human behavior impacts cannot be measured prior to making a decision. How do you measure the reaction of the public to something that has never been offered to them before? And very often one of the issues that comes up in regulation is that the product will not be offered unless there is regulation; for example, the air bag.

Actually General Motors did offer the air bag for three model years in a very limited way on ten thousand cars. If you talk to any of the people who have been involved in crashes with those cars, you will find the greatest advocates for this particular type of system. And they do not want to buy another car that does not have the bags. You do not know consumer reaction, however, until you have had the product on the market.

Ezra Mishan: Joan Claybrook speaks of two cases in which she would give an individual choice. The first is where the information is not sufficient to make a decision. The second is where the hazard is relatively small—although she did not discuss what relative meant. Now, anybody can say—and the bureaucrats would like you to say— that the information is not sufficient. It is never sufficient because our information is always changing. Therefore, it is quite reasonable to say to a person that we have no information on this, but you can take it at your own risk.

As an example, suppose someone takes hallucinogenic drugs. Although we have some evidence, I do not think it is very compelling. But give the information to him if he wishes, since we do not have any more. Then, if he wants to take the drug, let him take it. I am speaking as if I were Milton Friedman now.

The question of the hazard being relatively small is also an imposition in a way. Some of the sports that we like to engage in, for example, have very large hazards. In mountaineering or racetrack driving the risks are very great indeed. But, I think that if you did interfere on those grounds, you would find a great deal of public outcry.

The reason for government intervention that immediately comes to the mind of an economist is whether there is a significant externalities effect on other people. Like Joan Claybrook, I will take the liberty of not having to define "significant." But it is important because when one does intervene, there is a cost of intervening. There is a direct cost both in resources and in extending the bureaucracy that has to be taken into consideration. Therefore, the externality should be well known. This is the reason that would induce an economist to think of intervening.

Joan Claybrook: My list of reasons for intervention was not intended to be exclusive. It was used merely as a series of items that are considered in the course of trying to make an informed decision.

Nicholas Ashford: I think that there are two problems associated with the issue of value. We have dealt with one of them, which is the necessity for designing safety devices properly in order to identify the benefit. The plea that benefits be traceable to design of the safety device is sensible and I do not think that there is anything to be argued.

The second issue is getting people not to take risks. The question of the assumption of risk and the distribution of wealth was raised yesterday and, apparently, nobody wants to deal with it. It is a difficult question. Take a poor consumer who does not want to pay a lot of money for safety devices. He is valuing his life. He has perfect information. If you do provide by law that he has to expend his resources for the $50 child restraint, he cannot sell his wage off cheaply. The traditional response is that you have reduced his wealth. You have actually put him in a worse situation, because his evaluation of the risk he runs is such that he would rather have the other resources $50 could buy than have that particular kind of safety.

Let me suggest that this is a fallacious response because, in fact, what this health and safety legislation is doing is redistributing wealth. It is not making him poorer by not having money in terms of buying food and other things. We are mandating that he have a safe job, a safe consumer product, and a safe environment in which to live. Then society can no longer ignore the transfer payment that must be made for him to eat. If you give him palliatives by giving him his food stamps and making him poorer by the fact that he undervalues his life relative to the rest of society, you are creating shams and that is the kind of transfer we seemingly lean to and exercise.

Unidentified Speaker: You concluded that as a society there are certain transactions that we try to prohibit people from making because we do not like the kind of society that would result if they were able to make such transactions. I am not suggesting that this kind of thought process is systematically or neatly applied, or that we never violate it, but I think that it is a justification for telling poor people that they cannot expose themselves to a certain physical risk, even though they might benefit financially from so doing, just as we tell them that they cannot sell their votes, or sell their draft service during war time, even though it might financially benefit them.

David Harrison: That is the point that I tried to make in terms of this notion of whether it is societal or individual judgment. I guess the question is where you draw the line. The criteria that I suggested was the magnitude of the risk.

Unidentified Speaker: I want to ask Joan Claybrook if she believes that an improved, more extensive benefits analysis would have changed the introduction of the ignition inter-lock system that was later repealed by Congress.

Joan Claybrook: No. That was a political decision. The inter-lock system was not a decision of the National Highway and Traffic Safety Administration (NHTSA); it was a decision of the auto industry. They went to see Richard Nixon and said that they did not want to have to deal with passive restraints. They said that they had a good alternative, which would keep everybody quiet, that resolved the issue; this was the inter-lock device. The item was submitted to our docket and they showed that in Texas and in Florida people loved the lock device. The agency, therefore, decided that, under mandate from the White House, it was going to issue this requirement. The agency issued the regulation and Ralph Nader sued them, saying it was an inappropriate action. A year later, the auto industry went to the Congress and said, "This is terrible. People hate inter-locks." Then, without any hearings or discussion of it, with a quick floor vote, the day after Nixon resigned from office, Congress knocked out the inter-lock regulation. I think it was a bad decision to start with.

There was not really the consumer adverse reaction that many people thought there was. People just tinkered with the thing and undid it. So, I do not think that the benefit measurements would have had an iota of influence on this particular decision.

Robert Elder: I think that the same is true in regard to saccharine where the most elaborate benefit analysis would not have changed Congressional intent. One has to point out to the economist that as a regulator there are many situations where the most elaborate benefit analysis will be of little or no value because of a societal demand that is placed upon Congress.

Robert Rauch: I want to address the issue of regulation versus informing an individual's choice-making process. Two troubling aspects of this issue have been overlooked. First, there comes a point where the consumer reaches an information overload. A limit exists in how much one can tell consumers before they simply stop listening. We need to know how much information consumers can absorb before they reach that point.

Second, studies show that consumers think they are being protected by a paternalistic government regulatory process. When a consumer enters a store and looks at a product, he or she assumes, perhaps unconsciously, that someone in the huge federal bureaucracy has checked out the products and made sure they are safe. But perhaps no such tests have been performed and the public is making its choices based on the wrong assumptions. Thus, consumers are lulled into a sense of well-being when they should be examining more closely the possible effects of their purchases.

Joan Claybrook: I think that is very true. I tried to make that point when I said that it is very hard in a technological society to give people enough information. I think that the presumption of safety regulation has always been that there is a basic minimum level of risk that is not necessary.

Norman Waitzman: Professor Mishan has asked for criteria defining where government should intervene rather than letting consumers make their own choices. Joan Claybrook has given a list in response. I was curious as to why one of the criteria was not to counteract corporate paternalism.

The Consumer Product Safety Commission ran a survey of consumers asking what affected their choice of goods. A large majority said, "Because my neighbor has it, because other people accept and like it." Consumption patterns are guided, in other words, by what is generally acceptable within the community.

If the corporations, who have vast control over informational channels, are going to determine what is acceptable in my community, I want to have some countervailing power, such as the government, there to set the record straight. Maybe Pepsi does not keep me young; maybe certain cosmetics do not hold the key to increased popularity and happiness. In fact, maybe they are dangerous to my health and well-being, as the facts seem to show. But I am not going to give them up if my community still places a value on them. This area of corporate control over the information process—this corporate paternalism—is serious and frightening. The consumer is grateful to have the government to counteract these widespread influences.

Joan Claybrook: I accept your argument.

Henry Aaron: Typically, one is forced to use what information one has at a given point in time. Once a problem becomes current and relevant, regulators do not have the luxury of an extended time period before they need to make a decision. Particularly, the amount of time it takes to commission thorough research. I think of myself as a judge. I want to have all of the available evidence—every bit of it— and then, I will decide for myself whether I think the information is good or bad and what kind of a discount to put on it.

Ezra Mishan: The first thing to remember is that benefit-cost analysis is simply one more input into the decision process. We must not try to build too much into it. The second point is that we must make some decision about whether the uncertain factors are measurable: Can we determine the uncertainty?

Suppose we have five factors that can be determined within a range of probabilities. Then you would like to combine these five uncertainties to end up with a single probability curve from which you could then determine a 95 percent confidence interval—the confidence range would be from here to there. That would be your benefit. That would be the ideal. If you have uncertainties that do not have probabilities you cannot, quite obviously, do this type of analysis.

EPILOGUE

There are no ready answers to the issues raised in health and safety regulation. Although there was general concurrence at this conference that benefit assessment is a useful tool, many participants emphasized their belief that it is a tool of limited value, with a restricted role. There is confusion about the role of assigning monetary values to benefits, or costs. Some progress has been made in doing so and certainly work should be pushed in that direction, if for no other reason than to narrow the range of uncertainty about the worth of regulation, and in some cases to establish at least lower bound estimates of benefits. The fact that assessing benefits does not require their monetization needs to be emphasized. Some participants seemed to feel that inability to set dollar values on benefits somehow undercuts the whole concept of cost-benefit analysis. The facts that markets cannot take account of externalities, that they reflect the existing inequalities and, I would say, inequities in the distribution of wealth, that they are beset with inadequate and even misleading information, and that suppliers change consumers' preferences, means that observed market prices cannot in principle provide accurate measures of benefits. Hence, the need for developing methods of ascertaining and quantifying benefits (and costs) in physical terms emerges clearly. It is unreasonable to expect any single approach to the measurement of benefits to be adequate given the present state of knowledge and information.

The argument that economics can offer no guidance in cases of irreversible phenomena whose impacts fall on distant future generations requires serious consideration. Decisions as to whether to expand wilderness areas, permit greater exploitation of forests and mineral resources, or to dam streams, not to mention the possibility of catastrophic development of new materials not found in nature, have this characteristic. Mishan is surely right that present methods of discounting do not lead to accurate and reliable means of comparing present and future values. However, my own belief is that if the areas in which future impacts cannot be defensibly measured by present techniques are of major import, some progress can be made in improving the basis for judgmental decisions.

It is clear that in setting regulations political forces frequently dominate. For example, it was asserted that analysis would not have affected the saccharine decision. Similarly, the regulation requiring interlocking the ignition switch and seat belts was said to have been dictated politically by the automobile industry to the Nixon administration.

In general, regulators and activists felt that decisions were influenced predominantly by political considerations. Most appeared to think that this was appropriate, and virtually all felt that "economic" considerations, particularly cost-benefit analysis, should not lead directly to decisions. The economists tended to view political influence as verging on the illegitimate; that is, given the required information, cost-benefit analysis should lead to socially valid decisions.

At least two problems emerge here: The first involves divergent concepts of politics. One view is that the political process provides an expression of the popular will, with subjective but sensitive weighing of nonmaterial values. This view may be held in part by those who feel that their influence on the political process is greater than their influence on the market. The alternative view is that politics reflects special interest pressures and the distribution of power. This seems to be reinforced by the idea that regulatory problems are not amenable to nonanalytic solutions and the compromise is not likely to lead to optimality.

The second problem involves divergent views of analysis. Those who hold the view that cost-benefit assessment could be extremely valuable in making regulatory decisions appear to believe that it is possible to capture enough, if not all, values in suitable analysis and especially, that it is better to have an organized way of examining complex problems than to proceed without a reasonably rigorous structure.

Regulators and activists, on the other hand, seem less persuaded than most economists that the most important considerations can be captured in analysis or that the analysis will not be influenced by politics (in the derogatory sense) and by the selective provision of information by industrial protagonists, and further, that such influence will be concealed through the complexity of the analysis. In addition, the fact that economists tend to look toward market values for guidance was greeted with suspicion by some participants who see the market as dominated by the power of large corporations, and more of a source of problems than solutions.

There seemed also to be an implicit acceptance of the notion that where political considerations dominated, analysis was largely irrelevant. Nor was there any explicit discussion of whether the role of politics in affecting regulation is socially desirable.

A closely related idea was presented in two of the economists' chapters: the credibility and, therefore, the acceptability of regulatory decisions is likely to depend on the decisionmaking process itself. In light of the necessity of applying subjective judgments to the issues of values, and the great uncertainties about the nature of benefits, a process that relies on the presentation and weighing of informed but divergent views is more likely to be practical than one that adheres to simplistic application of an analytic technique, or that relies on legalistic proceedings with limited effective public participation.

From the floor discussion, some impressions about economics emerged. Perhaps the most obvious is that economists have failed almost completely to explain to the public and to decisionmakers that economics encompasses many facets of life that are popularly thought of as being "noneconomic"; that achieving efficiency is at least as apt to enhance the material well-being of the majority of the populace as to impair it; that concern with economic efficiency does not necessarily imply assigning dollar values to everything; and that economic analysis can, in fact, deal with human values and needs.

Many economists convey the idea that they believe that the market works, not just in the technical sense that it leads to efficient prices and outputs, but in a more operational sense—for example, that actual prices, outputs, and incomes are close to optimal, and that it does not lead to or depend on inequitable distribution of wealth or of political and economic power. Economists also often fail to distinguish adequately to the public between economic values and commercial or financial values and between the theoretical workings of the market and the actual practices of business, especially of the corporations.

Some regulators and activists seemed to perceive the main purpose of benefit analysis as justifying, rather than appraising, regulation. There is an interesting symmetry here with the implicit position that explicating the cost of regulation is an instrument for curtailing it.

In addition to producing informative substantive material, the conference provided an opportunity for economists, regulators, and activists to communicate their diverse points of view to one another and may have laid a foundation for future cooperation in creating regulatory policy.

APPENDICES

SUMMARY OF WORKSHOP DISCUSSIONS

The conference participants assembled on three occasions in small working groups to discuss specific issues raised in the plenary sessions. All the workshops were asked to explore the central concerns of the conference in detail as well as to probe lessons of individual cases drawn from the agency experience of their members. These discussions are summarized below by six workshop leaders. The issues covered in these workshops were as diverse as those covered in the preceding sessions.

Carl Gerber (Workshop 1): Our group spent most of the time discussing lead standards, and the functions of the Environmental Protection Agency (EPA) and the Occupational Health and Safety Administration (OSHA) in regulating lead. By focusing on a specific issue, we were able to bring some of our divergent attitudes and viewpoints toward cost-benefit analysis into focus. Our group did not really have a hardcore economist, but all other viewpoints were quite well represented. Although there were varying degrees of skepticism in the group, I think the conclusion, after some preliminary skirmishes, was that cost-benefit analysis is needed in the decisionmaking process, with certain qualifications.

There are numerous values for the decisionmaker in cost-benefit analysis. It is a tool that permits the decisionmaker to examine different policies and to see who will be affected by them. As a tool, it can also indicate gross differences—I want to emphasize the phrase "gross differences"—among different regulatory approaches, or between regulatory approaches and other types of incentive measures. It also has a value in setting rough priorities.

Good benefit analysis—presently lacking in the federal structure—would be a good counter-balance to the bias toward cost analysis that currently exists in the system. Obviously, cost analyses are, in many ways, easier to do; they relate more to engineering questions. It is also in the interest of those regulated to prove, for example, that the regulation is going to be very costly. At the present time, it is not quite as easy to evaluate the benefits.

There are some limitations that we believe are absolutely crucial to keep in mind in considering benefit analysis. One is that it is but *one* means to improve decisions. It should not be considered the only way to reach better decisions and it cannot be substituted for many other judgments and factors in the decision process. I think anybody here who has been involved in the regulatory process, realizes that the political aspects as well as the technical aspects are very, very critical to a final decision.

Another limitation is that benefit analysis does not now, and probably cannot in the foreseeable future, quantify or adequately reflect noneconomic drives. By this we mean behavior and certain subjective feelings such as pain. What is the cost of pain or the value of lack of pain, for example?

A third major limitation on benefit analysis is that the tools are presently very, very weak, and all we can hope to get out of it at the present time are gross analyses.

Given both the positive and negative elements of cost-benefit analysis, the question we tried to focus on, and inherent in all of our discussion, was how do you really get such analyses into the real world—into the decisions that are now going on and those that will be made in the near future?

We agreed that crucial to any establishment and improvement of cost-benefit analysis are adequate funds, properly trained people, and time. It is also necessary to deal with certain institutional restraints that currently exist; The Office of Management and Budget (OMB) and Congress are two very large institutions that were identified as posing major constraints to implementing a good cost-benefit analysis process. Equally important, though, is the crisis mentality or crisis management approach that exists in the regulatory agencies. Valid benefit analyses, particularly, will take time. They have to be foreseen and started long before you reach the final decision. This is something that the current system is not well set up to handle.

How can we overcome these institutional constraints? How can we deal with this problem? Although we ran out of time at this point in our discussion, I think the key here is planning, although not necessarily a gigantic, centralized type of system, which nobody really felt would solve the problem. However, within agencies that have regulatory responsibilities, within the Congress, and within the Executive Office of the President, probably some planning, some view of the bigger picture, that looks farther into the future is desirable. This might lead to defining the key problems or the key issues. For example, in pollution control, what are the key pollutants? What are the ones with the major economic and social impact? It might also identify key people in the process, both those affected as well as those who can do something about what is happening.

Basic to all this is the need for longer term studies. No one really knows, for example, the mobility of the hourly wage employee. The economists assume that if you close down a plant, then the person with a general skill can move to another plant or another location. But no one has systematically determined this. This is a case where a longer, general study should be undertaken to assure that this data is available for a cost-benefit analysis.

Another basic need is to do better epidemiology studies in health and many other fields. These, again, are studies that take time and basic resources. They cannot be done in the two years, six months, or three months that are available when writing a regulation. They must be started much earlier. How to fund these longer term studies, and who should do them, since it is not in the interest of a single agency to do them, became a subject of discussion. National Science Foundation (NSF) came up as the natural "Mother Lode" of funds for these less focused types of activities.

I think the interest is there; at least the academic people in our workshop agreed that they would do these studies if the funds were available. And the regulatory people in our group felt that it would be valuable to have the studies done. The real question is how do you fund them? Even if we design a perfect system, with better planning methods and longer term studies, how can the necessary work be accomplished?

Using the way that the government operates as an example, it would be best to wait for a crisis to occur before trying to implement some of these things. The crisis may be with us. I think the backlash, if you want to call it that, to regulation and to government control is fairly real at the present time. And the President is being forced on the inflation issue to address these problems more and more frequently. Therefore, this may offer the regulatory agencies a chance to use this backlash as a positive element to improve their systems or practices. On the other hand, they may get caught in the backlash and, though not necessarily abolished, could be very severely restricted in their missions. We believe the regulatory agencies should view the inflation fight, or the economic backlash, or the backlash against big government—whatever you want to label it—in a positive sense and try to come up with improvements in the way they make decisions.

An example of this might be the Fifth Circuit Court's decision to overturn OSHA's benzene regulation. If OSHA uses this decision constructively and does better benefit analyses in establishing future regulations, in the long run it may be better for OSHA and its regulatory process of the work place.

Maybe our conclusions are too pessimistic and there will not be any backlash. However, we feel that the regulatory agencies should be considering how they can improve their processes.

We must all look at how we can improve dealing with these problems through longer term studies, more and better planning, and more interagency cooperation. If we can do this and harness the current crisis, perhaps we can make some improvement in the system that will protect present and future key regulations and actually provide a better environment for the public in general.

Edwin Clark (Workshop 2):   An element of confusion that pervaded our workshop (and I think the entire conference) is that we have never clearly defined what we mean by "benefits" and what we mean by "quantification." If the conference was intended to focus on the question of incorporating benefit estimates into regulatory decisions, more emphasis should have been placed on defining what is meant by benefits at the start of the conference. George Eads's chapter was really the only one to address this issue head-on.

The terms "benefits" and "quantification" are used in a very confusing manner. The benefits in a risk-benefit analysis are the economic benefits that the hazardous substance is providing without its being regulated. These would be costs to the person undertaking a benefit-cost analysis of a proposed regulation. Confusion also appears when an economist speaks of benefits, because the regulator immediately thinks that the economist is talking about putting a dollar value on everything. However, I think that many economists here are not pushing that type of quantification. You can measure benefits in a number of different ways.

For example, if you have an ambient emission of a chronic chemical, emission reductions are a benefit that one can quantify. The next step is to look at the reduction in the number of people at risk—that is, the people who are exposed. This is another quantified measure of the same benefit. You could go a step further and try to weigh the number of people exposed by the amount that you are reducing their exposure. This is one more quantified benefit measure. If you want to go on to the next step, you can talk about a reduction in the number of tumors they would be expected to experience, another quantified measure of the same benefit. And, if you have real temerity, you can try to put a monetary value on that reduction in tumors.

All of these are perfectly permissible ways of measuring benefits and the question is not whether you should attempt to make some estimate, but rather how far down this road should you travel? In our workshop, we identified three major things to keep in mind. One is that as you move down the road the uncertainty associated with whatever number you come up with increases substantially. You might be able to estimate the reduction of air emissions by plus or minus 10 percent, and the reduction in the number of people exposed by plus or minus 30 percent; but your estimates of the reduction in tumors will only be by plus or minus 100 percent, and monetary benefits by plus or minus, say, 200 percent. So you have a substantial spread of uncertainty, and it gets greater as you become more elaborate.

Another thing to remember is that, in some cases, information actually decreases as you go down the road. An example of this fragility is provided by the benefit-cost analysis work of the Army Corps of Engineers on a water resources project in West Virginia. They came out with a very nice benefit-cost ratio, but when you looked at their analysis a bit, you found that most of the benefits came from recreation. Although recreation may be a fine thing, their number seemed surprisingly big. Upon further examination, to find where they got this number, it turned out there was an implicit assumption that every person within a radius of at least 250 and probably 500 miles from this dam, which included New York City, Washington, D.C., and Cincinnati, was going to visit the reservoir two to three times a year. This was the "information" that went into the analysis, but these underlying assumptions were lost by the time the effort produced a final benefit-cost ratio.

The final fact to remember in assessing benefits is that the impact of your estimate increases, but it becomes more uncertain and often is based upon less information as you proceed down the road of benefit estimation. If you come up with a number of $176,219,376, it has much more impact, particularly in Washington, than if you say you have reduced emissions by 50 percent. It may be less accurate and be less informative, but it has more impact. I think that this is something that we must be concerned about and that has not really been addressed adequately.

The next question that the discussion group asked was why do benefit analysis when you do not need to? Here, I think we essentially agreed with Workshop 1 that benefit analysis can help to make better decisions. However, there are also costs. One is that you may subject yourself to attack in Congress, in public, or elsewhere. There is also, in the economists' jargon, substantial opportunity cost in undertaking elaborate benefit-cost analyses. For one thing, all the time required to complete the benefit calculations means that there are damages incurred that could have been avoided. And, since every regulatory agency has limited personnel, if you are diverting funds to benefit studies, this means that you are not regulating something else that may be important. These costs can be quite high and I think that they tend to be ignored by the academics who see only benefits when doing benefit studies.

Another point the group raised was that regulators tend to be very impressed by the external benefits of regulations. These benefits occur because a regulation or an enforcement action often has effects outside the particular area that is being regulated or the particular plant that is being forced to comply. If you are enforcing a regulation, you initiate actions that will give you the most impact, not only, for example, in the amount of emissions reduced from a plant, but also in scaring other people to come into compliance. The group thought that regulators often put a substantial emphasis on such external effects of their decisions.

Another topic we covered was the whole question of the strategy of regulation. The first question we looked at was how risk averse regulatory agencies should be. For example, how many chemicals are you willing to ban in order to make sure that you do not miss some serious carcinogen? A demonstration of how people are naturally risk averse in incidences like this is provided by our reaction to razor blades in apples on Halloween. The probability of your child coming home with a razor blade in an apple is probably, in the United States, one in ten million. But how many families prohibit their children from eating Halloween apples because they do not want to take the chance?

The other question that was addressed under this general heading was how to decide how small a segment of the public to protect. We tend to think in terms of every regulation affecting everybody equally. But, in fact, regulations are made to protect particular segments of the population.

Much of our discussion focused on the balance between quantitative analyses, and the political factors involved in making regulatory decisions. Everyone admitted that economic analyses are not and probably should not be the major consideration in making regulatory decisions. Clearly, a major part of the decision is primarily political.

This raises the question of whether the regulatory agencies should not make greater efforts to inform the public about what they are doing and to develop the political support they need. Because of the importance of public support, it was even suggested that regulatory agencies might be better off taking the money they would spend on economic analyses and hiring good advertising agencies instead. The problems with informing the public were recognized by everyone. Information transfer has a number of characteristics: It is quite expensive (a fact often ignored by economists), it is very inefficient, and it is subject to rapidly diminishing returns. One could not hope to truly inform the public of all the relevant information pertaining to every regulatory decision.

A major problem with discussing regulatory efforts in the public forum is that the public usually only compares the way things are now to the way they were a few years ago, before the regulatory program was initiated. The important comparison, of course, is the way things are now to the way they would be if there were no regulatory program.

One of the work group members, for instance, had carried out a rather simple analysis of air pollution benefits. This was based upon some work done in 1974 estimating total damage costs from air pollution in 1970. These 1970 numbers were extrapolated into the future, first on the basis of how high the damages would have been if there had been no pollution abatement, and then on the basis of how high they are expected to be with pollution abatement.

The analysis indicated that the amount of benefits we are experiencing is in fact quite substantial. However, most of these benefits result from the fact that without pollution control things would have been much worse than they are now, rather than from the fact that with pollution control they are better than they used to be. This is a very difficult benefit to communicate, since it requires someone to imagine a condition that does not exist and never has existed, and then to compare the actual condition with this hypothetical one.

The final conclusion of our workshop, strongly endorsed by all the participants, is that economists are often their own worst enemy in promoting economic analyses. They seem to be profoundly unwilling to recognize the constraints and characteristics of the real world where these deviate from their theoretical models. They often seem to be more interested in impressing listeners with the profundity of their theories than in helping them to understand what they are trying to say.

Gil Thompson (Workshops 3 and 4):   Our group was very skeptical of the ability of benefit assessments to justify the very large costs that regulatory programs can impose on the industry being regulated or on society as a whole, because of the inherent problems in quantifying benefits to health or the value of human life. We are not necessarily looking for the most efficient program in an economic sense. We are looking to save human lives, many times whether it is efficient or not. Our group discussed benefit-cost analysis, or benefit assessment, as one tool for regulators to use when looking at their regulatory programs and choosing among the different places that they can put their resources. This is but one tool, however, and there are many other valuable tools, such as the number of complaints received from consumers or the number of calls from Capitol Hill. Communications from interested constituents are very well developed and have been used by Congress, which has made its own cost-benefit assessments, many times over the past two hundred years.

I am not certain about the need to develop a complex, new methodology—to invest substantial resources into developing benefit assessment as a system or technique. This is an academic consideration. On the other hand, there is another kind of danger in using benefit assessment. When an agency does a benefit assessment and finds, for example, that it is going to cost $4,000 per ride for a handicapped person on a subway system, this information is provided for public review. It can be a blunt and effective weapon in the hands of people who will use it unfairly to oppose this kind of program. Therefore, I am opposed to this kind of arcane methodology where it is used to talk about a program as a whole, rather than used in a particular agency's deliberating process to choose between programs. Do not think that you can use it when you are deciding, "Are we going to conduct this program?" When there is public debate about whether to proceed with a program or not, I think it is dangerous, because it inherently undervalues the human costs, benefits, and risks involved.

Kathleen Sheekey (Workshop 5):   We got into a very interesting discussion of the relatively minor influence in Canada of both outside groups and the press in the regulatory process. We compared this situation with the heavier roles played by outside groups and the press in the American process.

Benefit-cost analysis in the American system is but one element in a much wider spectrum of events. It is used primarily for choosing among alternatives, often before a regulation is proposed or for giving increased justification to that choice. However, the press is often the intermediary of a given benefit-cost analysis. And when a proposal is open to public debate, the influence of the press upon the people can make the benefit-cost analysis relatively useless. This is one set of circumstances that we have forgotten to discuss during this conference.

One example of the press's influence is the California Water Project, a much debated issue that was put to a vote several years ago in California. Very extensive benefit-cost analyses showed that the costs overwhelmed the benefits. In spite of this, the *Los Angeles Times* endorsed the project. Meanwhile, the *San Francisco Chronicle* opposed it. When the vote was taken, the Project won by a large margin because there were more voters in Southern California. The benefit-cost analysis served no purpose at all.

We also discussed the diminishing influence of outside groups on the regulatory process and examined some of the reasons for this diminishing influence. We talked about the defeat of legislation to create a Consumer Protection Agency, an agency that would have helped to correct the imbalance of representation that now exists at federal agency proceedings.

First, I think that out of our discussion came the feeling that we should not minimize the primitiveness of the current situation. It may be a bit premature to talk about the problem of comparability, of the value assigned a human life by different agencies, at a time when most agencies would resist the notion of even quantifying how many lives they are saving, much less making these quantifications comparable. Our general feeling was that in most agencies there is great reluctance to be explicit about benefits, there is some reluctance to be explicit about costs, and there is a total absence of any attempt to integrate or compare, or in any other way put together, the cost and the benefit elements of regulatory choices.

Second, there was a strong feeling that the best use of the kind of analysis we have been talking about is to provide insights to the decisionmaker, and maybe to set some rough parameters on the options.

I would disagree with Gil Thompson that because analysis may show that some decisions are outrageous, analysis is therefore bad. I think that such analysis is fairly useful, even though it does not tell you what the optimal decision is. You cannot take three or four realistic options and expect this kind of analysis to be precise enough, or for officials to have enough faith in it, for it to make decisions for you. It will not do this. The ultimate decision is a matter of politics, the values of the decisionmaker, and a variety of other things.

The third point is the distinction between looking at the benefits of total programs versus looking at the benefits of individual decisions. For example, the d'Arge and Kneese chapter looks at the benefits of a total program—the air pollution program. This is a different kind of analysis, done in a different way from setting out to do an analysis of the benefits of the SO_2 standard or options for standards for ambient lead.

There is a distinction between doing benefit analysis for total programs and doing benefit analysis for individual regulatory decisions. This distinction has not been made here, and I think it is important, because if you are after different things, you will do the analyses in different ways. We had some debate as to where the emphasis should lie; is the need greater for analyzing the benefits of total programs, or of individual decisions? There was some difference of opinion. In part, it is a question of where the political pressures will come. For example, will the political pressure, in the environmental area, be for a total weakening of the air pollution program or will the battles take place over individual air pollution standards?

Thomas Cohen (Workshop 7): Our group focused mainly on the decisionmaker, and what the decisionmaker looks for.

First, what is the value of the economic analysis? To answer this, you must know whether the policy is effective and whether certain political and legal requirements need to be met. Second, if the analysis has some value, how can the value be increased? First, you increase the amount of information in an analysis that does come in. As a decisionmaker you want all of the issues in front of you. To do this, you need to look at different analyses, especially given the uncertainty of each analysis. Henry Aaron made the point very clearly; you take the information in front of you and do the best job you can with it. The objective is to increase the pertinent information that is available to you.

A second way to increase the value of the analysis is to improve analytical techniques—better gathering of information, better methodology to categorize all costs and benefits—and then to quantify as much as possible. However, we must recognize the importance of the categories, rather than the numbers that are quantified. During the analysis, there is also a need to work with other professions: scientists, doctors, and people other than economists.

Finally, once you do the better analysis, what is the assurance that it will be taken seriously by the people in the agencies? First, the analysis must be timely—it must tie in to what the regulators or policymakers are doing at that time. This necessitates a close dialogue between the regulators, the economists, the scientists, and all the other groups participating in the process. The analysis must be practical in the present situation.

Deadlines must be imposed at all times. For example, if you miss a deadline for water regulation, the next opportunity for a project may be five years later. Therefore, you must get the analysis in at the proper time. It is also best to get it in early when the agenda is being set, so that you can help set that agenda and look at all the options and alternatives, and their consequences.

When considering how to get into the process, you need to distinguish between the agencies and Congress. Each works differently and your techniques of intervention must be thought out.

There is a need for review of current policy. Analysis certainly has a role here and the agencies should facilitate this analysis.

Mark Silbergeld (Workshop 8):   First, I think it was implicit in our group discussion that the benefit-cost analysis be understood as being only a tool—one tool for use by the decisionmaker. We felt that the question was not whether it is useful but in what circumstances it is useful and when it is advantageous to use.

It is most important to use benefit-cost analysis when there is reason to believe that the problem to be addressed involves a high magnitude of risk, a risk of a serious nature, choices in individual behavior that may help individuals to avert risk, and when the information that needs to be used in the analysis is likely to be sufficient. We felt that when one or more of these factors is absent, there is a less compelling need to engage in benefit-cost analysis. When talking about quantitative analysis—putting a dollar figure on everything— we also have a problem about using benefit-cost analysis in the absence of these four factors. However, there was less feeling against its use if one is simply talking about identifying factors of risk, or factors of benefits.

We discussed, in some detail, whether technological development since World War II had produced such a number of new health and safety risks with unmeasurable or unforeseeable consequences that the burden of justifying the risk should be placed on the manufacturer. This is presently true of new chemicals under the Toxic Sub stance Control Act and with new drug applications under the Food and Drug Act. Two factors that may play a part in answering this question are factors that benefit-cost analysis is designed to address; our group thought that there is a greater justification for reaching this risk avoidance strategy when the magnitude of the spillover effect is great and when there are intergenerational effects hypothesized as part of the risk.

Our group also discussed the introduction of collective risk. This includes such things as nuclear hazards or ozone layer damage that expose an entire population, regardless of whether there is direct exposure of each individual in that population, to a toxic substance.

In the case of the ozone layer damage, for example, people who do not use aerosol sprays and thus avoid being exposed to them directly, may nonetheless be exposed to the damage such sprays do to the ozone layer. We discussed whether this collective risk justifies placing the regulatory burden on the manufacturer or the industry that proposes to introduce the risk into the marketplace. The group also spoke of the cost of slowing growth in innovation by imposing this burden. Although we reached no conclusions on a risk avoidance strategy, we believe the question is extremely important.

Finally, we discussed whether one basis for regulation is a societal decision that the cost to individuals of avoiding risk—either a single risk from a single product or an aggregate risk from an aggregate of products, regulated by one agency or a multiplicity of agencies—is so great that society must reduce it by requiring or permitting its regulators to take steps to decrease the cost. This can be done by reducing the risk, by eliminating products in the marketplace, by setting standards for products, or by providing better information than the marketplace is currently providing, all of which reduce the cost of obtaining and processing the information.

We concluded that when this kind of basis is used for regulation, it is really a mixture of economic and political processes. It is most appropriate in two situations; one, when the public cannot obtain or cannot process the information needed to make individual decisions to avoid risk and, two, when there is an information overload. This overload may occur either when a particular risk is so complex that the public is not willing to deal with digesting and applying the information or when the number of identified risks is perceived to be so great that enough people prefer to reduce the opportunity costs through regulation.

COMMENTS FROM RONALD HIRSHHORN, OF THE ECONOMIC COUNCIL OF CANADA

Over the past few years, a very strong demand for an evaluation of regulation-making in Canada has arisen, largely in the context of the concern over inflation and the relationship that many people perceive between increased regulation and higher costs and prices.

A working group was set up in 1976 to examine the whole process of regulation-making in the area of health, safety, and fairness. The group concluded that while the system was not in the deplorable state that many people believed, there was much to be desired in terms of a more systematic and rigorous analysis by departments of proposed regulations. Also, there did not seem to be the sensitivity to the concerns of various interests and the opportunity for public input into regulatory decisions that many people thought there should be.

Subsequently, the Canadian government implemented a program that essentially required three things from departments implementing major new regulations in the health, safety, or information areas. A major regulation is defined as one involving social cost for the economy above some threshold level—initially set at $10 million in one year, or $30 million in discounted dollars over ten years.

The three steps essentially involve: (1) the preparation of a cost-impact or socio-economic impact analysis of the proposal; (2) publication of the regulation proposed and a summary of the cost-impact

251

analysis in the *Canada Gazette* (our equivalent of the *Federal Register*); and (3) provision of a time period for interested groups to respond to the analysis and to comment on the regulation. The cost-impact analysis is essentially a cost-benefit analysis plus. Departments are required to evaluate benefits and costs of the proposed regulation and of attractive alternatives to the greatest extent possible. Where this is not feasible, officials are required to try to indicate the direction and the probable size of an impact, or to otherwise describe the effects of the regulation as best they can. The analyses are expected to deal not only with the direct costs and benefits of regulatory changes, but also with implications for the distribution of income, industrial structure, international competitiveness and regional income disparities.

This reform just came into effect this summer and we have not had much experience with it. The new system is limited in three important ways. First, the new requirements only pertain to the federal level and they do not apply to the provinces, which are responsible for a large portion of the regulatory activity in Canada. Second, the system only applies to new regulations; there is no requirement that departments go back and look at the existing stock of regulations. And third, there is a form of escape clause in the system for emergency regulations, so that a department can implement a regulation where the situation is considered to be an emergency and, ex post, undertake the socio-economic impact analysis.

A central body formally known as the Technical Advisory Group was established to oversee the program. Its role is largely advisory — to develop general methodological guidelines for the socio-economic analyses and to assist departments in the preparation of their studies. One of its more important functions is to ensure that a common set of assumptions are used throughout the government with respect to general socio-economic variables such as the rate of discount, real economic growth, price trends, and demographic developments. However, this central group cannot impose its judgment on specific matters on the departmental officials who are responsible for a cost-impact analysis. And, unlike your own Council on Wage and Price Stability, it does not have the option of commenting publicly on an analysis or the regulatory proposal.

I think it was recognized that the analyses of social regulations were unlikely to be very sophisticated in the initial period. There is an important element of "learning by doing" and it will take some time for those involved, including both government officials and out-side interests, to become familiar with the new system and skilled in the techniques of analysis. There was also, I believe, a general appre-ciation, among those who designed this program, for the limitations of cost-impact analysis and of the fundamental problems of the sort that have been highlighted at this conference. It was hoped that the reforms would contribute to solving these problems by requiring de-cisionmakers to make their judgments explicit and by compelling politicians and officials to set out their reasoning for the critical scru-tiny of those who are to be affected by the decision. The requirement for greater openness and increased public participation in regulatory decisionmaking is one of the most important features of the pro-gram, and it is a reform that is of particular significance in the Cana-dian policymaking context.

I might briefly note that this new system for the evaluation of social regulations represents only a first, hesitant step towards regu-latory reform in Canada. There is considerable interest in this general subject in our country, as there is in the United States, and gov-ernments at all levels in Canada are reexamining many of their regulatory activities. The Economic Council of Canada is now em-barking on a major review of government regulation, which will extend to both rulemaking by various levels of government, and to the regulatory activities of such agencies as the Canadian Transport Commission and the Canadian Radio-Television and Telecommuni-cations Commission. There is a shortage of solid empirical evidence on the impact of regulatory activity in Canada, and it is hoped that over the next few years the Council can move some distance toward closing this gap. Perhaps it goes without saying that in this, as in our recent review of health, safety, and fairness regulations, we will be borrowing heavily from your country's experience and from the considerable body of research pertaining to regulation in the United States.

PROFILES OF AUTHORS AND PANELISTS

Henry J. Aaron was Assistant Secretary for Planning and Evaluation, Department of Health, Education and Welfare at the time of the conference.

Prior to that position Dr. Aaron served as a Senior Fellow at The Brookings Institution from 1968 to 1977. He taught at the University of Maryland as Professor of Economics from 1974 to 1977, and as Associate Professor from 1967 to 1974. Dr. Aaron has written numerous books and articles on housing policy, welfare, social security, taxation, and other aspects of public policy. Since the conference, Dr. Aaron has returned to The Brookings Institution and to the faculty of the University of Maryland.

Joan Claybrook, Administrator, National Highway Traffic Safety Administration.

Prior to her current position, Ms. Claybrook worked for Ralph Nader's public citizen group, Congress Watch, as a researcher and organizer concerned with health and safety matters. She served as Special Assistant to the Directors of the National Highway Safety Bureau from 1966 to 1970.

Ralph d'Arge, John S. Bugas Professor of Economics at the University of Wyoming.

Professor d'Arge has taught at Cornell, the University of New Mexico, and the University of California, Riverside and Los Angeles campuses. He has authored approximately seventy-five research articles, books, and technical monographs in the field of resource and environmental economics. He serves as editor of the *Journal of Environmental Economics and Management* and the *Natural Resources Journal.*

George C. Eads was Research Program Director of Regulatory Policies and Institutions Program at The Rand Corporation at the time of the conference.

Dr. Eads is now a member of the President's Council of Economic Advisors. His wide-ranging experience includes positions with The Rand Corporation, being Executive Director of the National Commission on Supplies and Shortages and an Assistant Director for the President's Council on Wage and Price Stability. He has served on the faculties of George Washington University, Princeton University, Harvard University, and Yale University. Dr. Eads's publications focus on transportation policy, telecommunications regulation, and the economics of regulation.

Robert L. Elder, Assistant Surgeon General, U.S. Public Health Service, and Deputy Associate Commissioner for Science, the Food and Drug Administration.

Dr. Elder came to this position from the Bureau of Radiological Health, having served as Deputy Bureau Director from 1974 to 1976 and as Director of the Division of Electronic Products from 1969 to 1973. In 1967 he was selected as a scientific advisor for legislative activities in the Environmental Control Administration, National Center for Radiological Health. Since the conference, Dr. Elder has assumed directorship of the Cosmetic Ingredient Review.

Allen R. Ferguson, President, Public Interest Economics Foundation (PIE–F) and its affiliate, the Public Interest Economics Center (PIE–C).

Dr. Ferguson has directed PIE–F and PIE–C since their founding in 1972. Before that, he was the Director of Policy Research of the Planning Research Corporation, Coordinator for International Aviation in the Department of State, Director of Research of the Transportation Center at Northwestern University, and Deputy Head of the Logistics Department of The Rand Corporation. He has contributed to the field of transportation economics in his writings and through organizing research activities, as well as through lectures, testimony, and in an advisory capacity. Other publications focus on environmental regulations and health services.

Cynthia L. Figge was Director of Education of the Public Interest Economics Foundation at the time of the conference.

Ms. Figge directed the Conference on the Assessment of Benefits of Health and Safety Regulations. She has also worked with the Wisconsin Office of State Planning and Energy concentrating on federal and state energy legislation. Since the conference, Ms. Figge has become a student at the Harvard Business School.

Roy N. Gamse, Deputy Assistant Administrator for Planning and Evaluation, Environmental Protection Agency.

Mr. Gamse joined the Environmental Protection Agency in 1972 and served as Director of the Economic Analysis Division in the Office of Planning and Evaluation before taking his current position. Prior to that, Mr. Gamse was employed in the Systems Analysis Department of the MITRE Corporation.

David Harrison, Jr., Associate Professor, Kennedy School of Government, Harvard University.

Professor Harrison teaches in the areas of energy and environmental regulation and public policy. He has been a consultant to the Environmental Protection Agency, the Department of Housing and Urban Development, and the Massachusetts Department of Environmental Quality Engineering. Professor Harrison has published a number of books and articles in the fields of environmental policy, transportation, and urban land use. Since the Conference, he was appointed to the senior staff of the President's Council of Economic Advisors (1979–1980) and has recently returned to Harvard.

Susan B. King, Chairman, Consumer Product Safety Commission.

Ms. King served as Executive Assistant to the Commissioner of the Federal Election Commission from 1975 to 1977. Prior to that she directed the Center for Public Financing of Elections and the National Committee for an Effective Congress.

Paul Kleindorfer, Professor of Decision Sciences and Management, the Wharton School, University of Pennsylvania.

Professor Kleindorfer has taught at the Sloan School of Management at the Massachusetts Institute of Technology, and has been a research fellow at the International Institute of Management in Berlin. He has published extensively in the field of decision sciences in the private and public sector with special emphasis on dynamic planning problems.

Allen V. Kneese, Senior Fellow, Quality of the Environment Program, Resources for the Future, Inc.

Dr. Kneese has been on the faculty of the University of New Mexico, the University of California at Berkeley, and Stanford University. He has published over eighty books and articles in resource and environmental economics.

Howard Kunreuther, Professor of Decision Sciences, Wharton School, University of Pennsylvania.

Professor Kunreuther's past experience includes positions as Research Advisor at the Pakistan Institute of Development Economics and the Institute for Defense Analysis. He was Assistant Professor at the Graduate School of Business, University of Chicago, before moving to the University of Pennsylvania.

Ezra Mishan, Professor, the City University of London.

Professor Mishan was Professor at the London School of Economics from 1956 to 1977. He has published books on economic growth and welfare economics. He is currently affiliated with the City University of London.

William Nordhaus was a member of the President's Council of Economic Advisors at the time of the conference.

Dr. Nordhaus became a member of the Cowles Foundation for Research in Economics in 1967. He spent a year at Cambridge University; a year at the International Institute for Applied Systems Analysis in Austria, and shorter periods with the National Bureau of Economic Research. His writings include numerous books and articles in the professional and general literature. Since the conference Dr. Nordhaus has returned to his post as Professor of Economics, Yale University.

Donald S. Shepard, Adjunct Research Associate, Kennedy School of Government, Harvard University.

In addition to this position, Dr. Shepard holds the position of Economist for the Veterans Administration outpatient clinic in Boston; Lecturer for the Harvard School of Public Health; and Member of the Center for the Analysis of Health Practices, Harvard School of Public Health. His research and publications focus on the cost-effectiveness and benefits of health care delivery programs.

Gus Speth was a Member of the Council on Environmental Quality (CEQ) at the time of the conference and has since become Chairman of the Council.

Before his appointment to CEQ, Mr. Speth was a staff attorney for the Natural Resources Defense Council, which he helped found in 1970.

James W. Vaupel, Associate Professor, Institute of Policy Sciences and Public Affairs, Duke University.

Professor Vaupel was Research Associate of the Harvard Multinational Enterprise Project. He has consulted with several private and public institutions and has lectured at the Harvard Business School and the Public Policy Program at Harvard University. He has published articles on multinational corporations, and more recently on decision analysis and "the prospects for saving lives."

Paul H. Weaver, Economic Communication Planning Director, Ford Motor Company.

Prior to joining Ford, Dr. Weaver was a member of the Board of Editors of *Fortune* magazine, Associate Editor of *Public Interest*, and Assistant Professor of Government at Harvard University. Mr. Weaver has written extensively on government regulation and the role of the press in American politics. In 1970 he was Editor-in-Chief in charge of the reports issued by the President's Commission on Campus Unrest.

Richard Zeckhauser, Professor of Political Economy, Kennedy School of Government, Harvard University.

Professor Zeckhauser teaches analytic methods in public policy at the Kennedy School in addition to giving instruction in organizations, decisions, and welfare in the Department of Economics, and law and public policy in the Law School of Harvard University. He has published a number of books and articles; major topics include benefit-cost and policy analysis, economic efficiency, and valuation of lives in the marketplace.

CONFERENCE PARTICIPANTS*

The Honorable Henry J. Aaron
Assistant Secretary for Planning
  and Evaluation
Department of Health, Education,
  and Welfare

Mr. Robert Anderson
Attorney
Environmental Law Institute

Professor Nicholas A. Ashford
Assistant Director and Associate
  Professor of Technology and Policy
Massachusetts Institute of Technology

Dr. John R. Ball
Senior Policy Analyst
Executive Office of the President
Office of Science and Technology Policy

Mr. Richard Bergman
Executive Director
Interagency Task Force on Work Place
  Safety and Health

Professor Stephen G. Breyer
Harvard University Law School

Dr. Alan Carlin
Senior Operations Research Analyst
Office of Health and Ecological Effects
Environmental Protection Agency

Dr. Edwin H. Clark, II
Special Assistant to the Administrator
Environmental Protection Agency

The Honorable Joan B. Claybrook
Administrator
National Highway Traffic Safety
  Administration

Ms. Rhea L. Cohen
Washington Representative
Sierra Club

Mr. Thomas Cohen
Attorney, Issue Development Staff
Common Cause

*Affiliations listed are those of the participants at the time of the conference.

Ms. Zena Cook
Economist
Public Interest Economics Center

Mr. Robert E. Copeland
Director, Office of Health and Disability
  Policy, Evaluation and Research
Department of Labor

Professor Ralph d'Arge
Department of Economics
University of Wyoming

J. Clarence Davies, III
Executive Vice President
The Conservation Foundation

Dr. George Eads
Research Program Director
Regulatory Policies and Institutions
  Programs
The Rand Corporation

Dr. Robert L. Elder
Deputy Associate Commissioner
  for Health Affairs
Food and Drug Administration
Department of Health, Education,
  and Welfare

Mr. Barry Felrice
Acting Assistant Administrator for
  Plans and Programs
National Highway Traffic Safety
  Administration

Dr. Allen R. Ferguson
President
Public Interest Economics Foundation
  and Center

Ms. Cynthia L. Figge
Director of Education
Public Interest Economics Foundation

Ms. Mary Ellen Fise
National Consumers League

Mr. William R. Fiste
Chief Relations Division
Bureau of Motor Carrier Safety
Department of Transportation

The Honorable Carol Tucker Foreman
Assistant Secretary for Food and
  Consumer Services
Department of Agriculture

Mr. Roy N. Gamse
Deputy Assistant Administrator for
  Planning and Evaluation
Environmental Protection Agency

Mr. Carl R. Gerber
Senior Policy Analyst
Executive Office of the President
Office of Science and Technology Policy

Mr. Paul Gorecki
Assistant Director
Regulation Reference
Economic Council of Canada

Professor David Harrison
Department of City and Regional
  Planning
Harvard University

Mr. Richard Heller
Special Assistant to the Chairman
Consumer Product Safety Commission

Ms. Sharon Higginbotham
Business Manager
Public Interest Economics Foundation
  and Center

Mr. Ronald Hirshhorn
Regulation Reference
Economic Council of Canada

Mr. Thomas Hopkins
Assistant Director for Operations
  and Research
Council on Wage and Price Stability

The Honorable James B. King
Chairman
National Transportation Safety Board

The Honorable Susan Bennett King
Chairman
Consumer Product Safety Commission

Professor Paul Kleindorfer
Department of Decision Sciences
The Wharton School
University of Pennsylvania

Professor Allen Kneese
Department of Economics
University of New Mexico

Professor Howard Kunreuther
Department of Decision Sciences
The Wharton School
University of Pennsylvania

Ms. Mary Kurkjian
Policy Analyst
Consumers Union

Ms. Laura Layman
Research Assistant
Public Interest Economics Center

Ms. Judith A. Nelson
Acting Chief, Toxics Economics Staff
Environmental Protection Agency

Dr. William Nordhaus
Member
Council of Economic Advisors

Mr. Michael R. Pollard
Coordinator of Health Policy
Office of Policy Planning
Federal Trade Commission

Mr. Warren J. Prunella
Acting Director, Economic Program
  Analysis
Hazard Identification and Analysis
Consumer Product Safety Commission

Mr. Robert Rauch
Attorney
Environmental Defense Fund

Mr. Richard Ridge
Economist, Regulatory Programs
Experimental Technology Incentives
  Program
National Bureau of Standards

Professor Ezra Mishan
Economist
City University of London

Dr. Laurence Rosenberg
Program Manager, Division of Applied
  Research
National Science Foundation

Ms. Kathleen Sheekey
Legislative Director
Consumer Federation of America

Dr. Donald S. Shepard
Kennedy School of Government
Harvard University

Mr. Mark Silbergeld
Director, Washington Office
Consumers Union

Mr. Kirk C. Smith
Counsel
Subcommittee on Oversight and
  Investigations
Committee on Interstate and Foreign
  Commerce
U.S. House of Representatives

Mr. Gus Speth
Member
Council on Environmental Quality

Mr. Gil Thompson
Attorney
Swankin and Turner

Professor James W. Vaupel
Institute of Policy Studies and Public
  Affairs
Duke University

Mr. Norman Waitzman
Corporate Accountability Research
  Group

Mr. Paul H. Weaver
Economic Communications Planning
  Director
Ford Motor Company

Professor Richard Zeckhauser
Kennedy School of Government
Harvard University

INDEX

ABOUT THE EDITOR

Allen R. Ferguson is President of the Public Interest Economics Foundation and Center (PIE–C/F), which he founded in 1972. He has devoted his professional career for thirty years primarily to analysis of the economic aspects of public policy. He has performed research and presented testimony on a variety of regulatory issues ranging from transportation to environmental, health, and safety regulation. Dr. Ferguson has a particular interest in information aspects of quality of life regulation which he has pursued by participating in the development of new decision-making processes for the Food Safety Council. His concern that explicit benefit assessment be included in regulatory decision-making led to the planning of the conference on which this book is based. The Public Interest Economics Foundation organized the Conference, and Allen Ferguson acted as moderator in several of the sessions.

ABOUT THE EDITOR